ALSO BY ISABEL VINCENT

*Bodies & Souls: The Tragic Plight of Three Jewish
Women Forced into Prostitution in the Americas*

*Hitler's Silent Partners: Swiss Banks, Nazi Gold,
and the Pursuit of Justice*

*See No Evil: The Strange Case of Christine Lamont
and David Spencer*

Gilded Lily

Gilded Lily

Lily Safra:
The Making of One of the
World's Wealthiest Widows

Isabel Vincent

HARPER

An Imprint of HarperCollins*Publishers*
www.harpercollins.com

HarperCollins books may be purchased for educational, business, or sales promotional use. For information, please write: Special Markets Department, Harper-Collins Publishers, 10 East 53rd Street, New York, NY 10022.

Library of Congress Cataloging-in-Publication Data has been applied for.

ISBN: 978-0-06-113393-0

10 11 12 13 14   ID/RRD   10 9 8 7 6 5 4 3 2

In memory of my mother

Contents

Contents

Gilded Lily

Introduction
"The Plot of a Great Novel"

THE DRAMA THAT would lead to the death of Edmond Safra began at 4:49 a.m. on Friday, December 3, 1999. That was when Patrick Picquenot, the night watchman at the Belle Epoque, first noticed the noise of the service elevator as it lumbered down from the fifth-floor back entrance to the banker's sumptuous duplex penthouse with its panoramic views of Monte Carlo. Moments later, the doors opened to reveal a man Picquenot had never seen before.

Perhaps he was a new member of Monsieur's staff?

It never occurred to the night watchman that the man might be an intruder because everyone who worked in the beaux-arts building on the avenue d'Ostende knew that Safra, one of the world's wealthiest bankers, was obsessed with security and had installed state-of-the-art alarm systems and steel doors and shutters in his residence above the Monaco branch of his Republic National Bank of New York, which was housed on the first floor of the Belle Epoque. The building also housed branches of Banque Paribas and Banque du Gothard. For all intents and purposes, the Safras' 10,000-square-foot penthouse, which contained two separate wings, was a bunker, impossible to penetrate.

The Safras also employed almost a dozen Mossad-trained security guards. Edmond himself suffered from a debilitating case of Parkinson's disease and was constantly attended by a team of well-trained nurses. And even though he lived part of the year in Monaco—one of the safest places on earth, where there are myriad surveillance cameras monitoring the streets, one policeman for every 100 of its 30,000 residents, and two hundred identity checks carried out by the authorities every day—Edmond refused to dispense with his extremely loyal security detail. But on that early Friday morning in December, not one of the members of his security staff was on duty at the apartment. They were all in Villefranche-sur-Mer, at the Safras' palatial summer home, which was a twenty-minute drive from Monaco.

Still, things were typically so quiet in Monaco that a lesser professional than Picquenot, a small, wiry man who was not armed, could probably be excused for nodding off on the job from time to time. In fact, Picquenot, who hailed from the sleepy town of Menton on the Italian border, was hard-pressed to remember a time when he had had to respond to any kind of robbery or break-in. He wasn't alone. A policeman who had spent twenty-two years on the Monaco force later confessed in court that he had never seen a gunshot wound. The only violence that he had witnessed, he said, involved an antiques dealer who attacked someone with a broken champagne bottle. Crime was rare in this luxe principality, known for its lavish casinos, Formula One racing, and generous tax breaks for its citizens, who are among the world's wealthiest people.

The truth is that Picquenot, at thirty-eight, had little experience when it came to dealing with any kind of violent emergency, which was why he was momentarily dazed when he saw the man—tall and lanky with dirty blond hair and a strange gleam in his piercing blue eyes. He hobbled out of the elevator doubled over in pain, his hands stained copper. He was shouting something in English, a language that Picquenot could barely understand. The man was clutching his stomach and limping, and blood, which appeared to be dripping from his stomach or his leg or both, was pooling on the Italian marble floor.

But Picquenot needed little translation to understand that something was terribly wrong at the Safra apartment. At first, he thought that the man had been shot, although he could not remember hearing anything resembling a gunshot in the moments before he appeared in the lobby. "I called the police," recalled Picquenot. "A little later, a fire alarm went off on the west side. I called the fire brigade. Very rapidly, the police and fire services arrived." But his recollection proved incorrect. There was no fire alarm until much later, a situation that was partly to blame for the chaos of that early winter morning in Monaco.

A few police officers reached the Belle Epoque at 5:12 a.m. and immediately began questioning the bleeding man, who Picquenot quickly found out was Ted Maher, an American and one of Edmond's nurses. Maher told the police officers that he had been the victim of two hooded intruders who had entered through an open window in Safra's penthouse. Before an ambulance arrived to take him to Princess Grace Hospital, the wild-eyed Maher, a former Green Beret with a sterling reputation as a neonatal nurse in New York, told police that the intruders were likely armed, and that Safra and another nurse, who huddled with the billionaire in his bunker-like bathroom, were in terrible danger. Maher was wincing in pain and bleeding profusely, and no one doubted his version of events. Not yet.

It was Maher's statements to police that would further contribute to the chaos of the next three hours and result in the horrible deaths of the sixty-seven-year-old billionaire banker and his night nurse Vivian Torrente, fifty-two. Perhaps, like Picquenot, police and firefighters in Monaco simply didn't have the experience of dealing with an emergency of this scale, so they took their time analyzing the situation, making sure that it was safe to send their own men to Safra's apartment to save the financier and put out the blaze that an hour later was still raging in Safra's bedroom.

They were careful to the point of stunning ineptitude, for when Safra's own chief of security showed up to help with the rescue op-

eration, a police officer promptly arrested him and told him to get out
of the way, even as he offered up the keys that would open the steel
doors in the Safra apartment.

As the sun rose over Monaco, billows of black smoke began escaping through the roof of the Belle Epoque. Edmond and his nurse
made frantic calls to police and family from the cell phone Maher had
given to Torrente before he fled the apartment to alert authorities.
Beginning at 5:00 a.m., Torrente would make six anguished phone
calls to her boss, head nurse Sonia Casiano Herkrath, begging her
to call police. Later, in her statements to police, Herkrath said she
advised Torrente to place rolled-up wet towels around the room. Torrente told her that the bathroom was filling with black smoke, and
that Safra stubbornly insisted they remain until he was certain that
the police had apprehended the hooded intruders. Safra, a legendary banker to whom the world's wealthiest had entrusted their funds,
had provided evidence for an FBI investigation into Russian money-
laundering a year earlier. Since then, he had redoubled his security
because he feared for his life.

"Enemies?" said his friend Marcelo Steinfeld. "Of course, Edmond had enemies. You don't get to make that much money and not
have any enemies."

Perhaps this explained why Safra huddled with his nurse in the
bathroom, shaking uncontrollably in his yellow pajamas. He must
have been terrified that these unnamed enemies, these shadowy "intruders," had come to exact their revenge.

"Telephone calls between third parties and the occupants of the
apartment, which was filled with smoke from the fire, apparently
did not convince the occupants to let the firefighters in," wrote the
medical examiner who was assigned to carry out the autopsies hours
later.

Edmond's first two calls were to his beloved wife, Lily, urging her
to leave her apartment, which was across the hall on the sixth floor,
and to get help immediately. Lily made a daring escape through her

bedroom window onto a balcony, and in a flowing nightgown with a navy school blazer that belonged to one of her grandsons draped over her thin shoulders, she appeared dazed and confused as she gingerly made her way down several flights of stairs to the lobby.

If Picquenot and the dozens of police officers who had by now assembled in the palatial lobby of the Belle Epoque noticed the rather frail and frightened banker's wife shivering in the ill-fitting blazer, few took any notice.

That would come later, after the funeral, and after the sale of her husband's bank to the Hong Kong and Shanghai Banking Corporation (HSBC) made the front pages of the world's financial papers. Of course, the chatter among the aristocrats and the socialites who moved in the Safras' rarefied circles began soon after the media trucks pulled up outside the Belle Epoque to film the blaze and report live from Monaco on the bizarre series of events that would leave one of the world's richest bankers asphyxiated in his own home. By 6:15 a.m., many could clearly see the blaze from their own stately apartments along the avenue d'Ostende and avenue John F. Kennedy. A torrent of intercontinental phone calls began.

"As soon as I turned on the television and saw that the penthouse was on fire, the phone rang," said one longtime resident of Monaco who could also see the Safras' burning penthouse from her own apartment. "The phone kept ringing with people calling me from London, New York, Paris, and Rio de Janeiro. Everyone wanted to know the same thing: 'Where is Lily?'"

Lily, one of the world's richest and most elegant women, was used to the chatter about herself. In many ways she courted it, propelling the media-shy Safra into society columns on three continents. Safra was her fourth husband, and her greatest catch, but he was less than enthusiastic about what seemed to be Lily's need to court publicity and appear at all the best parties.

"I saw their relationship as very unique," said Eli Attia, who had worked as Safra's architect for nearly fifteen years, beginning in 1978.

"She gave him a new angle on life. He was very shy and not comfortable in his dealings with people. They were very complementary to each other and you can't escape [the fact] that it was a great love story."

Safra, balding and stocky, with thick black eyebrows and sad eyes, moved slowly and deliberately. With his courtly Old World manner, he was in many ways the stereotype of the dark-suited prosperous banker, singularly devoted to his clients around the world. Lily once likened going to bed with him to attending a board meeting because "he would telephone his far-flung business associates all night." Still, Safra was clearly in love with Lily, "a slim blonde charmer," who was forty-two when they married in 1976. What she lacked in beauty in her later years, Lily made up for in elegance, sophistication, and extremely good taste. Safra, forty-four when he married her, was a legend in the banking community who was known for his sober discretion. The motto of his Republic National Bank in New York was "to protect not only your assets, but your privacy."

"No other major banker since the era of the Morgans and Rockefellers has been so successful as an entrepreneur," said *BusinessWeek* in a rare profile of Edmond Safra.

But the mighty banker allowed Lily to have her way—most of the time. Following their marriage, the couple regularly dined with such luminaries as Karl Lagerfeld, Valentino, and Nancy Reagan, and befriended *Women's Wear Daily* society columnist Aileen Mehle. One of the earliest mentions of Lily's entrée into Manhattan high society occurred in March 1981 at a dinner in the Safras' honor chez the Brazilian ambassador to the United Nations attended by Diana Vreeland, Bill Blass, the Safras' friends Ahmet and Mica Ertegun, and Nancy Reagan's "walker" and Manhattan society fixture Jerry Zipkin. "Lily answered a toast from her host with a sweet little speech, using one of the Plexiglas lorgnettes that Jerry Zipkin gives friends who are farsighted or nearing 40." Lily was a few months shy of her forty-seventh birthday.

Later, Edmond and Lily attended the same benefits and luncheons as Elton John, Blaine and Robert Trump, and the Monegasque royals. Mehle wrote that Lily and her friend Lynn Wyatt, the Texas billionairess, were among a large entourage "tagging along" with Prince Albert of Monaco during his visit to New York in 1997.

Lily became such a luminary in haute circles in New York that her name became a boldface fixture alongside more established high-society icons. At a luncheon in New York in 1994, Lily must have been thrilled to be mentioned alongside Brooke Astor, the doyenne of the New York social world for decades and a paragon of East Coast old money. At the luncheon, Brooke Astor "wore her sable hat, and Lily Safra wore her velvet one."

The Safras had "exquisite taste" and were considered important collectors. After Edmond's death, Lily sold their collection of eighteenth-century European furniture and decorative objects at a Sotheby's auction—a two-day event in New York that raised a staggering $50 million, double the pre-auction estimate.

But the superlatives were saved for the Safras' magnificent homes around the world. A house Lily bought in London after Edmond's death was "perhaps the most beautiful home in all of London with a swimming pool on the ground floor, surrounded by what looks like the Garden of Eden."

The jewel in the crown was surely their home in the south of France—a place *Women's Wear Daily* described as "one of the most wonderful private houses on the Cote d'Azur, maybe in the world." Lily and Edmond threw fabled balls and "intimate dinners" at La Leopolda, the sprawling seaside villa, named for the estate's first owner, King Leopold II of Belgium. Invitations to the villa, which was surrounded by orange groves and stately cypresses, were the most sought-after among members of high society during the summer social season on the Riviera.

When *Women's Wear Daily* featured one of her most sumptuous balls at La Leopolda in August 1988—a vernissage of sorts after lavish renovations—the magazine referred to her as "The Gilded Lily" in the headline.

By the time Edmond died, Lily was well on her way to establishing her high-society bona fides. But even before she married Edmond, Lily had already honed her reputation as an elegant hostess. In South America, where she was only a minor fixture on the social circuit, first as the wife of a hosiery factory owner in Argentina and Uruguay, and then as the wife of one of Brazil's wealthiest men, friends remembered her for her acts of generosity and her sumptuous parties.

"Lily was an extremely generous woman, a great hostess, with elegant manners," recalled Vera Contrucci Pinto Dias, who socialized with her in Rio de Janeiro in the 1960s. "She wasn't Princess Diana, but she was pretty close."

In October 2008, Lily's longtime friend Princess Yasmin Aga Khan, Rita Hayworth's daughter, honored her with an award for her work on behalf of the Alzheimer's Association. In her speech at the gala dinner at New York's Waldorf-Astoria hotel, the princess pronounced Lily "an extraordinary woman—someone I admire and am honored to have been friends with for nearly three decades. She has inspired many and because of her actions the world is a better place and the future is ever brightening." Lily herself donated a pair of ruby-and-diamond ear clips by JAR for the event's silent auction. The earrings were valued at $180,000 —by far the most expensive lot at the auction.

But hand in hand with generosity went sheer extravagance. This was a woman who thought nothing of sending a favorite hairdresser on a transcontinental flight from Rio de Janeiro to Geneva to do her hair for an event. In 1989 she hired a commercial jet to ferry her friends from New York to Rio for her eldest son's wedding, and renovated a floor of the city's elegant Hotel Meridien for the comfort of her out-of-town guests. The decorating bill for her bedroom (not including furnishings) at her summer home in the south of France was over $2 million. A recent public records search in Manhattan revealed that she has several vehicles registered in her name at one of her Fifth Avenue addresses, including a Bentley Brooklands Sedan and a rare BMW 750IL. One year, at Christmas, she sent out dozens of pairs of Manolo Blahnik shoes to friends.

But her most important characteristic—the one that has propelled her astonishing ascent in social circles around the world—is a steely determination.

"I think that since childhood her dreams had always been to marry into the British nobility or, second best, to marry a billionaire (which she did), but on the world stage, with Class and Pedigree," said Samuel Bendahan, her third husband. "I remember how truly annoyed she still was, months or years after the event, when she related to me that she was to have gone to some lavish function with J. Paul Getty, but that he had had to cancel and she never heard from him again."

Of course, money was always important to her, said Bendahan, "but nothing like being very rich and being, say, the Duchess of Marlborough or *faute de mieux* Mrs. J. Paul Getty."

Indeed, from an early age Lily knew what she wanted: wealth, power, and prestige. "Every girl dreams of her Prince Charming," said Ana Bentes Bloch, who knew Lily in high school in Rio de Janeiro. "Lily was no different. She was such a beautiful girl that you really couldn't deny her anything."

Others remember her differently. "She was a social alpinist," said one acquaintance from the 1950s. "Her parents prepared her from a very early age to marry a rich man."

Although she may not have always known exactly how to get the things that were most important to her, she knew instinctively how to take advantage of those around her who did. She has surrounded herself with an extremely loyal group of lawyers, financiers, and public relations advisers whom she rewards handsomely. But while they manage her financial and legal affairs on three continents, it is Madame who is clearly in charge.

On her own, Lily didn't achieve the wild success in business and finance that distinguished two of her four husbands. But like them she is largely self-made—a middle-class arriviste from the far-flung reaches of South America who built her own impressive empire in elite society. She is a skilled and much admired hostess and an important philanthropist in her own right. She is also a canny survivor, a street-smart society princess who knew how to use her relationships with men to get ahead.

"She didn't exactly lie around the house all day eating chocolates," recalled one of her acquaintances from the 1960s. "In many ways, I am completely repelled by her, but I also admire her greatly. She knows exactly how to take advantage of a situation."

And she lets nothing and nobody stand in her way. Her vindictiveness can be swift and precise. She has been known to change the seating of guests at her elaborate dinner parties when one of them has made the slightest faux pas. A guest could easily be removed from the place of honor at her table and be relegated to the outer reaches of the "children's table" if he had done something to offend Lily.

She hates Safra's brothers in São Paulo, who have never accepted her—someone they view as a lapsed Ashkenazi Jew with a *past*. Although they were very close to Edmond, for years they resisted allowing Lily into their tight-knit Sephardic clan. But in the end she got her revenge. According to the Safra family, in the final months of Safra's life, Lily convinced Safra to distance himself from his siblings even though he had pledged to honor a long-standing Safra family tradition to turn over his banks for them to run. Edmond, who had no children of his own, had made the decision long ago that his younger brothers would take care of his banks when he was gone.

Few details have emerged about her personal life, largely because most of her former employees are forced to sign strict confidentiality agreements. Ted Maher's agreement, which is dated August 16, 1999, reads in part: "You agree that during any period of the retention of your services and thereafter you will not disclose or cause or permit to be disclosed any confidential or non-public information . . . relating in any way to Mr. or Mrs. Edmond Safra, any member of their family, or any company owned or controlled by them or any member of their family . . ." The agreement goes on to say that "a breach of this confidentiality and non-disparagement agreement" will result in "immediate termination" and "the Safras shall have all additional rights and remedies available at law or in equity in the event of such breach." Many former employees reacted with silence when approached for interviews for this book; others passed on their regrets through their attorneys. Others agreed to speak only under the strictest confidentiality.

Many were afraid of potential lawsuits, and described Lily and her elite group of aides as ruthless when it came to protecting her reputation—the carefully edited biography that stresses only her generous philanthropy and her relationship to one of the century's greatest bankers. In many ways, she has decorated her own life's story in the same way that she has decorated her sumptuous residences around the world.

"Lily Safra litigates with a bottomless pit," said Lady Colin Campbell, a best-selling author and biographer of Diana, Princess of Wales. In 2005 Lily threatened to sue Lady Colin over her novel, *Empress Bianca*, which she felt was a thinly veiled roman a clef about her life.

"She's a narcissist who hungers for attention," said Lady Colin, who turned the tables on Lily and sued her for lost revenues when Lily's lawyers managed to pressure her publisher to remove *Empress Bianca* from stores in England and destroy any copies remaining in their warehouse. The lawsuit ended in "a Mexican standoff," said Lady Colin.

Still, Lily has attracted an extremely loyal following among her friends, although she has also managed to strike deep fear in the hearts of those who have fallen out of favor with her. Indeed, some of her friends not only refused repeated interview requests during the research of this book, they claimed they had never met her. "I didn't know her at all," said Carmen Sirotsky, a friend from Rio de Janeiro, who is listed as a witness at her wedding to Alfredo Monteverde in 1966—the second of the three times that they officially registered their marriage. On a trip to Rio de Janeiro in 1972, Lily introduced Carmen Sirotsky to Samuel Bendahan as "my best friend from Rio."

For all the column inches devoted to descriptions of her exquisite clothes, fabled parties, and philanthropy, little is actually known about Lily Safra. Strangely, more is known about her husband, who made it his life's mission to stay out of the media spotlight. Safra almost never gave interviews, largely because his business was built on utter discretion and loyalty to his ultrarich clientele, most of them Sephardic Jews and Arabs who had entrusted their money to generations of Safra bankers in the Middle East.

"He was one of the smartest people I had ever met," recalled Attia, who designed Safra residences around the world as well as the modern addition to the Republic National Bank of New York on Fifth Avenue. Attia met Safra at his offices in Geneva in 1978. During an epic meeting that lasted twelve hours and saw Edmond's dark-suited aides rushing into his office with breaking financial news on bits of white paper, Safra took dozens of calls from around the world as panic began to hit global markets, presaging one of history's worst recessions two years later.

"Milton Friedman called him on the phone to ask his advice," recalled Attia, referring to the Nobel laureate and leader of the Chicago School of economists. "It was amazing. It seemed like he was at the center of the world."

Safra unwittingly stepped back onto center stage as dawn broke over Monaco on December 3, 1999. As the fire raged inside the beaux-arts penthouse, the Safras found themselves thrust into an increasingly harsh media spotlight. Overnight, Lily went from being a glamorous hostess and a boldface name in the society columns to front-page international news. But the instant fame came with a price. It invited intense scrutiny—the kind of publicity that she could surely do without.

Marc Bonnant, Lily's longtime lawyer, asked her point-blank on the witness stand at Ted Maher's trial in Monaco in 2002, "What do you think about people saying you were the cause of the tragedy?"

"It is awful," replied Lily, impeccably dressed in a black business suit, her blonde hair cut stylishly short, her demeanor stoic. "I adored my husband. We were so united. Everyone around us knew that. We lived for each other."

Following several days of testimony from fifty-eight witnesses, Maher was convicted of starting the fire that led to the two deaths and later sentenced to ten years in prison.

In a public statement after Maher's conviction in December 2002, Lily's public relations team rushed out a press release that attempted to put the terrible events behind her, "Let us thank God for this moment when justice has been done: the guilty man has been punished and the full facts of that dreadful night exactly three years ago, which claimed the lives of my dear husband and his devoted nurse, have been laid bare for all to see."

But years after the end of the trial "the full facts" still remain elusive. Maher's defense team recently called for a full investigation after the French press reported that the trial may have been fixed and that legal authorities had met beforehand to work out Maher's conviction and sentencing.

In itself, Maher's trial raised more troubling questions than it answered: Why had the police and firefighters acted with such incompetence? Why had the servants and bodyguards been given the night off? Why did none of the servants have keys to the apartment? Why had Safra decided to sell his bank a month before his death? Who had made the decision to hire Maher? Why did Monaco authorities refuse to conduct a thorough investigation of the events leading up to Safra's death? Did Maher act alone?

As the São Paulo branch of Safra's family noted in their own competing and rather cryptic press statement following the verdict: "Those who were there at the scene on that fateful morning each know what they did and did not do. They must now live the rest of their lives with that knowledge."

The events of December 3, 1999, proved so intriguing that the legendary *Vanity Fair* magazine columnist Dominick Dunne noted six years later, "Some crime stories simply refuse to die, even after a trial and a guilty verdict."

But perhaps it was Ted Maher himself who would put it best: "This story is all about money, power, and corruption."

Just after six a.m. on that fateful Friday morning, Safra's night nurse Vivian Torrente made what would be her final call to her boss Sonia Casiano Herkrath. By then the bathroom was filled with inky black smoke. Herkrath would recall that Torrente's voice sounded strangely sleepy, her words garbled. Herkrath later told authorities that she knew that the nurse was on the verge of losing consciousness. She could also hear Safra coughing incessantly in the background. "I knew she was near the end," Herkrath told Monagesque authorities. "The line went dead."

It would take firefighters another hour and a half to put out the blaze that had already killed Safra and his night nurse. When they finally managed to gain access to the fortress-like bathroom, they found Safra seated in an armchair and Torrente slumped on the floor behind him. Their nostrils were filled with soot which was as black as the trousers that Torrente was wearing. Their skin had turned greasy gray.

Workers from the coroner's office began to remove the bodies at 10:00 a.m. for transfer to the medical examiners' office in Nice for the autopsies.

In the drafty lobby of the Belle Epoque, a police officer sought out Lily to break the terrible news. Leaning on her daughter, Adriana, and son-in-law, Michel Elia, who had arrived moments earlier from their apartment nearby, she made her way to the penthouse. The fire-fighters and police officers who had fumbled for hours in their efforts to save Edmond could now do little more than bow their heads: *Desolé, madame. Nos sinceres condoléances.*

A few weeks before her sixty-fifth birthday, Lily found herself a widow for the second time in her life. Like the first time, thirty years earlier, she also found herself in a uniquely privileged position. This time, the stakes were significantly higher and she would be described in the headlines that dogged her for years after Safra's death as one of the richest widows in the world. Days after the untimely death of Edmond Safra, Lily, an heir to her husband's immense banking fortune, received $3 billion from the sale of his bank. Coincidentally, a day before the fire, Monaco's Prince Rainier had signed the papers making the Safra couple citizens of Monaco. Acquiring citizenship in the principality is a long and complicated affair unless you are personally invited by the Prince, as was the case with Lily and Edmond, who had wined and dined the Grimaldis for years with this specific end in sight. Citizenship ensured that the couple's immense fortune would not be subject to any tax in the principality.

In the more fashionable capitals of Europe and in New York, there was shock and sadness at the horrible turn of events in Monaco. Initially, there was also a great deal of sympathy for Lily.

"I don't know how she has coped with so many things that have happened in her life," said Carlos Monteverde, Lily's adopted son, who considered Safra "a second father."

How would she cope?

Perhaps it was a question posed in the immediate aftermath of Safra's death. Perhaps it occurred to the Monegasque police and fire-fighters as they glanced at Madame, forlorn and shivering in the lobby.

"She is really the prettiest of women," a society columnist had noted about Lily some years earlier. "In a land of giants it's a pleasure to see someone who looks as though she's made of porcelain."

But Lily Safra is made of much stronger stuff.

In Rio de Janeiro, where family friends and acquaintances could still recall Lily as an upwardly mobile young woman in the 1950s with the single-minded goal of marrying a rich man, few people had any doubts about how she would cope without Safra.

"I have always believed that Lily is a woman of great luck and fortune," said Gastão Veiga, a family friend who had known Lily as a teenager and young adult in Rio de Janeiro. "Her life has always struck me as the plot of a great novel."

ONE

"The Most Elegant Girl"

G ASTÃO VEIGA, WHO knew Lily as a teenager before her first marriage, said he wasn't surprised that she had landed one of the richest men in Brazil before her thirtieth birthday. It was clear to him that the only daughter of Wolf White Watkins had been trained from an early age to marry up in the world. In the end, it didn't seem to matter how many times she needed to walk down the aisle.

"Lily was a social climber, it's true," said Veiga. "The Watkins family lived around the prospects of Lily marrying a wealthy man."

The Watkinses were well off by most standards, but they had fallen short of the wealth dreamed of by Wolf White Watkins, who had left his native London in his early twenties to seek his fortune in the wilds of South America. Wolf, an engineer by profession, settled first in Uruguay, where he met his future wife, Annita Noudelman de Castro. Annita, an Uruguayan of Russian-Jewish descent, was still a teenager when she married Wolf and became pregnant with the couple's first child.

At the beginning of the twentieth century, many Jews escaping hardship and persecution in Europe had moved to the southern reaches of South America, most of them aided by the Jewish Colonization Association. The organization was founded by the Baron

Maurice de Hirsch in 1891 to help Jews who were in danger of being targeted in anti-Semitic pogroms in Eastern Europe. The baron's organization gave the mostly Ashkenazi Jewish immigrants from Russia and Poland a plot of land and helped each settler buy livestock and a horse in agricultural colonies in South America where they could practice their religion without fear of persecution.

It's not clear if the Noudelman family arrived in Uruguay under the Baron de Hirsch scheme, but for many Jews fleeing persecution in Europe, Uruguay was not a destination but merely a stopover on the way to more prosperous communities in Brazil or Argentina. Although there are records of Jewish settlement in the country dating back to the 1770s, the Jewish presence in Uruguay in the early twentieth century was negligible. There were fewer than two hundred Jews in the capital Montevideo in the early 1900s and the first synagogue in the country was only established there in 1917. Still, the government of the day seems to have been extremely tolerant of Jews. At the San Remo Conference in April 1920, a post–World War I meeting of the Allied Supreme Council to divide up the former Ottoman-controlled lands of the Middle East, Uruguay boldly supported the establishment of a Jewish homeland.

Most of the Jews who decided to stay in Uruguay eventually gravitated to Montevideo, where they opened small businesses. The Noudelmans appear to have gone against the grain, settling in Rivera, a small frontier town in the northern part of the country, near the Brazilian border, where the small Jewish community worked as traders, gauchos, or farmers.

It's not clear how Wolf White Watkins ended up in Rivera, but it certainly wasn't religion that drove him there. The twenty-three-year-old dreamer headed to the New World after the First World War because he wanted to strike it rich.

"Watkins was a controversial figure," said Veiga, a business associate in the 1940s and 1950s, who, in later years, imported luxury vehicles, such as Rolls Royce and MG, to Brazil. "He was mixed up with everything and he was determined to earn money. Whether it was clean or dirty, he didn't care. The line in business that he followed was never straight."

Despite his fierce-sounding name, Wolf White Watkins was a slight, balding, and bespectacled man. The photo on his Brazilian identity card shows a rather mousy middle-aged man in a smart business suit who looks more like a mild-mannered accountant or schoolteacher than a tough, enterprising businessman who traveled across the world to seek his fortune.

In February 1919, Wolf and Annita, who were living in Rivera close to Annita's family, decided to move to Sant'Ana do Livramento in Brazil. It's not clear that they actually crossed a border since both Rivera and Sant'Ana do Livramento are twin cities with an undefined crossing. One could easily get lost in the outskirts of Rivera, only to find that he had unwittingly crossed the border into Brazil. In the early twentieth century, the region, marked by rolling hills, lush vineyards, and fruit trees, was a haven for smugglers, who could easily move contraband goods, such as petrol, tobacco, machinery, salted beef, leather, and precious metals, into Brazil and Argentina, where tariff barriers on imported goods were extremely high. Although Wolf's expertise lay in the construction of railway carriages, like most enterprising frontier residents, he also tried his hand at smuggling, says Veiga.

At some point, Wolf and his wife must have made the conscious decision to move to Brazil to start their family. Compared to rural Uruguay, which was at the time a sleepy agricultural backwoods, Brazil was turning into an economic powerhouse where the booming coffee trade was fueling rapid industrialization and attracting a steady stream of European immigrants who came in search of economic opportunities.

Less than a year after the couple established themselves on the Brazilian side of the border in Sant'Ana, nineteen-year-old Annita gave birth to the first of the couple's four children. Rodolpho Watkins was born in Sant'Ana do Livramento on January 1, 1920. His brother Daniel was born a year later.

The Watkins family's next move, in 1922, was to Porto Alegre, a relatively prosperous city of German and Italian immigrants where most afternoons gauchos in capes and faded cowboy hats gathered around the central plaza to share a gourd of maté, the strong herbal tea which is a staple in the Southern Cone. Porto Alegre, which was 250 miles away from Sant'Ana, was also becoming an important center of Jewish settlement, and by the time Annita and Wolf moved to the city, Ashkenazi Jews were beginning to settle in the Bom Fim neighborhood, a middle-class enclave dotted by kosher slaughterhouses and other Jewish businesses. In 1928, their third son, Artigas, was born in Porto Alegre. He may have been named in honor of General Jose Gervasio Artigas, the nineteenth-century hero of Uruguay's independence movement. Wolf must have felt a special bond with the long-deceased general because both of them began their professional lives as smugglers on the Brazilian border.

Six years after the birth of Artigas, Wolf and Annita's only daughter was born in Porto Alegre, on December 20, 1934. An opera buff, Wolf insisted upon naming the baby girl Lily in honor of the petite French soprano Lily Pons, who was at the height of her fame just as her Brazilian namesake was born.

By the time Lily was born, residents of Porto Alegre were keenly following events in the country's capital, Rio de Janeiro, where one of their own native sons, President Getúlio Vargas, a lawyer and former populist governor of Rio Grande do Sul, was turning Brazil into a fascist state. Vargas, a gaucho who had seized power in a coup d'état in 1930, began to consolidate his powers in the 1934 constitution, which cracked down on left-wing opposition, centralized the economy, and set up economic incentives to spur industrial development.

Wolf watched events in the capital with keen interest and wondered how this new Vargas "revolution," as it was hailed throughout Brazil, could make him rich. Watkins knew that in order to prosper even further he needed to leave Rio Grande do Sul, where promises of cheap land had drawn thousands of migrants from Europe at the turn of the twentieth century. Most of the Jews who were settling in Bom Fim brought their professional experience from the Old Country and were happy to be able to open up a small shoe store or tailor's shop. But Wolf wasn't interested in owning land or running a small business. His specialty was the railway, and he followed its development in Brazil, hoping to get rich.

Just before his forty-fifth birthday, in 1940, Wolf decided to uproot his family yet again, still in pursuit of the fabulous wealth he had dreamed about as a young man in England. This time, the Watkins clan headed to Rio de Janeiro, then Brazil's capital. At first they settled on the city's outskirts in the down-at-heels municipality of Mesquita, moving three times in their first year until Watkins established the Society of National Reconstruction, a company that specialized in building and fixing railway carriages, known by its Portuguese acronym SONAREC. Mesquita, the site of a large sugar plantation that had fallen on hard times after Brazil's Princess Isabel abolished slavery in 1888, was named for the plantation's owner Baron Jeronimo José de Mesquita. Although the rolling hills and lush landscape must have reminded the Watkins clan of Uruguay, Mesquita was no pastoral retreat populated by well-mannered European immigrants. The town was located in the mosquito-infested Baixada Fluminense, the lowlands north of the city of Rio. It was hot and sticky in the summers and endured punishing torrential rains in the winters. Most of the town's nine thousand residents were impoverished farmers, factory workers, and aging former slaves who had never left the ruins of the former plantation. There were few diversions in Mesquita, and the good schools were nearly an hour away by rail in Rio de Janeiro. It was hardly the place for an upwardly mobile businessman like Wolf and his young family.

By the time the Watkinses arrived in Mesquita in the 1940s, local businessmen had largely failed in their efforts to turn part of the baron's old plantation into orange groves for the production of orange juice. Still, Wolf saw opportunity. With its proximity to Brazil's capital, Wolf felt that it was only a matter of time before Mesquita would turn into a booming industrial center, especially as it was strategically located on Brazil's great Estrada de Ferro—literally "the highway of iron," or the railroad. Yet, in the early days of their life in Mesquita, the Watkins family must have faced some difficult times.

But it was there that Watkins began to make his important connections among Brazilian politicians and railway barons that would ensure his success for years to come.

Although Watkins did end up making a lot of money, the bulk of his earnings weren't exactly from the repair of railway carriages. From his base in Mesquita during the war years, when gas was severely rationed in Brazil, Watkins entered into a lucrative if not quite legal partnership with a powerful politician and military man named Napoleão Alencastro Guimarães. A former minister of transportation, the tall, dapper politician was also the director of the Central do Brasil train station in Rio de Janeiro, one of the country's largest transport facilities at the time. Alencastro Guimarães, an anglophile who was fond of bespoke suits and an habitué of the most elegant supper clubs in Rio, took an instant liking to the plucky Englishman. And so when he sent railway carriages to SONAREC for repair, they would arrive loaded with cans of petrol. Watkins, who had developed a healthy network of black-market contacts from his years spent in the towns strung along the border of Brazil and Uruguay, easily sold the petrol on the black market. He then returned the railway carriages empty to the Central do Brasil and divided the spoils with his friend Alencastro Guimarães.

"He made a tidy fortune," said Marcelo Steinfeld, who first heard the stories of Wolf White Watkins from Lily when she was living in Rio in the late 1960s. "But even though he was rich, Watkins was too much of a spendthrift to ever be successful."

Wolf's partnership with Alencastro Guimarães proved so profitable that he was able to move his family to a stately apartment in Rio at the end of the Second World War. Wolf managed to install his family in a large, ground-floor apartment on Joaquim Nabuco, a leafy residential street of some prestige in Copacabana, a block and a half from the beach. It was a good address, but far from the opulence of Flamengo and Laranjeiras, home to diplomats, high-ranking government officials, and the country's president—the seat of old money in Rio de Janeiro. Still, one of his neighbors on Rua Joaquim Nabuco recalled that Watkins's home was "nicely furnished and very comfortable."

In Rio, Wolf loved nothing more than showing off his wealth by tipping extravagantly and dressing in the custom-made linen suits he ordered from his tailor on the fashionable Rua do Ouvidor in downtown Rio, where the city's wealthiest businessmen and politicians all ordered their made-to-measure suits. Wolf thought nothing of tipping extravagantly, and friends recalled that he once gave an attendant the equivalent of $100 to park his car. When he invited business associates to lunch, it was always a lavish affair, and he wasn't content unless he invited six or seven people at a time.

Wolf also loved spoiling his daughter. At first, he bought her toys and Belgian and Swiss chocolates that he ordered from the Portuguese import houses in downtown Rio. But when she became a teenager, Wolf was determined to give his little girl—the apple of his eye—the most exquisite clothes that money could buy.

But Wolf's extravagances often landed him in debt. According to some of his business associates he moved from place to place in order to escape paying those debts—a rather dangerous proposition in twentieth-century Brazil, when many disputes over money and women were settled with a bullet.

Wolf was, however, nothing if not street-smart and wily, and he had become an expert at extricating himself from particularly difficult situations. For instance, when he wanted to hang onto the lucrative contract to repair railway carriages for Rio de Janeiro's Central do

Brasil Station, he knew his debts to a wealthy *coronel*, or local strong-man, threatened to sink his prospects. But Wolf was undaunted. He ignored the repeated requests for repayment and stalled, knowing that top-level officials at the Central do Brasil desperately needed his company's services after the Second World War. His strategy eventually proved successful. Eurico de Souza Gomes, who was in charge of the administration of the Central do Brasil between 1951 and 1953, and was a leading *coronel* in Rio, finally reached out to Watkins, through an intermediary, to collect part of the debt. Souza Gomes asked his friend Gastão Veiga to collect the money that Watkins owed him. If Watkins paid even part of the debt, the managers of the Central do Brasil would continue to do business with SONAREC.

Veiga had never met Wolf before, but soon realized that the distinguished businessman who mixed the King's English with guttural Uruguayan Spanish was his neighbor in Copacabana. Following Veiga's intervention, Wolf appears to have at least partially settled the debt he had with Souza Gomes. After his difficulties with the Central do Brasil, Wolf's company continued to repair an average of 360 wagons a year for the railway.

Wolf was so grateful to Veiga for his intervention that he grandly presented him with a gold Audemars Piguet watch, which was then an extremely expensive Swiss timepiece that was difficult to obtain in Brazil, especially as the fascist Vargas government had set up even more tariff walls on foreign products to protect local industry. But for Wolf the watch was a good investment: the way he saw it, Veiga had just helped break the impasse with his most important client, so he was worth more than his weight in gold.

The intervention also helped in other ways, for when Wolf required a letter of reference from the principals of the Central do Brasil in order to apply for Brazilian citizenship in 1950, they did not hesitate to write the nicest things about the transplanted Englishman. "For ten years we have worked with Mr. Watkins, who has always faithfully fulfilled the requirements of the railroad," wrote Hilmar

Tavares da Silva in a letter to Brazilian authorities attesting to Wolf's good conduct in business. "He is a person of absolute moral and material integrity."

It is not clear why Wolf saw the need to become a Brazilian citizen after living quite successfully in the country for nearly thirty-one years as a foreigner. Perhaps he wanted to consolidate his business and make sure that it survived after his death. In October 1950, Wolf and Annita began to collect the letters of reference and undergo the medical examinations that would enable them to apply for Brazilian citizenship. In the black-and-white photo pasted to his Brazilian identity card, Wolf wears wire-rimmed spectacles and has a receding hairline. Annita, fifty at the time, is a heavyset woman with a double chin and a short, tightly curled coiffure. Her severely plucked eyebrows lend her a hard, defiant air.

Part of the citizenship application involved describing their children's activities in Brazil. To this end, both Wolf and Annita focused on Lily, who was their only minor child at the time.

While the Watkinses sought their Brazilian citizenship, Lily was well on her way to making a splash in Rio society—at least as it was defined within the city's upper-middle-class Jewish and English-speaking communities. Lily was enrolled at the Colegio Anglo-Americano, a traditional British-American private school, housed in a handsome colonial building that had once belonged to a Portuguese duke. The school was next door to the Sears department store in the Botafogo neighborhood, where the country's best schools were clustered. Known as the British American School when it was founded in 1919, the school was re-christened with a Portuguese name after President Vargas declared—in a fit of nationalistic fervor during World War II—that all educational and religious institutions in the country had to have Portuguese names.

Margareth Coney, the no-nonsense British matron who founded the school, duly changed the school's name but continued to direct its strict programming until just before her death in 1968. Coney had arrived in Rio de Janeiro at the turn of the last century to work as a governess for one of Brazil's wealthiest families. By the time her contract with the family was over, Coney had begun to look for other opportunities. She bemoaned the lack of proper educational facilities for the growing colony of English-speaking immigrants in Rio de Janeiro and decided that the city needed a proper British school. The British American School soon became a tough training ground for the sons and daughters of British and American expatriates in the city, and offered Brazilian students the opportunity to become fluent in English, which was the working language of the school. Lily herself speaks a refined international English as well as Portuguese, Spanish, and French. Her multilingual skills would later prove excellent assets in elite society.

By the beginning of the Second World War, Coney had developed an impressive educational institution in Brazil that drew upper-middle-class students, although it never attained the social prestige of the elite Catholic schools, such as Notre Dame de Sion, Santo Inacio, and Dom Pedro, where the old money coffee and sugar barons sent their children.

The Colegio Anglo-Americano was particularly popular among well-to-do Jewish families in Rio who didn't want to send their children to schools with Christian affiliations, although Jewish children were welcome in the Jesuit-run institutions throughout the city. In many cases, Jewish parents who worried about their social standing in the city sent their children to the Catholic institutions, but insisted that they not participate in any of the religious classes. The Colegio Anglo-Americano was one of the few elite schools in Rio de Janeiro that had no discernible religious affiliation.

According to her parents' application for Brazilian citizenship, Lily attended the school from 1945, when she was eleven years old, until she graduated in 1951 at sixteen. In school, she was known as Lilly de Castro Watkins, using, as per Brazilian tradition, part of her mother's maiden name and signing her first name with a double *l*. Her older brother Daniel signed her report cards and the tuition receipts on behalf of Wolf, who still worked in Mesquita, an hour outside Rio, and was probably too busy to attend to the bureaucratic requirements at his daughter's school. Sometimes Annita Watkins's shaky signature appears on her report cards.

According to her school records, Lily's best subjects were English and the Portuguese language; she scored nine out of ten on both during a final exam in 1951. But she received failing grades in physics, mathematics, and chemistry, even though she appears to have been a diligent student. In one exam she copied a descriptive paragraph three times in her neatest handwriting before including a polished final version in her examination booklet. In "Description of the Engraving," Lily wrote about an etching that showed three people—two children and a woman. Interestingly, Lily, who was eleven years old at the time, didn't focus on the personalities of the people in her paragraph, but homed in on the interior design of the room and their clothing: "The little girl wears a little blue dress and white socks. Her shoes are brown. On the other hand, the boy's clothing is quite different. He wears brown trousers and a white shirt and vest. The woman wears a red dress with a white apron." The floors of the storeroom where they are posing were made of ceramic tile; there was a table and two stools, she wrote.

"She was a beautiful girl, with green eyes and light hair," said Ana Bentes Bloch, who hailed from a prominent Jewish family in the city and also attended the Colegio Anglo-Americano in the 1940s and 1950s.

But the black-and-white school photograph attached to Lily's registration shows a plump little girl with a shoulder-length bob and a very large nose.

"Children used to tease her at school because of her nose," recalled one of her acquaintances who did not want to be identified. "Everyone used to call her 'Lily *nariz*.'" The direct translation from the Portuguese is "Lily nose."

But despite her nose, others remember her as an extremely poised and elegant teenager. Perhaps Lily was so beguiling in her speech, gestures, and carriage that she managed to convey the impression of beauty. Although Bentes Bloch was a few grades behind Lily, she remembers her as a striking presence in high school. "She had beautiful clothes, and was easily the most elegant girl at the school," said Bentes Bloch. "Lily was really a pleasure to be around."

As a result, she was also the most sought-after girl at school socials and Saturday night dances at the Clube Israelita Brasileiro, known by its acronym CIB. The Jewish community center is located in Copacabana, down the street from the elegant Galeria Menescal shopping arcade and several blocks away from the grand Copacabana Palace hotel, where many of the girls at the Colegio Anglo-Americano attended the sumptuous balls during Carnaval in February. Inspired by the Hotel Negresco in Nice and the Carlton in Cannes, the Copacabana Palace was designed by the French architect Joseph Gire to be the grandest hotel in Rio de Janeiro, overlooking the Atlantic Ocean on Copacabana Beach. In the 1940s and 1950s, when Lily was growing up in Rio, the hotel was the focal point of upper-middle-class society in the city.

On the weekends, wealthy families gathered at the Copacabana Palace hotel for dinner at the Bife de Ouro, or Golden Beef, the city's most fashionable restaurant.

When a government edict shut Rio's casinos in April 1946, the hotel's Golden Room drew some of the world's biggest entertainers. The hotel became an important destination for fashionable society, even though its most popular feature was a nightly floor show featuring young women, known as the *emancipadas*, or "emancipated ones," because most of the showgirls were under eighteen, which meant that hotel officials had to seek special permission from the local government to allow them to perform in public. The resulting permissions, when they were granted, allowed the girls to be "emancipated" from the strict laws forbidding minors from performing in a bar. "At that time in Rio, there were very few places where you could gather to see a show," recalled Hélio Fernandes, a former owner of the *Tribuna de Imprensa*, one of the city's leading newspapers at the time. "The beauty of the dancing girls at the Golden Room became the stuff of local legend, and anyone with any means was flocking to the shows in the evenings."

Like many upwardly mobile Jews in Rio, Lily's family frequented the Copacabana Palace's Golden Room, although they likely never took in the rather risqué floor shows. The center of their social life was the CIB on Raul Pompeia Street. The club organized balls and other cultural events that were attended by most Jewish families of means in Rio de Janeiro. It was not uncommon for young Jewish women to meet their future husbands at the CIB socials.

In the late 1940s, CIB officials began the club's tradition of debutante balls for the daughters of their members. The balls were organized by Lygia Hazan Gomlevsky, the elegant wife of the club's then president José Gomlevsky. With her shoulder-length chestnut hair, porcelain skin, and smoky eyes, Lygia looked like a glamorous Hollywood movie star. And she was determined to inject a little bit of that glamor into the debutante balls, which were modeled after the sumptuous coming-out parties for high-society girls at the Copacabana Palace hotel. The annual debutante balls in the Golden Room of the Copacabana Palace, which began soon after construction was completed on the hotel in the mid-1920s, were considered the highlight of the Rio social season.

Lygia, herself a local socialite who attended all the best parties in the city, often showed up as a boldface name in the social columns, alongside her friends the Klabins, one of the wealthiest Jewish families in Rio de Janeiro. In black-and-white photographs of the balls, Lygia is shown ushering a group of young girls into the CIB ballroom. The girls are all beautifully dressed in puffy white taffeta or organza dresses. Every year, Lygia hired an orchestra for the annual debut and she personally chose twenty of the most beautiful girls from among the member families. One of those girls was a perfectly poised and elegant teenager named Lily Watkins.

"I can easily say that Lily was the most beautiful and the most elegant debutante we ever had at the club," recalled Gomlevsky. "She wore a magnificent white organdy dress embroidered with tiny white flowers on the sleeves. She was the chicest girl at the debut."

Although cosmetic surgery wasn't as commonplace in Brazil as it is today, perhaps Lily did manage to get a little "help" when it came to her features. Gomlevsky, for one, doesn't remember that Lily had a prominent nose by the time she was ready for her debut.

Although her family otherwise kept a low profile at club events, where they would sit together *en famille* at dinners, the Watkins girl turned heads wherever she went.

"Lily used to wear the most exquisite dresses at the CIB dances," said Bentes Bloch. "She had an absolutely wonderful lilac organza dress that was the envy of all of the girls. It was absolutely stunning."

José Behar seemed to agree. Lily met José, or Zeca as he was known to his friends and family, at a CIB dance. Zeca, a handsome Sephardic Jew, was slightly older than the teenaged Lily, and was already out of high school, working for his uncle's currency trading business on Avenida Rio Branco in the city center.

But any union with Zeca was severely frowned upon by Lily's upwardly mobile parents. Zeca might have been a nice young man with a good job, but he would never attain the fabulous wealth that the Watkinses dreamed of for their daughter.

"Lily and Zeca had a real romance," said a family friend who frequented CIB events in the 1940s and 1950s. "He loved her, but it was hopeless. Lily had been trained to marry money. She was educated to marry a rich man."

In fact, when Lily found herself falling desperately in love with another middle-class boy, her parents were quick to put a stop to the budding relationship.

Her new obsession was Izidor, a classmate at the Colegio Anglo-Americano. Izidor was tall, slim, and green-eyed. He also had a way with the girls.

"He would tease them relentlessly," said Bentes Bloch. "He knew he was popular and so he would string along all these girls who all had a mad crush on him. Then he would dump them."

Lily ended up being one of his many victims, but she still dreamed about Izidor as her own Prince Charming, and she pursued him relentlessly, recalled Bentes Bloch.

For his part, Gastão Veiga recalled that whenever Lily wanted to see Izidor, she would tell her parents that she was going to Veiga's home around the corner from the Watkins family's residence in Copacabana. During those fleeting meetings, hidden from outside view in Veiga's courtyard, Izidor might hold Lily's hand or touch her on the shoulder. If they felt particularly daring, she would allow him to kiss her on the cheek. In Rio's middle-class Jewish society, the most risqué events for teenagers involved boys from the lower classes invading one of the orderly school or CIB dances and drinking beer.

"We were all quite chaste back then," said Bentes Bloch, whose father, one of the country's first Jewish generals, had arrived in the Amazon as a thirteen-year-old immigrant from North Africa at the turn of the last century. "Dating didn't have the same connotations that it has now."

Lily was so much in love with Izidor that she fell ill. She desperately wanted to marry him, but her parents seemed to have other plans for her. Like Zeca, Izidor did not come from great wealth—not the kind of family that was suitable for their daughter. And so her parents decided that they had had enough of Rio de Janeiro and its loose morals for a while, and became determined to find a more suitable young man for their daughter among the members of their old Jewish community in Uruguay.

"Her parents were very strict, and it was important to them that Lily marry well," recalled Veiga.

But Bentes Bloch remembers things differently. She said that Lily was so heartbroken over Izidor's antics and how he toyed with her affections that her parents feared that she might do something rash. According to Bentes Bloch, Lily was determined to marry Izidor.

"Her parents must have been beside themselves," said Bentes Bloch. "What do you want for such a beautiful girl? You want to give her the most you can—the maximum."

When they realized that the relationship with Izidor was becoming too intense, the Watkinses decided to go on a long vacation, and get their daughter out of Rio de Janeiro, and far away from Izidor. During summer vacation in her last year of high school, the Watkins clan headed back to Uruguay to visit Annita's family. In order to dissuade their daughter from an improper match, they found her someone much more to their liking. Lily eventually did get over Izidor, and following the trip to Uruguay she returned to Rio de Janeiro already engaged to a handsome and older Italian-born Jew named Mario Cohen.

"Lily went on vacation for a long time with her parents, and when she returned we all heard that she was going to be married," said Bentes Bloch. "That's how we all heard about her first marriage."

Lily married Mario Cohen in Montevideo, Uruguay, on September 19, 1952, two months before her eighteenth birthday. Mario, who was nearly nine years older, came from a respectable family that had made a small fortune manufacturing hosiery in Argentina, where their company was based. Less than a year following the wedding, Lily gave birth to her first son, Claudio, on July 16, 1953. She had two other children—Adriana and Eduardo—in rapid succession.

After her pampered adolescence in Rio de Janeiro, life as a mother of three young children in Montevideo, far from friends and family, must have come as a bit of a shock. Although the Cohens lived amongst upper-middle-class Jews in Montevideo, the city and the country were growing increasingly unstable as the world market for agricultural products began to decline in the 1950s. In Montevideo there was massive unemployment and inflation coupled with increasing student militancy and unrest. The civil unrest led to the birth of an urban guerrilla movement known as the Tupamaros, who first made their mark robbing banks and distributing food to the poor. By the 1960s, the guerrilla group began to play a part in high-level political kidnappings in Montevideo.

If Uruguay was emerging as an increasingly unstable country, Lily Cohen took little notice. In the early days at least, she was the wife of a successful hosiery magnate who occupied her time organizing the servants, fixing her hair, and vacationing in Punta del Este, an upscale resort and casino town on the southern tip of Uruguay where upper-middle-class Jewish families flocked between December and February at the height of the austral summer.

But Lily, who seems to have inherited Wolf's passion for spending money, also indulged in what was to become her favorite pastime—shopping. During one memorable spree in downtown Montevideo, Lily managed to spend thousands on lingerie—an astonomical sum of money in the late 1950s. When he received the bill, Mario was so furious he ripped up all her new purchases, said a family friend.

"Mario wasn't like Lily's father when it came to money," said Marcelo Steinfeld. "I think he had very little patience when it came to Lily's excesses."

IN FACT, WHEN it came to money, Mario was the polar opposite of Wolf, which might explain why Wolf seemed to have little tolerance for his new son-in-law, who, he believed, failed to treat his daughter in the manner to which she had become accustomed in Rio. In Uruguay, where the young couple lived to escape the severe economic policies and other repressive measures directed at Jews during the presidency of Argentine leader Juan Peron, Mario bought his new wife a car. It was a Morris Minor, a British import designed for the working classes. Furious at his new son-in-law's miserly gesture,

which he viewed as a slap in the face to the entire Watkins clan, Wolf
ordered a Cadillac through his friend Gastão Veiga and had it shipped
to Lily.

THROUGHOUT THE DECADE she spent in Montevideo, Lily yearned
to return to the cosmopolitan city of her youth. She missed the family
dinners at the Bife de Ouro in the Copacabana Palace hotel and high
tea at the Confeiteria Colombo in her old neighborhood. She missed
the family vacations at the hot springs at Poços de Caldas and Cax-
ambu, where many well-heeled Jewish families escaped the month-
long frenzy of Carnaval in Rio. By the time she was pregnant with
her third child, she had already grown tired of Mario.

When her beloved father died of a liver ailment while on a visit to
Montevideo in March 1962, Lily was already plotting how she would
tell Mario that their marriage was over. She'd had enough of their
sleepy existence in Montevideo. She wanted to return to Rio, to recapture at least part of what now seemed such a glamorous life as a
promising debutante in her white organdy dress. In her late twenties,
her youth was slipping away, and life with Mario was not the fairy tale
she had envisioned it to be. Although he appeared to be a good father,
he was distant with the children, overwhelmed by his own concerns
with the Cohen family company. Often when Lily and the children
prepared for family vacations in Punta del Este, Mario was absent for
weeks at a time, tending to business in Montevideo and Argentina.

Although she yearned to return to her old life in Rio, Lily wanted
to do so in style. In the early 1960s, it simply wouldn't do for a respectable mother of three young children to leave her husband and set
off for another country, even if she could move quite easily into her
parents' sprawling apartment in Copacabana. No, Lily would have to
wait for another way out of her marriage to Mario Cohen.

Lily's escape route may have been made patently clear to her when
she met Alfredo Monteverde, the handsome owner of Ponto Frio,

Brazil's most successful chain of appliance stores. Alfredo was tall and worldly with a devastating sense of humor. He was also extremely wealthy. Friends say that it was on one of those long family vacations in Punta del Este that the married woman and mother of three began to flirt with the Rio millionaire after the two had been introduced by their mutual friend Samy Cohn.

After his second failed marriage, to a former Air France stewardess named Scarlett, Alfredo was ready for another relationship. He fell in love easily with Lily. She was beautiful and refined, and she would have none of Scarlett's difficulties of adaptation to life in Rio de Janeiro. Lily must have seemed to him practically a native.

"She was even more charming as a young mother," recalled Veiga, who saw Lily again at Alfredo's office for the first time since she was a fifteen-year-old sneaking into his courtyard to kiss Izidor.

Veiga, Wolf's former neighbor and valuable intermediary, also did business with Alfredo, who was planning to add car imports to his burgeoning appliance business. Veiga recalls finding out about the relationship between Alfredo and Lily during a business meeting at the Ponto Frio corporate offices in 1964. "I was completely stunned," recalled Veiga. "I saw Lily followed by three small children at Fred's office, and it was very clear to me that she and Fred were very much a couple. I knew from the way they were behaving with each other that they must be married or on their way to being married."

Alfredo married Lily in a civil ceremony at the Office of the City Clerk in lower Manhattan on February 26, 1965. According to friends and family, Mario was not happy about the divorce, and desperately tried to hold onto his young wife. Alfredo was forty and Lily had just celebrated her thirtieth birthday the previous December.

The following year, on October 16, 1966, they married again at a registry office in downtown Rio de Janeiro, attended by Lily's brother Daniel and her best friend in Rio at the time, Carmen Sirotsky. Carmen's husband Sani, an advertising executive in Rio, had worked on many of Ponto Frio's advertising campaigns and knew Alfredo well.

The Monteverde-Watkins marriage (on registry documents, she didn't acknowledge that she had once been Mrs. Cohen) was also registered in Brazil's new capital, Brasília, on April 5, 1967.

It is not clear why they felt the need to register their marriage in so many different places. As with his previous marriages, Alfredo made a point of registering the union in New York. Perhaps he felt that legal unions carried more weight when they were registered outside of Brazil, which was well known for its bureaucratic red tape and corruption.

Lily would have gladly married Alfredo twenty times over. She appeared desperately in love with her second husband, and tried to do everything to please him. And for a while at least, it seemed she did.

TWO

"Everything in Its Place"

Bᴙ ᴍᴏꜱᴛ ᴀᴄᴄᴏᴜɴᴛꜱ, it was initially a happy marriage. Alfredo, a striking European émigré with wavy brown hair and an easygoing manner, was head over heels in love with Lily—at least in the early part of the courtship and the marriage, while the conquest was still fresh.

For most of his adult life, Alfredo was known as a serial womanizer; he had been married twice before. But Lily was different, he told his family. Here was a beautiful woman and a wonderful mother whom he adored. The marriage to Lily had been a good decision, Alfredo assured his friends and family.

Alfredo João Monteverde, born Alfred Iancu Grunberg in Galati, Romania, on June 12, 1924, was the younger child of Iancu Grunberg, a prominent Jewish banker to the Romanian royal court, and his wife, Regina Rebecca Leff Grunberg. Alfred and his older sister, Rosy, lived a privileged life in Romania. Black-and-white family snapshots show the Grunberg children posing with their French and Austrian governesses and attending children's parties in a palatial family residence. In one photograph, Alfred, who appears to be six or seven, is dressed up as Mickey Mouse, after the popular Walt Disney comic strip that was first released in 1930. Although the Grunbergs were Jewish, the family was so assimilated that photographs show them posing in front of a beautifully decorated Christmas tree in their living room. Their aunt Josephine, on their mother's side, ended up joining the Catholic Church and becoming a nun.

From an early age, Alfred was extremely close to his sister Rosy. The two siblings shared a made-up language to confound their nannies, and were pretty much inseparable even as they were both sent off to the Millfield School, which was the first elite boarding school in England to become coeducational in the 1930s.

Tragedy struck the Grunbergs on November 21, 1937, when Iancu, forty-three, committed suicide while undergoing treatment for his severe depression at a hospital in Vienna. Following the death of her husband, Regina Grunberg, thirty-nine, decided to join her children in England. With a war looming in Europe, Regina packed up the house in Romania and traveled to London with the family's gold reserves. When Nazi Germany invaded Poland in the fall of 1939, the Grunbergs applied for permanent residency in England. Told that they would have to surrender their large fortune in order to stay, Regina and her teenaged children began to cast around for another country that would take them in without such a huge financial penalty. They applied for visas to the United States but were told that the wait would be long, and that there was no guarantee the American government would issue travel documents to Jews fleeing from wartorn Europe, no matter how wealthy they were. Then, as France, Belgium, the Netherlands, and England came under fierce attack by the Germans, the Grunbergs knew they were running out of time and needed to act quickly. When they managed to obtain visas to Brazil, they didn't hesitate for a moment even as the British government froze their assets after the outbreak of hostilities. In December 1940, as German bombs rained down on London during the Blitz, Regina, Rosy, and Alfred sailed from the port of Liverpool aboard the *Andalucia Star* to Rio de Janeiro.

It was a dangerous voyage and proved to be the ship's final Atlantic crossing before it was sunk by German U-boats in 1942. The Grunbergs spent much of their time at sea practicing lifeboat drills with their fellow passengers, dozens of Mormons sailing third class. Like many other moneyed refugees escaping the horrors of the war in Europe, the Grunbergs felt that the Brazilian capital was to be a temporary destination—a safe stopover, far from the battlefields and concentration camps and bombings—where they could wait in relative comfort until the U.S. visas they had applied for were issued.

But the U.S. visas never materialized and the family decided to settle permanently in Rio, which was rapidly becoming a glittering cosmopolitan city, the temporary home to a glamorous international crowd of spies, exiled royalty, and artists. They included the Austrian-Jewish writer Stefan Zweig, at the time one of the world's best-selling authors, who settled in Petropolis, a mountain town outside Rio, before committing suicide in February 1942.

After the strict confines of a British boarding school, Alfred and his sister entered an exciting new world. Alfred was sixteen, and Rosy had just turned eighteen two months before they sailed to Rio. They'd left behind the bitter damp and early darkness of an English winter, and arrived in the land of seemingly permanent summer—a tropical paradise, full of sultry women and artists and intellectuals from around the world.

While war was raging a continent away, Alfred and his sister practiced their Portuguese by volunteering at the Radio Nacional, the country's most important radio station. They helped translate the news from Europe, and later Alfred worked as a producer on other shows. They also became habitués at the Vogue nightclub—a popular spot in Copacabana founded by an Austrian refugee named Max von Stuckart. Known in Rio as the Baron, Stuckart had founded the Tour Paris nightclub in Paris, which became a regular haunt of artists, such as Pablo Picasso, and French politicians and intellectuals in the 1920s and 1930s. Like the Grunbergs, the Baron fled to Rio during the war. With the help of one of the city's wealthiest families, who were habitués of his Paris club, he founded the legendary Copacabana nightclub, whose slogan was "open from seven to seven." The Vogue rapidly became a de rigueur watering hole for the city's politicians, business leaders, and intellectuals. Many émigrés used its address—an art deco apartment block on Avenida Princesa Isabel in Copacabana—as a makeshift post office box for their correspondence from Europe. The nightclub featured some of the best black jazz artists (considered risqué in the 1940s) from the United States as well as Sacha Rubin, a Turkish pianist who played the piano with a glass of whisky next to the keyboard and a lit cigarette permanently dangling from one side of his mouth.

In the early 1950s, the club's most popular entertainer was a French singer whose stage name was Patachou. While crooning French songs, the sultry chanteuse would flirt with the male patrons, sitting on their laps and coquettishly cutting off their neckties with a pair of scissors. One night, a grandson of one of Brazil's former presidents exposed his penis in a drunken stupor and offered it up to Patachou's scissors. She politely declined, going for his tie instead.

After the club burned down on August 14, 1955, in a fire that left five people dead, Rubin opened his own bar in Copacabana, known simply as Sacha's. But although popular, the club never had quite the same mystique as the Vogue, especially as many of the politicians and intellectuals who frequented the famous nightclub began to head to Brasília, the country's new capital, in 1960.

But in the 1940s and 1950s, Rio de Janeiro must have seemed like a magical place, especially for young Romanian refugees transplanted from wartime England. Errol Flynn and Carmen Miranda regularly descended to the pool of the Copacabana Palace hotel, and Orson Welles held court at the Vogue when he arrived during the war years to work on a series of wartime propaganda films for the U.S. government.

After living in Rio for a few years, the Grunbergs could count themselves among the city's elite, many of whom lived like European royalty, attended by white-gloved butlers in their spectacular apartments overlooking Guanabara Bay. The Grunbergs were close to the Seabra family, one of Rio's prominent families at the time. The Seabras were so enamored of the Dakota apartment building on Manhattan's Central Park West that they ordered an architect to make an exact replica of it, complete with a private elevator to their ballroom, in Rio's elegant Flamengo neighborhood. The socialite Nelson Seabra, whose penthouse, with its stunning views of Sugarloaf Mountain, took up an entire floor of the family building and was filled with his collections of antique furniture and objets d'art from around the world, was also a keen collector of thoroughbred horses. He installed air-conditioned stables—a rarity in the 1940s—at the family's sprawling country home. On weekends, the Seabras flew their friends, including Rosy Grunberg, in their private airplane to their country estate for riding and elaborate parties. Later, Nelson Seabra divided his time between homes in Paris, New York, and Los Angeles. A Hollywood producer, he counted Kirk Douglas, Greta Garbo, and Grace Kelly among his closest friends. In 1980, his Red Ball birthday party in Paris attracted everyone from the Rothschilds to Andy Warhol and Mick Jagger.

Rosy and Alfred found themselves in this rarefied world of extravagance and rather loose morals. Rio's leading socialites, for example, never did their shopping in the city, but headed to Paris once a year to buy couture at Dior or Chanel. The clothes typically took three weeks to a month to be completed, and while they waited, they attended the wild soirees chez Prince Aly Khan, the Pakistani race horse owner and playboy, who married Hollywood star Rita Hayworth in 1949. During the day, these extremely well-brought-up daughters of the rich and powerful spent their time at the Café de la Paix, "doing the *trottoir*," or moonlighting as prostitutes, to amuse themselves in between fittings. "If the men were really good looking, they charged only a little bit," said one woman who was familiar with the pastime. "If they were ugly, they charged a lot."

Although he had a reputation as a bon vivant, Alfred was also determined to become a business success in his adopted country. In May 1944, four years after arriving in Rio, Alfred graduated from the Faculdade Nacional de Filosofia da Universidade do Brasil with a degree in chemical engineering. He worked as a producer at the Radio Nacional before taking a job as a technician at the Shell Mexican Oil Co. in 1945. He quickly recognized other opportunities in Brazil, a huge country with a largely untapped market for imported consumer goods. Using the Romanian gold that the Grunbergs managed to ship from England after the war, Alfred incorporated Globex Import and Export in 1946, with his mother and sister as partners. In the early days of Globex, the twenty-two-year-old entrepreneur headed out along the highway from Rio de Janeiro to Belo Horizonte hawking Firestone tires to truck drivers. Later, working from a dingy, one-room office on Winston Churchill Street in downtown Rio, he imported sewing machines and kitchen appliances.

But it was the Coldspot refrigerators imported from the United States that became his best-selling items and eventually gave rise to a chain of stores that bore their name. He began selling Coldspot, which translates as *ponto frio* in Portuguese, outside a popular movie theater before he opened his first store on Rua Uruguaiana, in the heart of the Saara, or the old Arab market, in downtown Rio. His mascot was an Antarctic penguin that had accidentally washed up on a Rio beach. Although the penguin died of heat exhaustion after a few days, Alfred had it stuffed and mounted so that he could display it in his office. Later, an artist's rendition of that unfortunate penguin would grace the company's newspaper ads and become part of the corporate logo for Ponto Frio—a symbol of the extreme cold generated by one of the company's refrigerators.

At the same time that he was laying the groundwork for what would become one of Brazil's most successful companies, Alfred decided that he needed to transform himself from a wartime Romanian refugee into a successful Latin American businessman. In 1946, Alfred and his mother embarked on the long, bureaucratic process of acquiring Brazilian citizenship, which they finally achieved in April 1948. Rosy would take a different route, applying for citizenship after marrying a Hungarian-born cameraman who had landed in Rio in 1941 to work on Orson Welles's project, *It's All True*.

A year after the Grunbergs obtained their Brazilian citizenship, mother and son applied to change their name to Monteverde, a literal Portuguese translation of Grunberg, which means "green mountain." By November 1950, the Romanian refugee Alfred Iancu Grunberg had successfully transformed himself into the Brazilian entrepreneur Alfredo João Monteverde.

"Fred was an incredible businessman with an incredible vision," said Victor Sztern, whose father was one of Alfredo's early business partners. Victor, who was in his teens when he met Alfredo, was co-opted into helping him set up a set of traffic lights in his office. A red light meant that Alfredo was thinking and his staff was prohibited from entering.

"Fred was brilliant," said Gastão Veiga. "He was the only person I knew who made money selling to the poor at discounted prices. He was also the only person I knew who could do percentages in his head."

Friends recalled that even at his summer home at Aguas Lindas, a stretch of pristine, white sand beach on Itacuruça Island, he was fond of mathematical brainteasers and absently worked on problems even while entertaining his guests.

"We'd be on his boat, and he'd be steering, and doing these incredible figures in his head, like that game Sudoku," said his friend Vera Contrucci Pinto Dias, who met Fred at Aguas Lindas when he was still in his early twenties. "There was no one like him."

A Rio newspaper referred to Alfredo as "one of the most important figures in commerce and industry." The editorial also noted that he was "an exceptional human being, a dynamic spirit," possessed of "a keen sense of accomplishment." Even decades after his death, his business associates and friends still marveled at his abilities, remembering his "violent intelligence," his constantly "buzzing" mind, and his legendary whimsy.

Alfredo's whimsy and irreverence—his "dynamic spirit"—were also legendary in Rio de Janeiro. For instance, to avoid rush-hour traffic, he bought himself an ambulance. With sirens blaring, one of Alfredo's chauffeurs would speed through stalled traffic as he reclined in the back, reading a newspaper or dictating notes to one of his secretaries. One day when the speeding ambulance was stopped by traffic police, Alfredo suggested they call his friend the governor. They did, and Alfredo was promptly released.

Once he asked a friend if he could borrow his Volkswagen camper van to transport a painting that he had bought in London. The painting, which would be arriving at the international airport in Rio, wouldn't fit in his own car. It was only when they arrived at the customs counter of the Rio airport that the friend realized that he would be driving back to the city with a priceless Van Gogh in the back of his clunky Volkswagen.

Despite his whimsy, Alfredo was a self-confessed workaholic who typically began his workday at seven in the morning and ended at eight in the evening. "I do not get tired, as I work with great pleasure—the pleasure of creation and because I love Globex as I would love my son," he wrote in a letter to his sister a few years after he founded Globex.

"Do not think if I work twelve hours a day it is to make more money," he continued in the letter. "I do this because I get so much satisfaction out of my work."

Alfredo had no qualms about rolling up his shirtsleeves and changing places with one of his sales staff on the Ponto Frio sales floor at the Rua Uruguaiana store. This way he could anticipate any problems experienced on the sales floor and deal directly with his customers. "Let's change for the day," he was fond of telling his bemused staff.

"You pretend you're me in the corporate offices, and I'll pretend to be you and deal with customers."

Most of his friends and business associates described Alfredo as a visionary. "He was talking about computers when no one talked about computers," said Sztern, who looked upon Alfredo as a substitute father after his own parents died while he was still in his teens. "He wanted to do things like recycle paper, and he wanted to create a popular bank for the poor because he sensed that Brazil was missing a popular instrument of credit."

While many of Alfredo's early clients were prosperous consumers like himself, it was among the ranks of the impoverished masses that his company was to have its greatest success. Alfredo made huge sums of money creating a system of credit for Brazil's working classes, who could not afford to buy appliances or other big-money items outright. The scheme led to a consumer revolution across the country in the days before credit cards were commonplace. It was a risk, to be sure. How could he be sure that the country's poor would ever pay off a refrigerator, which for many was as monumental as the purchase of a house or a car? It was a risk he was willing to take, for he fervently believed that the poor, so grateful to obtain credit on favorable terms, would rarely default on a payment. The poor, he was fond of saying, are better at managing credit than most people with money. Credit at Ponto Frio was easier to arrange than at banks, which charged enormous interest rates. When buyers fell behind on a payment at Ponto Frio, Alfredo simply lowered their monthly payments to an amount they could afford.

"Sometimes we had people who would come into the office and say they couldn't pay the monthly installment," said Maria Consuelo Ayres, Alfredo's first and most trusted employee, who began working for him in 1946. "He would lower the rate, and before you knew it the buyer would bring in a friend who also wanted to buy something on credit."

The installment system Alfredo pioneered in the 1950s is now commonplace in a country where the minimum wage hovers at just under $200 per month. In Brazil, prices are displayed in shop windows in multiples of the actual price, and the consumer can buy everything from clothing to appliances and cars in installments, the payment terms of which can range from five months to two years.

Laurinda Soares Navarro, Alfredo's housekeeper, was an early beneficiary of this new system of credit. Laurinda lived with her two young sons in the Parque da Cidade favela—a jumble of half-finished brick and stucco houses connected by a warren of steep stairs and concrete alleyways in the hills above Rio where hundreds of slaves had worked the coffee plantations of the Marquis de São Vicente in the nineteenth century. Like most of her impoverished neighbors—all of them squatters who had built ramshackle houses on the marquis's former estate—Laurinda had no refrigerator. Alfredo arranged for Ponto Frio to deliver a gleaming new Coldspot refrigerator to her home, and discounted the monthly payments from her salary until it was completely paid off.

Alfredo's success in business came with a well-honed sense of social responsibility. If the poor were his best customers, then Alfredo was determined to be their best friend, and give back to the community in a country with one of the world's biggest disparities between rich and poor, and an abysmal lack of government-financed social services. Shortly after founding Ponto Frio, Alfredo teamed up in Rio with a local priest who did charitable work among the city's poor, and paid to restore the Rosario Church next to his offices in downtown Rio. In one of his more memorable moments, Alfredo managed to block one of the city's main thoroughfares after he bought all the produce and livestock from a local farmers' market, and started to give it all away to the poor.

"People came from the favelas, blocking traffic and turning the day into a festive occasion," said one observer, who also recalled that law enforcement officials were not amused by the gesture. "Fred decided that the government wasn't giving the people enough holiday time, so he created his own national holiday. That was Fred."

He was also a hero to many. He was the first to step forward in August 1954 when the assassination attempt against journalist and opposition politician Carlos Lacerda resulted in the death of his bodyguard, the air force major Rubens Florentino Vaz. Although he was generally apolitical, Alfredo had a great deal of admiration for Lacerda, who was the most outspoken critic of the government of Brazilian dictator Getúlio Vargas. Alfredo insisted upon paying for the education of the young daughter Vaz had left behind.

The assassination attempt against Lacerda, on a residential street in Copacabana, had deep political ramifications for the Vargas government. A few weeks later, an independent commission of inquiry implicated Vargas's chief bodyguard in the death of Vaz, which eventually signaled the end of the dictator's twenty-four-year reign and drove Vargas himself to commit suicide. In his blue and white striped pajamas, the country's president shot himself in the chest in his bedroom at the presidential palace on August 24, 1954. Alfredo promptly stepped in again, this time to buy the dictator's Rolls-Royce.

There were other grand gestures. In 1961, Alfredo set up a fund to help the families whose loved ones had been killed when an arsonist set fire to a circus, resulting in more than four hundred deaths. Three years later, he bailed out Garrincha (Manuel Francisco dos Santos), one of Brazil's greatest soccer heroes, who helped lead Brazil to two World Cup victories in 1958 and 1962. Garrincha, who was in serious debt, was in danger of losing his home on Governador Island, on the outskirts of Rio. Alfredo paid off his debts, in recognition, he said, of Garrincha's contribution to Brazilian soccer.

He also created a private foundation to assist his workers, who grew from a handful of employees in the late 1940s to several hundred twenty years later.

At the Millfield School, his posh alma mater, in Somerset, England, Alfredo's generosity even made the local papers when, on a visit to the school, he bought £2,500 worth of tickets for a student production of the Sammy Davis Jr. musical *Golden Boy*. Funds from the sale of tickets were earmarked for the school's building fund. "Up rushed . . . Alfredo Monteverde, the Brazilian millionaire, who said he proposed to distribute the tickets among 'French students, Kenyan emigrants, nurses and the doorman at the Dorchester,' " said one report. "But really you didn't know whether to take the man seriously or not. Asked where he lived, he said 'The Moon.' "

Alfredo could be excused for his lunar preoccupations, especially after he was diagnosed with manic depression as a young adult. From the time he was in his twenties, his periods of whimsy and sheer euphoria alternated with periods of deep, dark depression. During one euphoric state, Alfredo tried to convince his accountant to allow Globex to buy forty homes for Ponto Frio workers. Maria Consuelo, his savvy secretary who was by then used to her boss's sudden acts of extravagance with company money, did not allow the deal to go through. However, other more costly ones did.

"I spent a lot of time undoing Fred's whims," said Ademar Trotte, the Ponto Frio accountant Alfredo hired in 1946 when he started the company. "When he went on a shopping spree, we had to convince people to give us his money back, or we had to re-sell the things Fred bought."

Alfredo went on mad shopping sprees for things like mills, warehouses, and large plots of land when he was in his euphoric states, and then would sink into a soul-crushing depression when he realized what he had done. On many occasions, when the deals became too complicated for his secretary or accountant to fix, Geraldo Mattos, the director of Ponto Frio, would be called in to try to clean up the mess. At one point, in an act of extreme folly, Alfredo handed over all of his own shares in his company to Geraldo.

"Geraldo had a difficult time trying to fix things up when Fred went shopping," recalled Lourdes Mattos, Geraldo's widow. "I think

Geraldo spent an awful lot of time just repairing the damage from those flights of euphoria."

But as bad as his depressions became, observers say they never seriously affected his ability to do business. "There was no one like him in business," said Marcelo Steinfeld. "Nobody could have ever put together the fortune he did so fast, even with all his psychological problems." Indeed, in just over twenty years, Alfredo built a sizable empire, with property and assets spread around the world.

By the late 1960s, Alfredo Monteverde had a staggering net worth of nearly $300 million. Although he had a long list of business interests in Rio, his most successful enterprise remained Ponto Frio.

But when his depressions became overwhelming, Alfredo was indeed forced to retreat temporarily from the daily responsibilities of running his businesses. Friends say that during one of those early bouts of depression, he tried to commit suicide. Regina knew that her son suffered from the same malady that had plagued his father, and she often told Alfredo that she feared he would end up killing himself if he didn't get the proper treatment.

During his worst crises, Alfredo checked himself into a luxurious suite at the beachfront Excelsior hotel or the nearby Copacabana Palace where a steady stream of specialists were admitted by his majordomo Caruso, who was dispatched to the local pharmacy with a small stack of prescriptions for antidepressants, vitamins, and sleeping pills, hastily scrawled on hotel stationery. In the early days, Rosy would fly into Rio from wherever she happened to be in the world, to help her beloved brother through his darkest hours. But later, when she was preoccupied with her own business and demands on her time, Alfredo was left pretty much to the mercy of his various psychiatrists and closest business associates when a depression struck. On occasion, a nurse would visit to give him regular injections of vitamins B_{12} and C, which were considered an early form of therapy for manic-depressives.

For despite his phenomenal success in business, there was always something missing in Alfredo's life—something money could never buy. In a letter to his sister written in the summer of 1956, Alfredo tried to come to grips with his depression when he wrote, "we really make little progress in finding our happiness. When I came back from [a trip to] the States I did everything to fill my life—worked hard, played hard, but of no use for I was unhappy inside of myself. I thought that it was my old spring disease that came again."

Perhaps it was the "spring disease"—a deep dissatisfaction with himself and those around him—that was to blame for the string of wives and girlfriends he seemed to collect over the years, like the mills and factories and plots of land he recklessly snapped up for Globex. The patterns rarely changed—the manic womanizing seeming to coincide with his periods of utter euphoria. He would fall madly in love with a beautiful woman, live with her for anywhere from a few months to a few years, and then send her packing.

"The women arrived at Fred's house with a suitcase, but they always left with an apartment, a car, whatever they needed," recalled his sister. "He always took care of them."

While still in his twenties, he became involved with Sylvia Bastos Tigre, a woman from one of Rio's most important legal families, who was nearly double his own age. Typically, he was enamored with her during the first several months of their courtship. Unlike the two others, who would come later, Alfredo did not marry Sylvia.

"Sylvia is wonderful," he noted in an undated letter to Rosy. "She does all to please me and help me. What she possesses, and nowadays is a rare jewel, is goodness [sic]."

Sylvia, who was extremely well connected in Rio society, encouraged him to behave like the important Brazilian entrepreneur he was on his way to becoming. She convinced him to buy a yacht and a vacation home at Aguas Lindas and join the important clubs in the city.

But the relationship didn't withstand the "spring disease," and Alfredo impetuously ended everything in a moment of depression. "We never understood Fred's attraction to Sylvia," said his friend and former employee Maria Luisa Goldschmid. "We thought it was some kind of strange mother complex because Sylvia was old enough to be his mother."

Aviva Pe'er, who had been crowned Miss Israel in June 1954, seemed more like the type of woman for Alfredo. At least she seemed to be willing to put up with Alfredo's zanier moments. On New Year's Eve, he invited Aviva and his friend Maria Luisa to a hotel bar in downtown Rio following the annual Ponto Frio party. It was three in the morning, and instead of leaving his car outside, he decided to drive it through the wide open doors of the hotel lobby. Alfredo parked the car, calmly gave the keys to the startled concierge, and headed in the direction of the bar with his shocked entourage.

"Fred drove right through reception," recalled Maria Luisa, adding that his actions were not the result of an overindulgence in alcohol. "It was just Fred. This was the kind of thing he loved to do. Of course, it caused all sorts of confusion. The police were called, and Fred had to pay a huge fine. But we all had a great time."

In 1955, following his dalliance with Miss Israel, he married a woman named Zani Roxo in New York, only to divorce her less than a year later in Florida.

Marie Paule Flore Delebois, a pretty Frenchwoman whose mother Charlotte had worked for the French Resistance during the war, was next. Alfredo fell in love with Scarlett, as she was known in Rio because of her flaming red hair, and flew her to New York where he married her in a civil ceremony in July 1959. A year later, the couple adopted an infant girl and boy, both of whom had been abandoned at a local orphanage on the outskirts of Rio de Janeiro. A case of adulthood mumps had made Alfredo sterile. But the marriage didn't last. "Fred fell in love with an image, and the image didn't quite correspond to reality," said his sister Rosy, referring to his breakup with Scarlett.

In February 1962, the marriage to Scarlett was annulled. At the time of the breakup Scarlett agreed to custody of the little girl, Alexandra. Mother and daughter left Brazil for good, and took up their new lives in France. Alfredo, a newly single father, was left with the son, Carlos.

Single again, Alfredo headed back into his familiar nightly routine. He frequented Sacha's in Copacabana and hosted all-night poker games at his beachfront penthouse, which was considered the largest apartment in Rio at the time with over 10,000 square feet of space and stunning views of the ocean on the city's fabled Avenida Atlantica, next to the elegant Copacabana Palace hotel.

"We'd be playing poker at his penthouse on Avenida Atlantica when a little after midnight Caruso would put out this magnificent buffet feast that was simply fantastic," said Alfredo's friend Al Abitbol, a French émigré, who began to build his clothing empire in Rio at the same time that Alfredo started Ponto Frio.

"He was a crazy genius," said his friend Marcelo Steinfeld, who recalled how Alfredo once lost $200,000 at a poker game. "In those days, that was a staggering amount of money. Alfredo got up and calmly informed his opponents that he would indeed pay out what he owed, but he insisted upon doing it at the local police station. Of course, after that, everyone just begged off and told him not to worry, that it was just a game, after all."

After his failed marriage to Scarlett, the handsome thirty-eight-year-old businessman once again became Rio de Janeiro's most eligible playboy.

"Every woman in Rio turned her head when Seu Alfredo walked by," recalled Alvaro Pães, a flower vendor who managed the large flower market below Alfredo's office on the Rua do Rosario—Ponto Frio's new headquarters in the 1960s. "He was rich and he was good looking, and he had what every woman wanted. He knew how to make them crazy."

Although he could have any woman he desired in Rio, true happiness eluded him. "He talked in riddles about his life," said Alvaro. "It was as if he was searching for something he couldn't find."

Alvaro didn't get involved in Alfredo's personal problems although he always knew when he was in the grips of a new romance. For Alvaro, it always coincided with the times that Alfredo ordered copious amounts of flowers. He ordered yellow roses for his third wife—the blonde divorcée Alvaro knew only from a distance as the elegant Dona Lily.

"He was in love, but then he was always in love," said Alvaro. It's true that Alfredo often wore his heart on his sleeve.

In his euphoric states, Alfredo would drive up to the flower market, throw the keys of his car to Alvaro, and tell him he could take the car wherever he wanted, provided it was back by the time he needed to drive home at the end of the day. Some days, he would invite Alvaro up to his office for coffee and chocolate. The two would talk about politics and listen to music.

Ironically, just as he sensed his life spinning out of control, Alfredo would take up his favorite samba. "Everything is in its place / Thank God, thank God," he used to sing out loud to Alvaro. "When I come home from work / I say to God, many thanks / I sing samba the whole night / And on Sundays and holidays."

The harmony celebrated in the samba he loved so much would elude Alfredo for the rest of his life. It was not available to him at any price.

YET HE SEEMED so happy in February 1965 when he walked out of the Office of the City Clerk in lower Manhattan with his beautiful new bride on his arm. In fact, friends recalled that he was deliriously happy after the marriage to Lily Watkins Cohen. Alfredo celebrated their wedding by taking Lily to the French jeweler Boucheron and buying one of the biggest diamond rings in the store.

In the early days of their marriage, they acted like a happy, upper-class family. The four children—Alfredo's adopted son, Carlos, and Lily's two sons and daughter—were enrolled in good schools in Rio, and Lily hosted wonderful dinner parties for family and friends. Most weekends, the Monteverde clan headed to Alfredo's summer retreat at Aguas Lindas, where they went sailing and snorkeling.

In a family portrait taken of Lily and the children soon after their marriage, Lily is the very picture of the well-to-do matron—slim and smiling, with perfectly coiffed hair, a fashionable silk foulard tied loosely around her neck—surrounded by four beautiful children.

For her part, Lily was relieved to be back in Rio, which was decidedly more cosmopolitan than Montevideo, a quiet backwater where it was nearly impossible to find a Parisian-trained hairdresser and a good bottle of champagne, among other luxuries she could now simply never do without.

Alfredo appeared to be a dream come true. Not only was he handsome and a good father to her children, he was one of the richest men in Brazil. With Alfredo, Lily was living the fairy tale she had dreamed of as a teenager at the Colegio Anglo-Americano. Now they not only vacationed in South America, but Alfredo took her on expensive tours of Switzerland, Italy, and France. She could now shop in Paris and New York, and lounge on the French Riviera. When Lily complained to him that she had little to do during the long, hot afternoons in Rio, he helped her launch a boutique in the most elegant part of Copacabana, next to the Metro Theater and a few blocks from the Copacabana Palace hotel where Lily now frequented the hotel's lavish hair salon several times a week.

"We set up the store as part of Fred's larger company," said Trotte, the accountant. "It was a diversion for Lily."

The store was named Galati, after the city in Romania where Alfredo was born. It sold only the finest Baccarat crystal from France, imported jewelry, and other objets d'art.

"She had the best of everything in her store," said her friend Vera Contrucci Dias. "But it wasn't really a serious business. It was just something Alfredo had opened for her so that she had something to do during the afternoons."

Although the store became a favorite haunt of Rio's young social-ites, Lily and Alfredo were never part of the elite crowd in the city. "They were never among the first team," said Danuza Leão, who has chronicled Rio society for years. "Of course, everyone knew who Al-fredo Monteverde was, but he didn't frequent any of the high-society events. Lily and Fred weren't exactly boldface names in those days."

With four young children to raise and a rich man's house to run, perhaps the pretty debutante in the white organdy dress at the CIB balls in the 1950s was now simply too busy to worry about high so-ciety. Moreover, Alfredo was not the kind of man who cared about appearing in the social columns, even though many of his friends in Rio belonged to the city's richest and most prominent families.

Indeed, Lily seems to have been too wrapped up with more mun-dane things, like shopping, to work on her entrance into high society. That would come much later.

Like Mario, her first husband, Alfredo quickly learned about his new wife's extravagance. Alfredo could never understand why Lily insisted upon ordering bottles of champagne from Le Bec Fin, then Rio's finest French restaurant, rather than just buy them directly from the liquor store, which charged significantly less. Or why she would order the restaurant's elaborate French meals and try to pass them off as her own creation. In a society where servants were plentiful, and wealthy women like Lily were rarely judged by their husbands on their cooking or housekeeping abilities, Alfredo could never figure out why Lily tried so hard to make herself into the perfect house-wife.

"She had this geisha complex," said one of her acquaintances from the 1960s. "She went out of her way to please men."

In Rio, they had busy social lives that revolved around their chil-dren and friends, even if they were far removed from the grand soi-rees and balls that Lily would have loved to attend. Alfredo's weekly poker games continued, complete with the midnight feasts, this time orchestrated by Lily, with a little help from the French chefs at Le Bec Fin, who also helped her organize sumptuous dinner parties at the Monteverde residence.

It was to one of those dinners that Alfredo invited his friends, the Safra banking brothers—Joseph and Moise. Together with their older brother, Edmond, they had set up their banking business in São Paulo. Edmond now spent most of his time in Geneva, running his Trade Development Bank.

Edmond Safra was well-known to Alfredo, and Brazil's other wealthy Jews. He was the banker they sought out when they wanted to hide money offshore, far from the reach of Brazil's military dictatorship. According to his business associates, Alfredo was among the biggest depositors at Edmond's bank in Switzerland and also did business with the Safra Bank in São Paulo.

In addition to the soirees she organized for Alfredo's business associates and the couple's friends in Rio, Lily was also much admired for her children's parties, complete with magicians, clowns, and crowds of happy children. "She threw these great parties for the kids," said Maria Luisa, who later moved to the United States after her marriage to a fellow Ponto Frio employee in Rio. "It was Lily who gave my daughter her first Barbie."

In addition to her hostess skills, Lily also tried to be supportive of Alfredo, especially when he was in the grips of a terrible depression. At one point, in an effort to show solidarity with her husband, Lily checked herself into the exclusive São Vicente Clinic in Rio's upscale Gavea neighborhood for a sleeping cure, which was a popular form of therapy for mild depression in the 1960s. Alfredo, who was deeply concerned that his new wife was suffering from depression, decided to surprise her when she arrived at the clinic. He loaded his car with a hammer, some nails, and the couple's Van Gogh that he had asked a friend to transport from the international airport in a Volkswagen camper van. He took seventeen-year-old Victor Sztern with him to help him hang the painting in her room.

"He could move heaven and earth for the people he loved," said Sztern, who recalled looking over his shoulder to keep hospital personnel out of the room while Alfredo hammered the nail into the wall of the hospital room and put up the Van Gogh. "He just wanted to surprise Lily, to make sure that even for the short time she was going to be in the hospital she would be happy."

Although she eagerly encouraged her new husband's indulgences, especially when they involved gifts of exquisite jewelry, Lily was guarded about her own extravagances and never told her second husband what she regularly spent, especially on clothing—her passion. Perhaps she worried that Alfredo would react in much the same way Mario had reacted when she spent thousands on lingerie.

"Money was just paper to her," recalled Abitbol, who owns an upscale chain of boutiques called Elle et Lui in Rio. "Lily was my best customer. She would go into my stores and buy ten or fifteen dresses, at about $200 each."

Although he was thrilled with his best customer's shopping habits, Abitbol also felt extremely uncomfortable about the terms. "'Don't tell Fred.' That's what she always said to me," recalled Abitbol. "It was always our little secret how much of Fred's money she spent."

After one of Lily's afternoon shopping sprees at one of his boutiques, Abitbol found himself dining with Alfredo and Lily the same evening. He was surprised to see that Lily was not wearing any of her latest purchases from his store.

"Didn't you like any of the dresses you bought?" asked Abitbol, in a whisper, while Alfredo was out of earshot.

Lily replied that she was going to give all the dresses she had bought to her friends. Lily's generosity and her good breeding were well known in the couple's social circle. In the late 1960s Alfredo asked his architect to sell a piece of beachfront property that he owned in the

Ipanema neighborhood. The architect, Fernando Pinto Dias, managed to sell the property for well above the asking price. It was Lily who insisted that Alfredo pay Fernando a commission on the sale of the property.

"Fernando didn't even think of charging them a commission, but it was Lily who insisted that Alfredo treat him fairly," said Vera, Fernando's wife, and a good friend of the Monteverdes at the time. "Lily was extremely well brought up, and she was always thinking of others."

Even Alfredo's mother, the domineering matriarch Regina, was extremely fond of her new daughter-in-law at first. "Regina always said that Fred needed a good woman, and that Lily seemed to care about him and could help him when he was sick," recalled Masha Monterosa, Regina's friend and bridge partner in Rio.

Many of the couple's friends at the time agreed. "We finally thought that Fred had found the best woman for him when he married Lily," said Maria Luisa. "She was very sweet. She had her feet firmly planted on the ground, and she had Fred's total trust."

But she didn't have it for long. Barely three years into their marriage, Alfredo started to have serious doubts about Lily, according to friends and business associates. Maybe it was those elaborate French dinners, prepared by someone else.

Despite what appeared to be a happy married life, there were tensions. Lily could never quite understand the close relationship that Alfredo enjoyed with his sister, even though Rosy spent most of her time abroad in New York and Italy after she divorced her first husband.

Whenever brother and sister were together, Lily felt like a complete outsider, recalled Rosy. Sometimes they used the secret language they had invented as children in Romania, confounding whoever happened to be in their presence.

Their preferred mode of entry into the Ritz hotel in Paris or the Dorchester in London was by pretending to lean on a flower. Alfredo and his sister would drive up to the entrance in a Rolls-Royce, wait for a doorman to open the car door and, feigning great fatigue, they would lean on a lily or a rose and enter the building, laughing later at the incredulous expressions on the faces of the hotel staff.

During one such surreal exchange between Rosy and Alfredo in Paris, Lily had been so exasperated by their antics and role-playing that Alfredo took pity on her and ducked into Boucheron to buy her an exquisite diamond ring to make amends.

But while he indulged Lily with expensive surprises, he also loved to indulge his sister. He once wrapped a square-cut blue white diamond ring in crumpled toilet paper and tossed it carelessly on Rosy's coffee table at her apartment in New York.

Throughout Alfredo's life, Rosy remained his most important confidante. "Rosy dear, as usual I am filling a whole letter about me," Alfredo wrote to his sister in one of the frequent letters he sent to her in New York and Italy, alternating between English, Portuguese, and sometimes Romanian. "Forgive my selfishness but somehow I feel like telling you how I feel."

The relationship between brother and sister was troublesome to Lily, said one family friend, who did not want to be identified. "Lily was clearly jealous of Rosy," she said. "She tried to outdo Rosy when it came to everything. If Rosy had redecorated her apartment in New York, then Lily would come up with the same color scheme to redecorate the family home in Rio."

It's not clear whether Lily took her cue from her sister-in-law when she insisted that she needed to hire an architect and interior designer to redo their new home in Rio de Janeiro. Shortly after marrying Lily, Alfredo gave up his stunning penthouse in Copacabana and bought a sprawling modern house on a leafy residential street, with a garden in the back for the children and their dogs. The Monteverdes moved into the house at 96 Rua Icatu, in an exclusive hilltop neighborhood in Rio, in 1968, after the home had undergone extensive renovations overseen by Lily and their architect Fernando. The house was deceptively small at its rather demure front entrance, which was partially hidden by tropical foliage. A visitor had to drive farther up Rua Icatu, a winding road that snaked up a mountain, to appreciate the home's full size. The bottom floor featured floor-to-ceiling windows in the sunken living room and a tremendous view onto the tropical garden in the back. Guests enjoying an afternoon glass of champagne in the living room had a view of lush foliage, lilac and white orchids, and flaming pink hyacinth. The tranquillity and quiet were so complete that guests might be forgiven for thinking that they were lounging at a country retreat far from the urban chaos of Rio de Janeiro. On the second floor, where the bedrooms were located, Alfredo helped design a large office that led into the master bedroom suite, where a large picture window overlooked the garden.

After the final renovations were complete, Alfredo did not want to stop. He set out to create an annex to the property so that he could house his household staff. Unlike most of his peers, Alfredo was extremely dedicated to his staff. Shortly after moving in, he confessed to his housekeeper Laurinda that he had bought a vacant plot of land near the Icatu house. He wanted to expand the house, he said, and construct separate quarters to accommodate more live-in servants.

"I want to be able to walk a short distance when I need to talk to you," he told Laurinda, with a wink, ducking into the kitchen, as he did on most days, to sample the meals the servants cooked for themselves.

"Seu Alfredo ate filet mignon, but he loved the poor people's food," said Laurinda, recalling how Alfredo would savor the smell of a steaming pot of bean stew in the kitchen.

On weekends, Alfredo took the children, along with Laurinda's two boys, Adilson and Ademir, to the Rio Yacht Club or the exclusive Caiçaras Club in the city's upscale Lagoa neighborhood.

"Seu Alfredo treated everyone like part of the family," recalled Laurinda. "Everyone loved him."

But as it turned out, not everyone was enamored of Alfredo Monteverde.

For one thing, the rich man who was so kind to his household servants could also act with swift brutality when confronted with their disloyalty. About a year after moving into the Icatu house, Alfredo fired one of his longtime servants. Anita was a single mother from the impoverished northeastern state of Bahia. While Alfredo and Lily were away on vacation in Europe in June 1969 Anita had been put in charge of the house. She was to allow Laurinda and the other servants in to maintain the property. But Anita, who was not well-liked by the others who worked in the house, refused. When the Monteverdes returned and the house was dirty, Anita blamed it on the others, saying that they had not appeared while the family was away on vacation.

Laurinda had nothing but contempt for Anita, who often lit candles and made strange offerings to the Afro-Brazilian gods (known as *orixas*) in the black-magic (known as macumba) ceremonies that she had brought from her home in Bahia. "I told her, Anita stop smoking up the house with your spells, but she just kept on doing it," said Laurinda.

Anita's lies to her employers about the other servants were the last straw for Laurinda, who also accused Anita of trying to turn the children against her. Feeling cornered, Laurinda left the house on Icatu without a word to her employer, who was at his offices downtown. When Alfredo heard of the resignation of his favorite housekeeper, he drove to the Parque da Cidade favela to find out what had happened. Laurinda was livid. When he tried to convince her to return to work, Laurinda told him that she refused to work alongside Anita. She related the black magic and the duplicity, but Alfredo wasn't listening. He opened the door of his convertible and sped to his house to get rid of Anita, whom he fired on the spot. He gave her five months' wages, and five minutes to collect her things and leave the house.

Anita, who moved slowly at the best of times, took her time, and before she left the house, she may have taken her revenge on her boss. After Anita left, the servants discovered Alfredo's favorite shirt—white with pink stripes—which had been hanging to dry in the small outside area near the servants' quarters. The shirt was tied over and over again with twine and hidden under the wash basin.

"If I'm not staying, no one else is going to stay in this house," said Anita in a menacing tone to the other servants as she walked through the kitchen and climbed the garden stairs to the servants' entrance through the garage.

Coincidentally, Anita's ouster occurred simultaneously with Alfredo's decision to get rid of Lily.

"Tell me," he said to Maria Consuelo Ayres, his closest confidante at Ponto Frio. "How do you go about separating from your wife or husband?"

Maria Consuelo was used to such hypothetical, third-person questions from her unpredictable boss whenever he was having difficulties in his personal life, and knew it signaled the end of a romantic relationship. However, she does recall being a little bit surprised that Alfredo, whose ability to marry and divorce seemed to come so easily, was seeking marital advice from her. She knew right away that he was having trouble at home. Calmly, she told him that if one is indeed having marital problems, one must discuss them calmly with one's spouse. Maria Consuelo put the conversation out of her mind and assumed that all was well when Alfredo, Lily, and Alfredo's mother, Regina, took off on their European holiday in the summer of 1969. But when he returned, Alfredo matter-of-factly informed Maria Consuelo that her advice had not worked.

"By the way, what you said about calm, rational discussion," said Alfredo during the course of a business day. "It didn't work."

The crisis in his personal life became so overwhelming that he mentioned it to several friends, family members, and business associates. "Fred commented to my husband that he wanted to separate from

Lily," said Lourdes Mattos, referring to a conversation that Alfredo had had with her husband, Geraldo, Ponto Frio's chief director.

For his part, Geraldo was also used to such pronouncements from his boss, and when he heard nothing further, he assumed that Alfredo and Lily had ironed out whatever differences they had, said Lourdes. Besides, at the time, Alfredo was on so much medication to treat his depression that Geraldo assumed that he wasn't thinking straight.

Alfredo also must have confided his marital difficulties to his mother, who told her bridge partner that all was not well with Lily. "Shortly before Fred died Regina told me that she was completely wrong about Lily," said Masha. "She said, 'That's not a marriage for Fred.'"

Alfredo had also spoken to his accountant about an imminent divorce. "I didn't really deal with Fred's personal tax matters," said Trotte. "But as the divorce would involve issues directly affecting Ponto Frio, he told me that he and Lily would need to make some financial arrangements, pending their divorce."

But other than his family and closest business associates, few others knew anything about their imminent divorce. They didn't fight or raise their voices, at least not in front of the servants.

Perhaps Lily was hoping that Alfredo would change his mind. After all, most of her family now depended upon Ponto Frio for their income. Her brother Artigas Watkins worked as a security guard at a Ponto Frio warehouse when the Watkins family's business fell apart after Wolf's death in 1962. Her mother, Annita, and the other Watkins siblings also had their expenses paid for by Ponto Frio, said Trotte, who included the Watkins family's expenses in Ponto Frio's accounts. "It was a bit of creative accounting when it came to the Watkins family's expenses," said Trotte. "We received their bills, and we charged them to the company as expenses."

But below stairs, the hired help only found out that things were not well with their boss when they found Alfredo's cursed shirt. It was

Nelly, the maid who worked with Laurinda at Icatu, who found the striped dress shirt.

When Nelly showed Laurinda the shirt, she knew immediately that some kind of macumba curse had been put on her boss. Laurinda doused the shirt in hot water and cut the twine.

"But it was the wrong thing to do," recalled Laurinda with great regret many years later. "Hot water only makes the curse stronger. I should have put cold water and salt on it to kill whatever macumba curse had been put on Seu Alfredo. But I did the wrong thing. I made the curse stronger."

THREE

"She Behaved Beautifully"

THE NIGHT BEFORE Alfredo Monteverde died, Laurinda dreamed that she had fallen down the main staircase at the redbrick house on Rua Icatu. It was Alfredo himself—tall and handsome, in his pin-stripe suit and his favorite pink and white striped shirt, smelling of sandalwood—who rushed to her rescue in the dream. "Did you hurt yourself?" he asked her, staring intently into her eyes. But before she could answer him, she woke up crying.

"When you wake up crying from a dream, it always means death," said Laurinda. "The dream told me that Seu Alfredo was going to die. It couldn't have been clearer what was about to happen."

On the morning of Monday, August 25, 1969, Laurinda woke at dawn, prepared her children for school, and set off from her modest home in the hillside shantytown where she lived. By the time she hopped on the series of crowded buses that would take her to Alfredo's home, Laurinda had forgotten about the terrible dream that presaged the death of her beloved boss.

Icatu, a sleepy residential stretch of road that curls up a mountain, is surrounded by lush tropical forest in Rio's Humaita neighborhood. There are brightly painted colonial-style homes at the foot of the

street, but the farther you climb into the forest, the grander the homes
and gardens.

In the early mornings when the street is quiet, tiny tamarind monkeys, their long tails dangling beneath them, dart out of trees, balancing themselves like skilled tightrope walkers on overhead electrical
wires. For a split second at a time, they seem to stare in rapt attention,
their small bulging eyes scanning any passersbys who have stopped
to catch their breath in midclimb before attempting the last steep in-
cline to number 96.

On that fateful Monday morning, the monkeys didn't stray from
their routine. In the silence of the early morning, they startled Laurinda with their chatter as she climbed the last, steepest part of the hill.
Catching her breath, the diminutive, roly-poly housekeeper stood to
watch them gathering bits of rotted papaya and banana. Then she
rounded a corner and headed into the cul de sac high above the street
where the servants' entrance was located through the garage at the
back of the Monteverde house.

Looking back, Laurinda couldn't remember anything amiss. When
she reached the back of the house, Waldomiro Alves, the gardener,
already had the garage door open and was cleaning the interior of
Alfredo's car—a white 1966 Oldsmobile convertible with red leather
seats. Laurinda waved to Waldomiro as she headed down the steep
set of stairs that took her through the lush garden with its caged macaws. She patted Barbarella and Sarama, the two Irish wolfhounds, as
she walked towards the servants' part of the house, off the kitchen.

Laurinda nearly collided with her boss. In his charcoal gray pin-
stripe suit, neatly pressed white striped shirt, and striped black and
brown tie, he was heading up the garden stairs, taking them two at a
time, and humming the melody of his favorite samba: "Everything is
in its place / Thank God, thank God / We shouldn't forget to say /
Thank God, thank God."

Rushing up the stairs after her husband was Dona Lily, blonde and
elegant even in her bathrobe, which opened slightly as she ran to re-

veal a silky nightgown. As she did most mornings, Lily accompanied Alfredo to his car to kiss him goodbye. Laurinda didn't actually see them kiss that morning, and for about a split second she wondered why Dona Lily was running after her boss, rather than walking by his side, as she usually did. But then she heard the car speed away and saw Lily walk back down the stairs and head back to the bedroom. She didn't give it another thought.

It was 7:30 a.m., and time for Laurinda to change into her maid's uniform and begin her work.

However, Laurinda did recall that there were a few things amiss on that fateful Monday morning. For one thing, the children didn't go to school. Lily informed her that she was taking her children to the Copacabana Palace hotel for the day to see their father, who had recently arrived from Buenos Aires. Alfredo's son, Carlinhos, as he was known to Laurinda, would stay behind at the house.

After Lily and the children left for the hotel with the chauffeur, Lily's brother Artigas dropped by in the late morning, lounging in the garden.

"Seu Artigas was at the house for a very long time," said Laurinda, adding that it was not unusual for members of Lily's family to drop by unannounced. "I brought him juice, coffee, and water."

Despite this unexpected visitor and the enforced school holiday, everything else appeared to be in its place at 96 Rua Icatu on the day Alfredo Monteverde died.

ALFREDO WAS IN good spirits when he arrived at his offices in downtown Rio, recalled Maria Consuelo. "He wasn't in one of his depressions," she said. After twenty-three years of working alongside Alfredo, Maria Consuelo was familiar with the silence and irritability that always seemed to accompany one of those rapid downward spirals.

Shortly after arriving, Alfredo disappeared into a lengthy business meeting with his chief executive Geraldo, but before he did, he asked Maria Consuelo to make reservations at the Copacabana Palace hotel for lunch. He would be dining with Lily, and her first husband, Mario, he told her. He wanted to discuss what would happen to Lily's three children after they divorced. In the four years that he had been married to Lily, he and Carlinhos had grown very attached to Claudio, Eduardo, and Adriana. He wanted to maintain a relationship with the children, and needed to make arrangements with Lily and their father.

"He told my husband that he was having lunch with Lily that day to discuss the fate of her children," said Lourdes Mattos, Geraldo's widow. "In fact, this was the whole purpose of the lunch." At the meeting with Geraldo, Alfredo discussed plans for opening several more stores, recalled Lourdes.

Most of Alfredo's executive team at Ponto Frio knew that he was planning to divorce Lily. He had also confided his intention to Rosy, and on the weekend before he died he had made plans to join her at her home in Italy for a short holiday.

But if he was at all worried about the lunch with Lily and Mario, he wasn't showing it. Shortly after arriving at the Copacabana Palace hotel at midday, Alfredo bumped into his friend Michael von Lichnowsky, the personal assistant to Octavio Guinle, then the owner of the hotel. Von Lichnowsky later told Rosy that Alfredo emerged from the newspaper stand at the hotel, joking and brandishing a copy of the latest *Time* magazine. He wasn't the least bit anxious or depressed, Von Lichnowsky told Rosy.

Still, lunch must have been a tense affair for Lily, who was not in agreement about the divorce. "I know that Lily did not accept the divorce," said Maria Consuelo. "Lily didn't want to separate from Fred."

Indeed, Lily, who had spent her life trying to land a rich man, was now faced with the prospect of losing everything. No good could come of this divorce for Lily and her entire family.

Although they were by no means destitute after Wolf's company folded, the Watkinses relied on their monthly stipends from Ponto Frio to continue the comfortable lifestyle to which they had all become accustomed when Wolf's business was at its most profitable during the Second World War.

While it is not clear what took place at the luncheon, Alfredo seems to have emerged from the meeting with a headache. Instead of heading straight back to work, he decided to return home for a short nap. Alfredo appears to have headed straight for the second-floor master suite, and told one of the servants to wake him at three in the afternoon, which would allow him enough time to return downtown for an afternoon business meeting.

Alfredo was so tired that he didn't bother to change his clothes when he reached the bedroom. He removed his jacket and his shoes, pushed aside the satin-covered pillows Lily was so fond of clustering on the bed, and appears to have casually flipped through the pages of *Time* before drifting off to sleep, according to police reports.

Downstairs, the servants had gathered in the kitchen for a hearty lunch of rice, beans, and manioc. Their animated conversation, and the transistor radio, which played the latest sambas, must have drowned out the two loud pops on the second floor when the gun was fired.

Alfredo was already dead by the time Laurinda began calling the extension in the master suite.

"I thought he had a headache and had gone upstairs to lie down," said Laurinda. "But I knew when he didn't answer the phone that something bad had happened." It was just after three in the afternoon when Laurinda began to make the calls to the private extension in Alfredo's bedroom. Moments before Laurinda began to call the extension, Lily had called to say she was still at the Copacabana Palace hotel, just finishing up with Alain, her hairdresser.

Where was Seu Alfredo? Lily asked. Laurinda didn't find the question strange. Whenever she went out to the hairdresser or to her boutique in the afternoons, Lily called the servants to tell them where she would be, just in case someone needed to speak to her. She sometimes did this several times a day. Lily had already called his secretary Maria Consuelo, who had told her that he was expected back at the office for a meeting.

Laurinda only knew he had retreated to his bedroom for a nap because Djanira Nascimento, one of the other housekeepers, had seen him arrive. Laurinda found it strange that he had not come through the servants' quarters as he usually did to have a chat.

After repeated attempts to reach Alfredo on the telephone, Laurinda walked up the stairs, through the second-floor office and hallway alcove, and knocked loudly on the door.

"Seu Alfredo? Seu Alfredo? Are you there?"

No answer.

What was he doing in his locked bedroom? Had he mixed his medications with the Mandrax that he was so fond of taking, especially when he needed a deep sleep? Mandrax, a powerful sedative, was initially marketed as a sleeping pill but became extremely popular as a recreational drug in the 1960s and 1970s, especially in Brazil. The drug, which was a precursor to Quaaludes, could send the user into euphoric states. One pill a day for a month was likely to cause physical dependence, severe headaches, irritability, and mania. Alfredo, of course, suffered from all of those symptoms, and the Mandrax, upon which he had become so dependent, seemed to exacerbate all his physical and mental problems.

Laurinda knew firsthand the effects of Mandrax. When she was having trouble sleeping, she decided to help herself to a bottle from Alfredo's collection. One pill had been enough to convince her that nothing good could come of taking the drug. The Mandrax knocked her out so completely that days before his death, she flushed the rest of the pills that she had swiped from his bedside table down the toilet.

"When Seu Alfredo had one of his headaches, he didn't talk to anyone," said Laurinda. "He just went upstairs to lie down. I thought he must have been suffering from another headache, or he had fallen asleep."

When Alfredo was in the grip of one of his headaches, the servants were warned to tread lightly, the caged macaws in the garden were covered with towels or blankets so that they wouldn't screech, and the children were told to keep quiet.

As she walked down the stairs to the main floor, Laurinda was convinced that something awful had happened to her boss. Panic-stricken, she grabbed nine-year-old Carlinhos. Laurinda hoisted him up outside the second-floor bedroom window, which was wide open. Straining to reach the windowpane as Laurinda held his legs, Carlinhos shouted, "My father's sleeping!"

And then, as he had a better look, and perhaps noticed the blood staining the satin bedspread, he screamed, "My father is dead. He's angry. He's dead!"

Terrified, Laurinda tried to calm herself as she called for Waldomiro to fetch a ladder and climb in through the open window to investigate. Waldomiro leaned a ladder against the wall and climbed up to the window.

"Everyone in the house stopped working at that point," said Laurinda. "We all knew that whatever had taken place with Seu Alfredo, it was nothing good."

Waldomiro stepped over the window ledge and entered the room where Alfredo lay on his back on the bed, his head propped up on a pillow, thick, dark blood oozing from his open mouth.

Stunned, Waldomiro moved as if in slow motion to unlock the bedroom door as he tried to take in the scene in front of him. Alfredo's jacket was neatly folded on one side of the bed; his shoes were also neatly placed near the bed on the polished wooden floor. Alfredo was in his stocking feet. Waldomiro could still make out the sweat marks on the soles of his dark-gray socks. There were various bottles of medication on the bedside table, and the latest issue of *Time* magazine. Rolled-up towels from the bathroom were placed underneath the doors. With his left hand, Alfredo appeared to be pulling at his shirt collar. His mouth was slightly open. If it hadn't been for the blood, Waldomiro might have easily imagined that Alfredo was in a deep sleep.

Just as Waldomiro took in the scene, he heard Lily rushing up the stairs followed by Laurinda. As she passed through the study that led to the bedroom, Laurinda saw Lily stop to open the drawer of the cabinet that stood in the hallway alcove just outside their bedroom. Was she checking for their revolver, which was kept in the drawer of the hallway cabinet?

It's not clear why the Monteverdes kept a revolver in the house, especially since it was well known that Alfredo suffered from manic depression and had tried to kill himself in the past. But everyone who worked for him seems to have known where it was stored. Perhaps Alfredo was concerned about his family's security. After all, he was one of the twenty richest men in Brazil. But the Brazil of Alfredo Monteverde was a relatively calm, safe place, under the iron grip of the military junta that ruled the country. The urban violence that is associated with Rio de Janeiro today was almost nonexistent in the late 1960s.

Laurinda recalled that Lily visibly stiffened when she rifled through the drawer. Perhaps she realized that the revolver wasn't there. Dressed in a black dress with thin shoulder straps, her blond hair beautifully coiffed and smelling of hairspray, she entered the room where Waldomiro was standing as if momentarily frozen.

"I'm afraid it's not good news, Dona Lily," said Waldomiro, as Lily tried to get past him. "Seu Alfredo is dead."

It was the elevator operator at the Ponto Frio offices on Rua do Rosario in downtown Rio who informed Vera Chvidchenko, a secretary at Ponto Frio, that her boss was dead. Vera was rushing back to the offices for a meeting with Alfredo when she heard the news that was spreading throughout Rio's business district like a brush fire in a dry forest.

At the office, people were weeping.

Shot himself in bed?

But he was just here! He was in a good mood!

A stone-faced Maria Consuelo was gathering her things and preparing to go to the house on Rua Icatu to help Lily with the funeral arrangements. Geraldo, the director of the company, had offered to drive her. Company lawyer Conrado Gruenbaum would drive himself to the house later. Felix Klein, another executive who would prove invaluable to Lily in the future, began the process of sorting through Alfredo's complex financial arrangements in Brazil and Switzerland immediately after receiving instructions from Conrado.

"Eventually, everyone left the office. I just couldn't bring myself to go to the house," recalled Vera. "It was too painful. I was too upset."

Alfredo's friend Abitbol was among the first to arrive at the house. "I saw him lying on the bed, but I only took it in for a split second, because I rushed out to get help," recalled Abitbol years later. "It was so strange because we had played poker the night before, and he was in great spirits."

Trotte, the accountant, showed up soon after, accompanied by Geraldo and Maria Consuelo. "I saw Fred stretched out on the bed with blood covering his chest," he said.

In the space of a few hours, dozens of friends, business associates, and family members began arriving as news of Alfredo's death spread throughout the city. "I came as soon as I found out about his death on the news," said Victor Sztern. "The house was full of people."

Anita, the fired servant, appeared up at the house ahead of the police. "Is he really dead?" she asked Laurinda as she made her way to the servants' quarters.

"I wanted to know how she knew he was dead, and what she was doing at the house," recalled Laurinda. "But she just kept repeating the question with a mad look in her eye: 'Is he really dead?'"

Anita didn't need to see the body to know her former boss was dead. The distraught strangers crowding the living room and back garden must have immediately answered her question.

Carlinhos was dispatched to a friend's house, and the other children, who had been at the Copacabana Palace, were picked up by one of the chauffeurs and taken to the home of a family friend.

Maria Consuelo and Geraldo made their way to Alfredo's second-floor office where Lily was lying on a couch, attended by one of the servants, and speaking on the phone.

Maria Consuelo gingerly entered the bedroom. Perhaps it was the severe shock mingled with a deep sorrow at seeing her beloved boss splayed on the bed, the blood still oozing out of his mouth, or perhaps it was her meticulous secretarial instinct that propelled Maria Consuelo to do what she did next. Whatever the reason, she was hard-pressed to explain to police why she picked up the revolver that was lying on the floor on the right-hand side of the bed and placed it neatly on the bedside table, where the officers assigned to the investigation would find it later.

The Ponto Frio executives who assembled at the house immediately began the process of carrying out Lily's orders. Alfredo's will, which was drafted a year after their marriage, put her effectively in control of the company, and divided his assets between Lily and Carlinhos. Regina was mentioned in a separate legacy, but her take was relatively minor. Alfredo had left his mother a handful of shares and the sprawling apartment she occupied in Copacabana.

Although grief-stricken at her husband's sudden death, Lily was completely in control, especially when it came to consolidating Alfredo's financial holdings around the world. Securing Alfredo's fortune became the first order of business.

For except for Abitbol, who rushed out to get help, nobody at the house on Rua Icatu thought to call an ambulance or the police, even though under Brazilian law a suicide must be reported to authorities immediately.

It would be several hours after they found the body that Conrado would be dispatched to the local police station to report the death. Conrado calmly drove to the Tenth District Precinct in nearby Bota-fogo to file a report. According to that report, Conrado showed up at the police station at 9:45 p.m. to inform the duty officer that Al-fredo had killed himself in his bedroom at approximately three in the afternoon—nearly seven hours earlier.

In his initial report, Mario Cesar da Silva, the police constable who recorded Conrado's version of events as well as Alfredo's medical history when the lawyer showed up at the police station on that fateful Monday night, notes that Alfredo was undergoing regular treatments with a psychiatrist named Dr. José Leme Lopes, whose office was around the corner from Rua Icatu. Conrado told the officer that Al-fredo was a manic depressive, and a possible suicide.

But Conrado didn't tell the police the whole truth about Alfredo's personal life. For it was from Conrado's testimony that the officer concluded that Alfredo's "family life was tranquil." Perhaps Con-rado was not aware that Alfredo was planning to divorce Lily, even though it was common knowledge among his business associates. If everyone from Ponto Frio's accountant, secretary, and chief director were already making provisions for the divorce, then it seems highly unlikely that Conrado, the company's chief counsel and Alfredo's personal attorney, did not know.

It's not clear why Conrado left out important details about Alfre-do's personal life in his report to police. Perhaps he realized that fol-lowing his boss's death, his new allegiance needed to be to his widow, who would inherit Alfredo's staggering fortune, valued at almost $300 million. Perhaps he felt that the widow would not appreciate a messy police investigation, especially if it appeared that Lily herself had a motive for wanting one of the richest men in Brazil dead.

The police themselves were among the last visitors to arrive at the house on Rua Icatu. Detectives knocked on the door close to midnight, and hauled metal cases full of equipment—cameras, notebooks, measuring tape, and fingerprint kits. As they climbed the stairs to the second-floor bedroom, they had every reason to believe that they were off to investigate a suicide, not a homicide.

Nevertheless, they spent hours analyzing the room where the body was found. They seemed meticulous in their investigation, stripping Alfredo and affixing plastic arrows directly onto his body to show the wounds and the trajectory of the bullets. They took copious black-and-white photographs—of the body, the bedroom, the neatly folded suit jacket on the left side of the bed, the satin-and-brocade bedroll that appeared to have been thrown diagonally across the width of the bed. There is a photograph of Alfredo's shoes placed neatly under the bed. They even photographed the *Time* magazine carefully placed on the bedside table along with several bottles of medication.

They also photographed the weapon, which they placed on the floor just under the right-hand side of the bed, according to Maria Consuelo's description of where she had originally found it.

They demanded that Laurinda, Waldomiro, and Djanira remain in the house during the investigation, since they were important witnesses. They had been present at the time of the shooting, and police interrogated each of them separately about the day's sad events.

In the police report, handwritten on lined paper in a tight scrawl, da Silva described the corpse of a forty-five-year-old white male, wearing a white shirt, charcoal gray trousers, white underwear, gray socks, and a black and brown striped tie. "The first five buttons were open on his shirt and his tie was loosened with the knot to one side, and the left sleeve rolled up," noted the report. "On his mouth, on the left side, blood was flowing, and had coagulated on the pillow and the bed."

Alfredo Monteverde had been shot twice with a .32-caliber, Brazilian-made Taurus revolver. A bullet entered Alfredo's body at close range on the left side of his chest, leaving a circular wound that measured five centimeters in diameter. According to the report, the first bullet seems to have traveled through his body, exiting on the left side of his back.

"On or about three o'clock in the afternoon, he locked himself in his bedroom, and committed suicide with two shots to his chest on the left side, with both of the two shots entering the same orifice and exiting in different directions," said the police report. "One of the shots was piercing, with the bullet traveling through the right side of his back and embedding itself in the mattress of his bed. [He] committed suicide lying down and holding the revolver against his chest."

Yet no one who was at 96 Rua Icatu had heard the shots "because of the vast dimensions of the house," noted the officer after questioning the three servants. Since there were no signs of forced entry, and the servants had not reported anything unusual—the Irish wolfhounds Sarama and Barbarella would surely have alerted them if a stranger had attempted to break in—the police concluded their investigation.

But there were obvious gaps in their report. The police failed to interrogate any of the neighbors who may have heard the gunshots, even after one of the next-door neighbor's servants volunteered that she had indeed heard the gunshots. Similarly, the police did not seek out Artigas Watkins, who had been at the house earlier that day.

"He wasn't there when we discovered the body, that's for sure," recalled Laurinda. "He had disappeared, without informing anyone that he was leaving."

There were other elements missing from the police report. Why had the detectives not recorded their observations about the bedroom and the rolled-up towels they found under the doors, even though Laurinda and the other servants overheard them discussing all of these amongst themselves while they were at the house? As they gathered in the kitchen to drink cup after cup of sugary *cafezinho*, police puzzled over why Alfredo would have taken all the fresh towels from the en suite bathroom, rolled each of them up, and placed them underneath the door and the other openings in the room.

If Alfredo had committed suicide, perhaps he didn't want anyone to hear the sound of the gunshots. Clearly, the towels were placed around the room to muffle any sound. But if he was going to kill himself anyway, why would he care if anyone heard the noise? Obviously, the question did occur to police, which is why it is strange that they did not note it in their official report.

Nor did they enquire about Alfredo's habits. The police photographs show a dead body in a strangely immaculate bedroom setting. Yet anyone who knew Alfredo well would have been immediately suspicious of those photographs. Alfredo was a notoriously messy person, and it was unlikely he would have taken the time to arrange his blazer just so, or put his shoes away. This was a man who was accustomed to living with several servants who picked up after him. He was careless with his clothes, regularly leaving them in a heap on the bathroom floor, recalled Laurinda.

Of course, someone as meticulous as his secretary Maria Consuelo could have cleaned up the room before the police arrived at the scene. But why not also clean up the sheet of crumpled newsprint that police found on the bedside table? According to the police, the newsprint had been used to wrap the revolver while it had been in storage in the hallway cabinet.

The police photograph of the gun is probably the most intriguing piece of evidence gathered in the investigation because the most startling conclusion of the initial police report was not that Alfredo Monteverde had committed suicide by locking himself in his bedroom and shooting himself in the chest. What was more shocking was that somehow he had managed to shoot himself twice.

In the black-and-white photograph of the weapon, a police officer's hand points to the revolver's six-bullet chamber, showing four bullets intact and two missing.

"He shot himself twice," said Alfredo's friend Abitbol. "He really must have wanted to die."

Samy Cohn, another wealthy Romanian-born businessman whose wife Ruth was one of Lily's closest friends and who had introduced Lily to Alfredo years before, noted about Alfredo's passing that "we were all very heartbroken when he had to give [sic] two shots in order to die."

SHORTLY AFTER REPORTING Alfredo's death to the police, Conrado began the grim task of informing Alfredo's mother and sister. Regina was on a European cruise, and could not be reached, and Rosy was on vacation. After several phone calls to her home in Lake Como, Conrado finally tracked her down to the seaside villa of Camillo Olivetti, the Italian industrialist, who owned a magnificent vacation villa near Antibes, next to the legendary Hotel du Cap. Rosy and her husband were unpacking their bags when the telephone rang, no doubt echoing through the cavernous Mediterranean villa.

Rosy picked up the phone with some annoyance. She had left strict instructions with her secretary and the household servants in Italy not to bother her on vacation, and under no circumstances to give out her number in Antibes—unless it was an emergency, of course. What could possibly be so urgent at this hour? Why were they already bothering her when she hadn't even started this desperately needed rest cure?

But when she heard the voice on the other end of the phone pronounce her name with a familiar Brazilian-Portuguese inflection— "*Rozee*?" said Conrado—she knew immediately.

"How?"

Momentarily dazed, she could barely take in what was being said to her.

"Suicide," he said. "With a revolver."

Do you want the body embalmed? We can wait for you, for your mother, for the funeral. But even as Conrado said this to Rosy, he knew that they couldn't really wait. Regina's ship would not dock in Rio for another week. Rosy felt the shock would simply be too much for her mother if they telegraphed her with the news aboard ship.

Lily had given Conrado specific orders. She did not want to wait to bury her husband. Although Alfredo was not a practicing Jew, he would be buried as one, and Jewish law required that the burial occur almost immediately after death.

How are the children? How is Lily? Rosy asked. She told Conrado that she would leave immediately for Rio, but would not make the funeral. She told him to proceed without her.

Still in shock, she hung up the phone and went to inform her husband, who arranged for a taxi to take them back to Italy. They were simply too tired and too startled to drive themselves. She mentally planned their route to Brazil: She could arrive at Lake Como by dawn, take a taxi to the Milan airport, and catch the first flight to Rome, where, by the end of the day, she could be on her way to Rio de Janeiro.

Yes, that was what they would do. The planning cleared her head. She was temporarily relieved to have a series of logistical problems to solve.

But the relief was temporary. The cab was rickety and the driver tuned his radio to a rock-and-roll station, possibly to keep him alert as he drove along dark and winding coastal roads through the Alpes Maritimes. She politely asked him to turn off the music, preferring the sound of crashing surf and the occasional speeding car as she tried to come to grips with the fact that her dear younger brother, Fred, was really dead.

The thought suddenly turned her stomach, and she demanded that the driver stop the car at a seaside hotel. She walked purposefully through the darkened lobby and to the ladies' room, where she threw up, staying for a few minutes to press her head against the cool marble walls before heading out the door.

Although she was always ready to listen to her brother's problems, she seemed increasingly unable to play an active role in Alfredo's life. Besides, he had seemed so much better after marrying Lily. Still, she felt that he had not quite been himself when he had come to Italy to visit her in June, two months before he died.

In the only surviving photograph from that 1969 family vacation, Alfredo is pictured standing at a café or restaurant behind his mother, Rosy's husband and his own wife. A relaxed and suntanned Lily is laughing into the camera, her sunglasses pushed back on her head. Regina is wearing dark glasses and lots of gold jewelry—the very picture of the wealthy matriarch on vacation. Alfredo, casual in a white, open-collared shirt, is standing slightly stooped with an arm around his sister, pointing a finger at the unknown photographer. His sister is stiff and rigid beside him, in a buttoned-up blouse, her hair conservatively pulled back.

Perhaps it was the medication he was taking that made him seem at times slightly inebriated. Alfredo had also told his sister that he was in the early stages of diabetes. He had put on weight. But Rosy didn't think much of it. Her mind was on her own business. Then, several weeks after he returned to Rio, Alfredo called her at her villa in Italy. Had it been the day before he died? Yes, it probably had been the day before he died. Things were not good, he had said. He was having trouble with the business, with Lily. He wanted a divorce. He needed to figure out how to deal with the children, to lessen the trauma of separation, and had invited Lily's first husband to lunch the following day to discuss the situation.

Rosy hadn't had much time to talk to him. She was in a meeting, rushing to finish her work because she was heading out on vacation the next day. Perhaps she should have invited him to meet her in Europe, to get out of a situation he was finding increasingly difficult to handle. But maybe he didn't sound so desperate after all. Whatever the problem, she would deal with it after her vacation, have a good long chat with Fred.

But now it was too late.

AS ROSY AND her husband were racing to catch a flight to Rio, many of Alfredo's friends who had assembled at the house on Rua Icatu watched in stunned silence as two brawny officers carried his body out of the bedroom. Fighting back tears, Paulinho Guimarães, one of Alfredo's best friends, raced into the bedroom and grabbed one of the blood-soaked sheets to cover the body, which was loaded into an idling police van parked outside the front door of the house. Alfredo's remains were then driven to the Instituto Médico Legal—the coroner's office in downtown Rio de Janeiro—where the medical officer on duty waited to perform an autopsy.

The Ponto Frio executives worked into the wee hours of the morning to arrange the funeral, and more important to secure the deceased's financial holdings, which were scattered throughout Brazil and around the world.

"It's just like Fred to give us work even after he's dead," quipped Conrado, who was charged with convincing Jewish authorities to give Alfredo a proper burial. Suicides are against Jewish law, and the victims are usually buried against the back walls of a cemetery with little ceremony. Conrado would have to offer a sizable "donation" to the Jewish authorities who oversaw the cemetery on the industrial outskirts of Rio, in order to ensure that Alfredo received a proper Jewish burial.

"We had to pay a great deal of money to get Fred buried," said Maria Consuelo, adding that shortly after they discovered the body Geraldo was dispatched to various banks in the city in order to gather the cash.

"It was a huge headache for Geraldo," recalled his wife Lourdes. "Geraldo ran around looking for cash soon after Fred was found dead. Geraldo said that Fred's death was very strange and could not have happened the way it happened."

Indeed, the autopsy and a half-hearted police investigation would leave some difficult questions.

On the morning of Tuesday, August 26, a day after Alfredo's death, as final preparations were underway for the funeral, his secretary Vera received a call from the coroner's office in Rio's Lapa neighborhood. Could she come immediately? The medical examiners had some urgent questions. "When I arrived, the medical examiner told me that he found it very strange that they could find no traces of gunpowder on Fred's hands," she said.

Indeed, in the initial police investigation and the subsequent autopsy report there is no mention of gunpowder residue on Alfredo's hands. In a suicide with a revolver, one of the first things a medical examiner will inevitably record is the gunpowder residue on the victim's hands.

"Then they asked me another question," said Vera. "They wanted to know if Fred was left-handed. I couldn't figure out why they would want to know that, but I answered right away that Fred did everything with his right hand."

The coroner shook his head and asked her if she was certain. Vera told him that in the nine years that she had worked for Alfredo, she had always known him to be right-handed.

"Then he couldn't have shot himself."

If the statement shocked her, she kept it to herself, too frightened to carry its implications to their logical conclusion. Vera remained silent for nearly forty years after Alfredo's death. But there were others who were unaware of the coroner's pronouncement but were never convinced that the owner of Ponto Frio had taken his own life.

Hélio Fernandes, owner of the *Tribuna da Imprensa*, was one of them. "The newspapers omitted most of the details of his death," said Fernandes, whose newspaper was the only media outlet to resist the strict military censorship of the time. "The incident was never properly investigated."

Geraldo never believed that his boss had committed suicide. On the morning of August 25, Alfredo was full of plans for Ponto Frio's expansion. Until his death in 2006, Geraldo repeatedly told his family and friends that it was impossible for Alfredo to have killed himself.

Others, like Alfredo's friend Paulinho, who covered his body with the sheet, also refused to believe the official version of events but seemed powerless to do anything about it, except beg Alfredo's sister to demand a homicide investigation.

Shortly after Alfredo died, there were some rumors that police officers had been bribed in order to suppress the investigation. Lourdes said that part of the money that her husband gathered in the hours after Alfredo's death went to pay off investigators—a dirty deed that haunted Geraldo for the rest of his life, according to his wife and daughter. Lourdes recalls that $80,000 changed hands. Such a bribe paid to counter bad publicity or shelve an investigation would not have been unusual in military-era Brazil, where corruption was widespread. Death was bad for business. However, there is no hard evidence to suggest that the police accepted bribes in order to suppress the investigation into Alfredo's death.

But who would want Alfredo Monteverde dead?

Could his social activism have caused him to run afoul of Brazil's military rulers? After all, the country was in the dark years—the so-called "years of lead"—of a military dictatorship when Alfredo died. In 1968, a year before his death, the dictatorship entered its most brutal phase when military police fired on unarmed students who decided to protest against the quality of the food and hygiene at their university cafeteria in Rio de Janeiro. On March 28, dozens of police, armed with machine guns, tear gas, and grenades, invaded the Calabouço student restaurant, near downtown Rio. In the ensuing melee, police killed Edson Luís Lima Souto, an eighteen-year-old student from the Amazon state of Para. The following day there were 50,000 people at his funeral, which set off student protests across the country. The government reacted immediately and with force, passing Institutional Act Number 5, which closed Congress, suspended all civil rights, and made it legal for the military to throw civilians in jail without trial.

Deeply moved by the tragic events of March 28, 1968, which became known in Brazil as the Calabouço, Alfredo publicly offered to pay half the expenses of rebuilding the cafeteria, provided that all the authorities were in agreement on its reconstruction. But they weren't, and the cafeteria was eventually forgotten.

Despite his social activism, Alfredo was a businessman at heart and knew it wouldn't do him any good to alienate Brazil's military rulers. Even in the years that he admired opposition politician Carlos Lacerda, Alfredo never became actively involved with any political parties. He knew he needed to remain on excellent terms with the government of the day in order to continue to thrive in an economy that was becoming increasingly centralized and controlled by the state. In a country that was beginning to impose huge import duties on appliances and other manufactured goods, Alfredo and Ponto Frio needed to have friends in high places in order to circumvent the duties and remain profitable in a business that concerned itself with import and export.

"He was a very popular man, and a great formulator of public opinion," said Sztern. "When [former president Alencar] Castelo Branco died, Fred paid for a full-page ad in the papers in which he wrote what a great president he was. But mostly he was pretty much apolitical."

Castelo Branco, who was one of the leaders of the March 31, 1964, military coup that ushered in more than two decades of military rule in Brazil, became president in 1964 and died in a plane crash shortly after leaving office in 1967.

While he supported social activism on the left, Alfredo also supported the military governments. In fact, the only trouble that Alfredo appears to have had with the military authorities was in December 1967 when he had been called into a meeting at the Ministry of Revenue. The meeting, at the cavernous ministry building in downtown Rio, went on for several hours, during which he was questioned about his taxes and how he imported foreign products into Brazil, then one of the world's most protected markets. "I have no idea why they wanted to see me," said Alfredo to Sztern.

While he may not have wholeheartedly supported Brazil's military regimes, it is unlikely Alfredo worked against them to the point that he would be a target for murder.

If investigators ever demanded to know who benefited from Alfredo's death, they had only to look to his wife and son. According to a 1966 will that Conrado produced on the day of his death—a document he swore was Alfredo's last will and testament—Lily and Carlinhos were the main beneficiaries.

But neither Lily nor Carlinhos pulled the trigger. Lily was away from the house, and Carlinhos was a month shy of his tenth birthday.

Still, someone else could have grabbed the gun in the hallway cabinet, entered the room, and shot him at point-blank range in the chest while he was sleeping. Alfredo's lifelong battle with manic depression would have been the perfect cover for murder.

In theory, in order to make the murder look like suicide, the murderer could lock the door from the inside and leave through the open window. Alternatively, if the assassin had the key to the bedroom door, he or she could easily lock it from the outside and leave the house, being careful not to disturb the rolled-up towels.

Despite the coroner's obvious concerns, he nevertheless released Alfredo's body for burial hours after the autopsy. Strangely, the investigating officers were also quick to surrender two of their most valuable pieces of evidence—the bullet and the revolver, which they seized after their investigation at the house.

"Received the revolver, four bullets intact, two spent cartridges and one bullet," reads the handwritten scrawl on one of the margins of the original police report. The sentence is followed by initials that are difficult to decipher.

THE FUNERAL TOOK place a day later, and drew more than two thousand people to the Jewish Cemetery at Caju, on the industrial outskirts of Rio. All the managers of his twenty-two stores attended, as did the majority of the six hundred employees of Ponto Frio. The flags at the Rio Yacht Club, where Alfredo had been a member for years, remained at half mast for three days in his honor.

"I think so many people went to the funeral to see if he was really dead," laughed Marcelo Steinfeld. "You could never be sure with Fred if he was playing another practical joke." Indeed, at the time, the rumor making the rounds of the business community was that Alfredo had filled his coffin with rocks and disappeared to start another life far away from Rio de Janeiro.

Alfredo was buried in what a reporter for the *Jornal do Brasil* described as a hasty ceremony, barely lasting more than three minutes. But it was thanks to Alfredo's status as one of the richest men in Brazil that the ceremony lasted as long as it did. Since suicide is considered a grievous act under Jewish law, brief prayers are said but there is often no eulogy, which is why none of Alfredo's closest friends or business associates were allowed to make any kind of public statements at the cemetery.

Later, when the dates were carved into his marble tombstone, Lily would make her own public statement: *Merci d'être né, Puchi.* ("Thanks for being born, Puchi.") It was typical of Lily, of the playful notes that she left in several languages for her loved ones, and contrasted sharply with the more somber "Eternal remembrances from your wife, son, mother, sister and niece" engraved just below it.

Many saved their remembrances of Alfredo for the lavish reception Lily threw at the house on Rua Icatu. On August 27, the day that Rosy and her husband arrived from Italy, Lily was preoccupied with ganizing a luncheon for twenty-four friends and family, to honor Alfredo's memory. Of course, Rosy and her husband were welcome to stay.

As usual with Lily, every detail was carefully attended to, down to the long-stemmed yellow roses that filled the house. A few years earlier, Lily had singlehandedly organized the renovations of the Icatu house, redoing the bathrooms, the sitting rooms, and sprucing up the terraced garden.

Now, on the day after her husband's funeral, the grief-stricken widow had organized an elegant luncheon and had even thoughtfully sent a car to pick up Rosy and her husband at the airport and drive them to the house on Rua Icatu.

"I don't know how she managed to do anything, really," recalled Laurinda. "Dona Lily just shriveled up after Seu Alfredo's death. She got thinner and thinner until she was nothing more than a twig. From that day forward, she never took off her mourning clothes."

But in Montevideo and Rio de Janeiro, the twig was famous for throwing a good party, even if Rosy and her husband arrived to what appeared to be a disorganized scene at the house on Rua Icatu. The house seemed filled with Lily's friends and relatives from Argentina and Uruguay—people Rosy had never met and would never see again. Everyone seemed to be speaking Spanish at once, and although it was a somber occasion that had brought them all together, the air was definitely festive. Had it not been for the preponderance of black suits and dresses, Rosy might be forgiven for thinking she had walked into a reception for a wedding or a family reunion rather than the aftermath of a funeral.

Despite Lily's ordeal of the last forty-eight hours, Rosy thought her sister-in-law looked stunning in a simple dark dress, her hair perfectly coiffed. After exchanging hugs and condolences, Lily escorted Rosy to the master bedroom to show her where her brother had died. There were no bedclothes on the bed. Laurinda and the other servants had stripped them off and buried the satin-and-brocade bedspread in the back garden since there was no way to remove the bloodstains completely.

Earlier, the servants had removed the bloodstained mattress, and scrubbed every inch of the room with strong smelling disinfectant, which assaulted the visitors' nostrils as they made their way inside. Rosy was vaguely aware of Lily speaking in the background. Was she talking to her? It was a slightly apologetic tone, informing Rosy that all of the other bedrooms in the house were already occupied with her many guests, but if Rosy and her husband wished to stay, she could ask the servants to make up this one—the master bedroom—for them. Rosy never dreamed of staying at the house, and she was surely not going to sleep in the bed where her brother had died two days before. Lily, however, had thought of everything, which was probably why the driver didn't bother to remove Rosy's luggage from the car when they arrived at Icatu. It would probably be more comfortable at this point to stay in a hotel, Lily told her sister-in-law. Which is why Lily had taken the liberty of making a reservation for them at the Copacabana Palace.

The consummate hostess, Lily asked them to stay to luncheon. As Rosy recalled years later, the food and wine were perfect, and it was Lily herself who organized the waiters brought in for the occasion.

"It was the day after her husband's funeral, and she behaved beautifully, receiving people and organizing everything like the bloody undersecretary of state," recalled Rosy.

But Rosy had other things on her mind besides the food and the people she didn't recognize—were they really Fred's friends?—at her brother's home. How would she break the news to Regina Monteverde, her mother, who was arriving September 1—in four days' time—from her cruise?

In the end, Rosy arranged with Lily and Maria Consuelo, Alfredo's faithful secretary, to have a physician present to sedate her mother when they finally broke the news that Regina's beloved son was dead. Maria Consuelo would take a launch to meet the ship at the port of Rio, and speed Regina through customs and then into a suite of rooms at the Copacabana Palace so that she could have a day to rest before facing the grim news. They would tell Regina the following day, when she was comfortably ensconced in her own apartment.

On the day Regina arrived, Maria Consuelo picked her up as planned. "Why didn't Fred come to meet me?" asked the heavyset matriarch as she moved rather unsteadily onto the motor launch, Maria Consuelo holding her cherished lap dog. "Where's Fred? He's always here when I return from a trip." A tense Maria Consuelo mumbled something about work and ferried Regina to the port. Regina's own chauffeur was waiting to take her to the Copacabana Palace. The following day, Rosy, her husband, and Alfredo's widow were already waiting at Regina's well-appointed Copacabana apartment to break the news. A physician and his assistant waited in the servants' quarters for their cue to administer the sedatives.

Regina seemed well rested and calm when she entered her own apartment, although she must have immediately found it strange to see her family sitting in the living room. Just what could have brought her daughter back to Rio? And just where was Fred? But the questions barely had time to register. Immediately, she sensed something was very wrong, which is why she might not have seemed all that surprised to hear the news that her beloved son was dead.

Regina let out a long, piercing animal scream that echoed throughout the ten floors of her apartment building. That was when the physician moved in with the injection to ease the shock.

But Regina, who loved Alfredo above everything else, including her own daughter, would never recover.

"She had a passion for her son," said her friend Masha. "When Fred died, it was the end of Regina."

In some ways, Regina had been bracing herself for her youngest child's death for years. Regina was well acquainted with manic depression and suicide. Her own husband had jumped off the roof of the sanatorium in Vienna where he was undergoing treatment for his own depression before the war. On several occasions, she told Alfredo that like his father, he wouldn't survive into his mid-forties, that he would do exactly what Iancu had done. Just like your father, she would say.

Perhaps it was an internal defense mechanism. For Regina recognized all the signs—the mood swings, the euphoria, the withdrawal, the blinding headaches. Maybe she was so afraid that her precious son would end up taking his own life that she felt she had to speak out about it. Maybe by acknowledging the problem, Alfredo might be so frightened into imagining the consequences of suicide that he wouldn't have the courage to go through with it. Still, over the years she had reassured herself that he might be getting better. Alfredo had seemed to be so much better when he had married Lily in 1965. Of course, that was short-lived. In the last year, she had seen a steady decline. He seemed constantly glassy-eyed and weak. What kind of medications was he taking? Did he need to take so many pills? Alfredo was clearly not well.

But like so many others who questioned the circumstances of Alfredo's death, in the end his mother simply did not accept that he had taken his own life.

After Alfredo's death, friends urged his mother and sister to conduct their own independent investigation.

A few months after Alfredo's death, Regina and Rosy hired a team of lawyers and demanded that they do everything possible to reopen the investigation into Alfredo's death, even if it meant disinterring Alfredo. It was their intention to force authorities in Rio de Janeiro to reopen the case as a murder investigation.

But as the investigating lawyers would find, re-examining the facts of Alfredo Monteverde's death proved difficult. They were hit full force with the weight of Brazilian bureaucracy and came face-to-face with cynical homicide detectives who refused to help. Was this a cover-up or just the usual Byzantine bureaucracy and negligence associated with most official matters in Brazil?

No one would ever find out.

Yet the lawyers commissioned by Regina and Rosy seemed to think that there was some merit to the case, and in a letter dated March 18, 1970, they wrote: "Considering the story that [Regina's son-in-law] presented to us concerning the personality of Mr. Alfredo João Monteverde, of his wife, his business partners and some friends, as well as the multiplicity of his commercial interests and in relation to the events that took place at the time of his death, we understood from the beginning that the case really did have aspects that needed to be better understood."

But the truth was elusive. For instance, it was impossible to find the ownership of the weapon, even though the revolver appears to have been a fixture in the Monteverde residence. "Although we tried with great diligence to obtain the ownership of the weapon at the Department of Political and Social Order (DOPS), it was not possible to obtain this information," the investigators note, referring to a branch of Rio de Janeiro's military police that normally dealt with political prisoners during the military period.

But if the weapon wasn't registered in Alfredo or Lily's name, whom did it belong to? Why keep a gun in the house of a well-known manic depressive who had tried to commit suicide in the past?

"There could have been inducement by possible third party beneficiaries in his death," said the investigators. "The proof of inducement, however, is always one of the most difficult based on its complexity. In this particular case, considering the people, the circumstances, the inheritance issues and the lapse of time since the event, it will be difficult and doubtful to see convincing proof to justify any judicial initiative."

In the end, much surrounding the death of Alfredo Monteverde remained a mystery. The report commissioned by Regina and Rosy did almost nothing to clear up the unanswered questions surrounding Alfredo's death, even though all the investigations completed by police, medical examiners, and ballistics experts were submitted to an independent medical examiner for what was to be a grand reassessment.

"Although the initial police report conducted by a competent officer states that there were two bullets fired, there was only one bullet found," writes Alexandrino Silva Ramos Filho, the medical examiner hired by Regina and Rosy's husband to analyze the police and autopsy reports, months after the fact. "Only one bullet fired from a firearm was observed at the scene, lodged in the mattress where the victim was lying." He went further to note that "it left a circular wound with a dark deposit (gunpowder) that had all the characteristics of the entry of a bullet at short distance. On the dorsal [part of the victim], in the left dorsal region next to the line of the vertebrae, a wound was found with irregular borders that characterized the exit of the bullet."

Finally, Silva Ramos Filho closed his own report with the following observation: "[I]t is extremely rare in a process of auto-elimination that two bullets should be fired into the same orifice of entry. Given the above, we also conclude that in this case we are dealing with a process of auto-elimination."

But why was the first officer who entered the master bedroom on Rua Icatu so certain that two bullets had been fired into the body? *"On or about three o'clock in the afternoon, he locked himself in his bedroom, and committed suicide with two shots to his chest on the left side, with both of the two shots entering the same orifice and exiting in different directions."*

The police officer went on to write, "I put away the revolver, the two spent cartridges, the four bullets left in the chamber and the bullet that came out of his back."

Presumably, the second bullet must have stayed in Alfredo's body, but it wasn't noted in any of the autopsy reports. Where was the second bullet? Unfortunately, this important disparity, which could have changed the course of the Monteverde family history, was never properly investigated.

"Our conclusions, based on the information we have, is that there was in fact a suicide," wrote the lawyers.

But Regina refused to accept the conclusions. She would spend the rest of her life trying to prove that her son was murdered, and trying to recoup Globex, which had started out as a family business, financed by the Grunberg-Monteverde fortune.

Regina, who was unaware of Alfredo's 1966 will until its contents were revealed after his death, wanted to know why he had not made his sister Rosy a beneficiary, as well as Rosy's daughter Christina, his beloved niece. After all, Globex and Alfredo's other business interests had all been considered family enterprises, controlled by Alfredo, Regina, and Rosy since their founding in 1946. Maria Consuelo, his closest business associate, who was by his side when he founded the company in 1946, was also surprised her boss had not included her in his will.

"I was completely shocked," she admitted shortly before her own death nearly four decades later.

Could Alfredo, known for his goodwill and generosity, have been so ungenerous to his own family in his last will and testament, leaving nearly everything to his most recent wife? Although the will was signed by five witnesses, among them Conrado, Alfredo's good friend Paulinho, and some of Alfredo's most trusted associates, there was something not right about it, at least for Alfredo's closely knit family.

For Regina, Alfredo's death would dominate the rest of her life, and she would use every available legal means to try to thwart Lily's efforts to take over her son's business and inheritance.

For Lily, Alfredo's death marked the beginning of a new life. Two months shy of her thirty-fifth birthday, she began her transformation into one of the world's richest and most glamorous women.

"After Fred's death, she wanted to remake her life," said her former schoolmate, Ana Bentes Bloch. "And she clearly transformed herself into a major high-society figure."

Remarkably for someone unschooled in the ways of international finance, Lily acted swiftly and with great efficiency in the hours after Alfredo's death to secure the Monteverde family fortune.

But the speed and alacrity with which this grieving widow set the next phase of her life in motion surprised even her closest friends. Shortly after Alfredo's death, Ponto Frio executives canceled the powers of attorney that Rosy and her husband held on Alfredo's accounts at banks in Switzerland and Lily began making arrangements to leave Brazil.

She was in such a hurry to leave the country that she didn't bother to pack any of her clothes. When Lily's friends Marcelo and Klara Steinfeld bought the Icatu house from Lily in January 1973, they found everything intact—her clothes were still hanging in the closets and the family's furniture was still in place. Everything, except a few valuable paintings, was left at the house on Rua Icatu under the watchful eye of Waldomiro Alves and the Irish wolfhounds. Lily took the four children, moved into a suite of rooms at the Copacabana Palace, and began the mad preparations to settle in London.

At one point, Lily asked Laurinda if she wanted to accompany her to England. Laurinda declined, saying that she needed to remain in Rio to look after her two boys, Ademir and Adilson.

"That's when I told her about my dream, and the macumba on Seu Alfredo's shirt," said Laurinda. "I felt it was important for her to know what might have happened to Seu Alfredo." Laurinda also told her that a recent tarot card reading had shown her that Lily would end her life as a widow in mourning.

Laurinda thought she was imparting important information to her employer at what must surely have been the most difficult moment of her life. Lily smiled weakly and thanked the housekeeper for her concern. But she wasn't superstitious, she informed Laurinda. She didn't believe in dreams, in tarot cards, and certainly not in macumba curses, she told Laurinda.

But Laurinda's warning—that she would be doomed to wear mourning for the rest of her life—would come back to haunt her.

"I tried to warn her because I saw that she was really suffering, and she just kept losing weight," said Laurinda. "You could tell that Seu Alfredo's death had really knocked her out."

Or pushed her forward. On September 15, less than a month after Alfredo's death, the grieving widow was on her way to London, where she would move quickly to ensure by every legal means available to her that she was in complete control of the entire Monteverde family fortune.

In England, she executed several brilliant tactical, legal, and investment strategies that would duly catapult her into the exclusive billionaires' club. There would be other strategies too, of a much more personal kind, all of them engineered by a short Lebanese-Brazilian banker.

Edmond Safra was one of Alfredo's most trusted bankers, and, after his untimely death, he would become the most important man in his widow's new life.

FOUR

"Edmond Said He Would Fix Everything"

Edmond was, of course, well known to Alfredo. Like other wealthy Jews who had fled to Brazil during the war years, Alfredo had entrusted a large part of his assets to the Safra bank in São Paulo, which Edmond founded shortly after immigrating to Brazil in 1954. Later, when Edmond's Trade Development Bank in Geneva officially began to accept deposits, Alfredo was among the largest account holders. Fearing endemic corruption and political instability in Brazil, Alfredo had also scattered his assets in other Swiss banks and invested in property abroad.

"Every Jew had money outside the country because we were a generation of refugees, and you never knew when we would need to leave in a hurry," said Marcelo Steinfeld, whose father had the distinction of being one of Edmond's early depositors after he started building the Swiss arm of his banking operations in 1956.

"For years, Fred was Edmond Safra's biggest account, and I know that they worked together for many years while Edmond was in São Paulo," said Maria Luisa Goldschmid, who worked as Alfredo's assistant between 1954 and 1957.

In the early days, at least, Alfredo seems to have put a great deal of confidence in the Safra bank. Joseph Safra was a close friend and frequent visitor to the Ponto Frio offices in Rio de Janeiro, recalled many of Alfredo's business associates. And Edmond's new enterprise in Switzerland, the cradle of private banking, was the perfect place for Alfredo to safeguard a big chunk of the family fortune.

But Alfredo probably never imagined that Edmond would take care of him in other ways. For years the Monteverde family has wondered just what role Edmond played in the series of events that led to some of Alfredo's ill-conceived business decisions just before his death.

It's not clear how Lily met Edmond. Some claim that the two met at his brother Joseph Safra's wedding in São Paulo in the late 1960s. Others insist that they met immediately after Alfredo's death, when the distraught widow needed financial advice on how to run Ponto Frio. Still, others insist that Edmond and his brothers were frequent visitors at the Monteverde home on Rua Icatu. Alfredo's business associates recall that the Monteverdes had invited the Safra brothers for dinner on several occasions. On one of those occasions, Edmond was visiting from Switzerland and might have tagged along with his brothers.

"We all encouraged Edmond to visit Lily and give her his sympathies after Alfredo died," recalled a Safra family member in São Paulo who did not want to be identified. "That's when they met for the first time."

But wherever that first meeting took place, Edmond Safra fell hard for Lily Monteverde.

Their friend Albert Nasser swears that his friend the Lebanese banker locked eyes on Lily at Joseph's São Paulo wedding, where Alfredo had been asked to be the best man. Lily, in a green satin dress, her hair in a chignon studded with diamonds, looked absolutely beautiful, he recalled. When Joseph introduced Lily to Edmond, "they looked at each other as if the world did not exist around them," recalled Albert, who was also a guest at the wedding. "Edmond fell in love with her instantly," he said.

Nasser says that he is certain the love affair only started months after Alfredo's death in 1969. The way Nasser remembers it, a mutual friend in Rio, businessman Samy Cohn, who had also introduced Alfredo to Lily years earlier, had suggested that Lily call Edmond in New York to help her with some of the financial issues after Alfredo's death. Nasser says that within a few weeks after the funeral, she flew to New York for a meeting with Edmond, telling him that she had no one to help her with the business she had just inherited. It was only then that the two became lovers, Nasser insisted.

"Edmond said he would fix everything," said Nasser.

But Nasser's version of events does not coincide with accounts of those who were much closer to Lily and Alfredo at the time. According to family friends, Alfredo's business associates, and servants at the house on Rua Icatu in Rio, Lily traveled almost immediately to London, not to New York, after Alfredo's death. "We all thought that when Fred died, Lily would marry Safra," said a Rio socialite who knew the couple.

The careful planning that saw Lily take almost instant control of Alfredo's entire fortune may have been executed by Edmond himself. After all, he was one of Alfredo's bankers. Many marveled at how rapidly a grieving widow with little experience in the ways of international finance was able to so quickly secure her late husband's assets.

"My son died on August 25, 1969," said Regina Monteverde in court papers filed against Lily and Edmond in England in 1971. "On the 26th of August, my power of attorney on a joint bank account was canceled. I returned to Rio on September 1, and only then did I realize how miserable my life had become."

According to some business associates of Alfredo and his family, it was Edmond who took immediate control of Lily's business affairs— surely an arrangement that could only have been possible if a relationship of deep trust had already existed. It was Edmond and a team of his most trusted lawyers and international financial advisers who instructed Lily to move to London where she could take advantage of favorable tax loopholes for foreigners. They also guided her through the important process of adopting Alfredo's son, Carlos. Under Brazilian law, children are automatically heir to half of the deceased's estate. As a result of Carlos's adoption, Lily could control the entire Monteverde fortune.

Lily rented temporary quarters at 6 Hyde Park Gardens, a "good address" in high-society parlance, across the street from Hyde Park and in the neighborhood of Kensington Palace. The flat itself was expensively furnished but by no means opulent, not in the grand style for which Lily would later become famous. There was an apartment below for the three boys, which also seemed to be expensively furnished, "but in the manner that a railway baron would buy leather-bound books by the yard," recalled one visitor. Lily immediately enrolled Carlos and Claudio at Millfield, Alfredo's old boarding school in Somerset. Eduardo chose to live in Buenos Aires with his father. Adriana lived with her mother in the upstairs flat and attended a day school in London.

Of course, these were only temporary rented quarters, hastily arranged in the frantic days after Alfredo's death in Brazil. Lily tried to make the best of slight inconveniences. Her bedroom, for example, was too small, and did not have enough space to accommodate her extensive wardrobe. The solution was to keep her clothes in an adjoining bedroom. An opening between the two rooms had been constructed to make it appear en suite. But it was awkward. The opening was only five feet high, forcing her to duck whenever she moved from one room to the other.

Still, she pampered herself now that she was a wealthy widow. She leased a Rolls-Royce and a Mercedes convertible, and hired a driver to take her on frequent shopping forays in Knightsbridge. She also bought herself exquisite new clothes, and began to jet to

Paris to order her wardrobe for each season from the finest couture houses.

Lily lived quietly in London, although she frequently threw dinner parties for visiting friends from South America, and dined often at such elite restaurants as Annabel's, especially when Edmond was in town. Lily also traveled frequently to Geneva to see Edmond and take care of her financial affairs, recalled Ponto Frio executives who were summoned to Edmond's offices in the Swiss city for regular business meetings. Lily was careful not to declare herself a resident of London so that she wouldn't be taxed on the inheritance until all of it was squirreled away in Switzerland. Instead, in the fall of 1969 she maintained her Brazilian citizenship and established residency in Switzerland, using Edmond's address on the rue Moillebeau in Geneva as her own.

The intricacies of such artful tax maneuvers would have been lost on a Brazilian socialite with limited experience of the world of high finance, but Lily clearly had the best legal and tax advice money could buy.

"She wasn't exactly an intellectual, but it's fantastic how quickly she learned," said Rosy. "You really have to admire the unemotional part of Lily. She's coolheaded. The day after the death of her husband, she immediately canceled all his bank accounts."

While she was in London, Edmond gave Lily a generous weekly allowance in cash and forbade her from buying property or applying for a credit card until her residency was formalized. In many ways, Lily's legal and financial issues became his own, for Alfredo's fortune must have represented one of the most important assets in his own growing banking empire.

In a series of expensive legal actions that played out for years in British courts, Alfredo's surviving family tried to establish a strong professional and personal link that they believed existed between Lily and Edmond.

For Lily, Edmond Safra was not only a future marriage prospect, he was the ultimate repairman, fixing all the tangled legal and financial details that emerged soon after Alfredo's death and threatened her newly acquired fortune.

Edmond said he would fix everything.

And, in many ways, he did.

EDMOND SAFRA WAS born into a tight-knit clan of renowned Sephardic bankers and currency traders in Beirut on August 6, 1932. But his origins can be traced to Aleppo, the Middle East's most important ancient trading center, where the Safras, a prominent clan of Syrian Jews, first carved out their banking empire nearly a century before.

Located midway between the Mediterranean and the Euphrates—the crossroads of Europe and the Middle East—Aleppo was a thriving business capital where for hundreds of years merchants conducted a bustling trade in the world's finest spices, textiles, and precious metals deep inside the city's fabled souks. Commerce was traditionally dominated by the Halabim, as the Syrian Jews from Aleppo were known, who were skillful traders and financiers.

Safra Frères et Cie. was a respected firm well-known throughout the Ottoman Empire and as far away as the Persian Gulf. In the days before the opening of the Suez Canal in 1869, the bank financed the camel caravans to Iraq and Egypt. The bank, overseen by Edmond's great-uncle Ezra, also had branches in Istanbul and Alexandria, each of them run by a trusted member of the Safra clan.

Born in Aleppo in 1891, Jacob Safra, Edmond's father, cut his teeth at the family banking house after his own father, a local *sir-eh-feen*, or "money changer," died when Jacob was a boy. Jacob was taken in by his uncle Ezra, and by the time he was a teenager, was working at Safra Frères in Aleppo. But as the city fell on hard economic times with the decline of the Ottoman Empire and Jews began to be conscripted for military service, Jacob was dispatched by his cousins to Beirut to open a new branch office of the family bank in 1914. As conditions grew worse in Aleppo, hundreds of Halabim also made the trek to Beirut. Although Jacob tried to resettle in Aleppo at the end of the First World War, he found the city much changed. The Jewish population had dwindled and after the victorious Allies divided up the Ottoman Empire, Aleppo lost its importance as a major trading route. The Safras scaled back their banking operations in Aleppo, and the cousins focused most of their efforts on the branches they had set up in Istanbul, Alexandria, and Beirut.

The Syrian Jews who made their way to Beirut after the First World War became Jacob Safra's most important clients, although he also took in deposits from Arabs and Druse clients when he opened his new bank in 1920. But while the Jacob Safra Bank took in deposits, it did not make very many loans, which was in keeping with the conservative philosophy of banking that has infused generations of Safra bankers. Trading was the main activity of the bank, and Jacob traded commodities, foreign currencies, and especially gold. The gold business soon proved so lucrative that Jacob became one of the wealthiest Jews in Beirut. In 1918, Jacob married his cousin Teira Safra. The couple would go on to have eight children, beginning with the birth of their first child, Elie, in 1922.

Edmond, Jacob and Teira's second son, was born ten years after Elie, and from an early age seemed the natural heir to the family business. A banking prodigy by the time he was eight, he began accompanying his father to the souks of Beirut to check on the Safra bank's depositors. Jacob taught Edmond to look people in the eye, as a person's character was often more important than a financial statement. Would he repay a loan? How well was he doing in business? How much did he give to charity?

Jacob's manifesto for success became legend among the Safra family, and to this day is quoted on the Web site of Grupo Safra, the Brazilian branch of the Safra empire. "You need to build a bank like a ship, solid to weather storms," goes the Safra motto. "You also need to maintain a high level of liquidity because sometimes Jews have to flee in a hurry, and never be the biggest because lightning always hits the highest trees."

In rare interviews given when he was an established banker in Switzerland and the U.S., Safra called banking "a simple and stupid business." He told one reporter that his father had always said, "May God send you intuition in life." Jacob also warned him "that you should never take a loan that you cannot afford to have in default."

"You need honesty and hard work and you don't need intelligence," Edmond said in an interview with the *Jornal do Brasil* in Rio in 1978. "The more intelligent the man, the more dangerous he turns out to be."

In another interview, he noted, "My father taught me that if you loan a man too much money, you turn a good man into a bad man."

These seemingly simple rules of running a bank were drilled into Edmond by his father, who also warned his son that he must always maintain a low profile—never call attention to his family's wealth or business success. Among the Halabim, modesty was considered a necessity. They believed that it was of paramount importance not to tempt the *ayin harah*, or the "evil eye," which would bring bad luck and hardship. For years, Edmond did what generations of men in his family had done—he carried around shiny blue stones in his pocket to ward off the evil eye. He also avoided becoming too exposed, too prosperous in the banking world. As he noted in a 1994 interview, he had the opportunity in 1990 to buy up Chase Manhattan stock and earn a controlling interest in the largest bank in America, but, the ultimate outsider, he held back. Jews should not own the biggest bank in a non-Jewish country, he told the reporter. "That is what my father taught me. I told that to my brothers in Brazil, too. Never become the largest bank."

Jacob's decision to take Edmond under his wing at the bank was a huge blow to his elder brother, Elie. In Sephardic tradition, the eldest son typically inherits the family business. But while the decision to promote Edmond was painful for Elie, the Safras broke with tradition because Edmond seemed such a born financier.

His friends noticed the same kind of emerging business acumen. In the summer of 1942, while he was vacationing at the resort town of Aley in the mountains outside Beirut, he convinced his father's chauffeur to take his friends up the steep mountains for a fee that he and the chauffeur split between them. When the boys' families began to complain to Jacob that Edmond was exploiting the children, the Safra patriarch laughed and said he was very glad that his son knew how to make money, and gave him his blessing to continue ferrying passengers up the mountains for cash.

But while Edmond may have been destined to become one of the world's great businessmen, he was by all accounts a terrible student. Friends recall that he was one of the worst pupils at the Alliance Israélite in Beirut. One of his teachers, Madame Tarrab, used to chide him for being the class clown, and once told him, "Edmond, you are going to grow up to be a shoeshine boy because you know nothing, and you will never know anything!" Years later, Madame Tarrab swallowed her own words when she traveled to New York to ask Edmond for a loan to save the Jewish school where she worked in Montreal. Without an appointment, she entered the Republic National Bank of New York, took the elevator to the top floor and told the receptionist that she wanted to see Edmond, who was in a meeting.

"Tell him that Madame Tarrab is here to see him," said the elderly teacher, who took a seat in the waiting room.

Minutes later, she was ushered into Edmond's opulent office. "Madame Tarrab, I have thought a lot about you over the years, please tell me what I can do to help you," said Edmond, hugging his old teacher.

He didn't flinch when he wrote her a check for $100,000 that helped save the school. He also gave her a small package that he told her to open when she was back in Montreal. But curiosity got the better of her and she opened the package on the flight from New York. She was shocked when a perfectly cut diamond ring tumbled out onto her tray table.

Edmond's lack of academic success seems not to have troubled his parents as higher education among the Halabim was not especially welcome. As one expert on Sephardic culture has noted, "Sephardic assimilation was slowed . . . by the tendency of many, especially those of Syrian background, to stay within the business community and not to send their children to universities, eliminating a major force that encourages the abandonment of traditional ways." Edmond left high school to go into the family business when he was fourteen.

The Safras lived a life of luxury in Beirut, a cosmopolitan, French-speaking seaside center often referred to as the Paris of the Middle East. Under the French Mandate, and even during the Second World War, a tight-knit community of some five thousand Jews lived relatively comfortable lives, buffered from the rabid anti-Semitism that was raging through Europe. As a teenager, Edmond had his own valet. His father was considered an important patron in the city, called upon to resolve disputes between Jews and to contribute to synagogues and Jewish schools. He even paid for the construction of a mosque for Beirut's Muslim population, across the street from his bank.

But the prosperous peace was shattered after the end of the Second World War as Jewish refugees began making their way to Palestine and clamoring for the establishment of a Jewish state. Across the Middle East, angry mobs of Arab nationalists turned on the Jews. In 1947, marauding Arab nationalists burned Jewish businesses, including the old Safra Frères offices and the synagogues in Aleppo. A year later, Jews in Syria became victims of fierce anti-Jewish laws that prevented them from selling their property and froze their assets. The violence and anti-Semitism soon took hold in Beirut as angry Arabs began to picket Jacob Safra and his bank. Still, the Lebanese government was tolerant of Jews; it did not punish them for the "sins" of the Zionists and, after the founding of the state of Israel in 1948, continued to grant citizenship to new immigrants.

But following the anti-Semitic picketing in front of his bank in Beirut, Jacob felt it was time to leave. He split up the family, sending his two youngest sons, Joseph and Moise, to boarding school in England. Edmond was entrusted with the important task of finding a secure haven somewhere else in the world where the clan could become citizens and do business in peace. At sixteen, Edmond boarded a plane for the first time in his young life. He headed for Italy accompanied by his valet and Jacques Tawil, one of his father's most trusted bankers. After settling in the Italian financial capital Milan, Safra and Tawil set up a small trading company that dealt in commodities and gold across the Middle East and Europe. The business was a success, but the young Edmond clearly felt like a second-class citizen in a country where he was forced to check in with immigration authorities every three months to renew his visa. Feeling particularly nervous before his first such meeting, Edmond consulted a friend who told him the best way to handle any situation was to give out as little information as possible—a philosophy that would serve him well the rest of his life, as he shunned publicity to protect himself and his clients.

"If they ask you how you came into the country—was it through the window?—your answer is 'No,'" the friend said. "Just no. Not, 'I came in through the door.'"

Edmond searched for a stable country where he could easily come in through the door and establish a family business that would grow and prosper for centuries. "I'm in no hurry to make money," he told *BusinessWeek* in 1994. "I want to build a bank that will last 1,000 years."

After visiting a client's paper mill in Brazil, Edmond wrote his father a long letter urging him to settle in the resource-rich, then stable, and prosperous country in the Southern Hemisphere. The Safras moved to Rio de Janeiro, arriving just after the annual Carnaval celebrations, on March 3, 1954. While the seaside cosmopolitan city must have reminded them of their home in Beirut, Jacob, the sixty-three-year-old patriarch, was not impressed. He quickly determined that Rio de Janeiro was not a serious capital of international finance. He uprooted the family and moved to São Paulo, where they joined a large wave of Sephardic Jews escaping violence and anti-Semitism in the Middle East.

The Sephardic clans kept to themselves in São Paulo and had little to do with the more established Ashkenazi Jews, from Russia and Poland, who had arrived earlier and established the synagogues and religious schools in the region. As they had done for centuries, the Sephardim created their own religious communities, which continue to function independently of the Ashkenazi Jews. For centuries, the two groups have regarded each other with some mistrust. Ashkenazi Jews from Europe, some of whom consider themselves to be the more enlightened and educated of the two groups, often view their Sephardic counterparts as poorly educated, extremely clannish, conservative, and prone to superstition. The Sephardic label was first applied to Jews who were expelled from Spain and Portugal after 1492, but later came to include Jews who lived in the Middle East and North Africa. Within the Sephardic community, the Halabim, like the Safras, set themselves even further apart. In São Paulo, the Syrian Jewish immigrants founded their own closely knit synagogues and schools, and generally married within their own tight circle. By the mid-1980s, there were 50,000 Sephardic Jews in Brazil, the second largest community outside France.

In 1957, three years after arriving in Rio de Janeiro, Edmond, just shy of his twenty-fifth birthday, became a Brazilian citizen. But his ambitions lay elsewhere, for even as he was petitioning for citizenship, he was flying off to Geneva to establish a new bank. Borrowing money from family and a group of Brazilian investors, Edmond had laid the groundwork in 1956 for what would become the Trade Development Bank—a financial institution that did what generations of Safra banks had done in the past: protect Sephardic and Arab in-

vestments. When it officially began to accept deposits, the bank attracted hundreds of wealthy Halabim and other Sephardic Jews who
had fled the Middle East and Africa to re-establish themselves in Milan, Rio, São Paulo, Paris, Buenos Aires, and New York. The bank
also welcomed Arab depositors. Those who needed a safe place for
their funds knew that they could trust the Safra name, especially now
that it was behind a bank in the primary haven for flight capital from
around the world.

For the Halabim, Safra's new business venture in Switzerland, with
its strict laws ensuring secrecy, was simply irresistible. In an early
advertisement in a Brazilian newspaper for the Banque Pour le De-
veloppement Commercial, as the bank was known in French, Safra
offered "accounts in any currency; investments; and buying and selling of shares in all international markets." For clients in Brazil and
Argentina, countries that forbade offshore investments, the TDB offered numbered accounts to protect their assets. There were also so-
called hold-mail accounts that forbade any correspondence between
the bank and the account holder. Discussions were carried out with
the depositor in person or by telephone. "The rules on hold-mail accounts were considered sacrosanct, since a single errant letter could
well get a depositor thrown into prison." According to the ad, the
representative in Brazil for the TDB was Joseph Safra in São Paulo.

But Edmond needn't have bothered with any advertising. As with
his father and uncle before him, clients were brought in to the Safra
universe by the current account holders. The bank's reputation for
utter discretion and secrecy spread largely by word of mouth. Correspondence was sent to account holders in unmarked envelopes
and new depositors had to be vetted beforehand. The standing joke
among bankers in Switzerland was that the switchboard operator at
the TDB would answer the phone with a cautious "hello" rather than
reveal the name of the bank. No one simply walked into the bank,
located on the rue Chantepoulet before moving to more permanent
headquarters at the elegant place du Lac. Clients had to make an ap-

pointment and show proper identification when they arrived. Most clients in far-flung places around the world preferred to speak by phone, but account officers, known at the bank as *garants*, were only allowed to speak to the depositor at the other end if they knew their voice. Often, phone calls were conducted in code, with depositors only speaking in numbers. Later, Edmond opened branches of the TDB in Nassau, London, and Chiasso, on the Italian-Swiss border.

Discreet and extremely low-key, the Trade Development Bank, which Edmond started with a loan of $1 million, would explode into an enterprise worth $5 billion by 1983, the year of its sale to American Express. By 1962, as the TDB began to take in increasing numbers of Halabim depositors fleeing Arab discontent in the Middle East, Edmond had decided to concentrate full time on his Swiss venture. He sold his Brazilian holdings to Moise and Joseph. A year later, Jacob died, and Edmond's younger brothers took over control of the family business in Brazil.

Grief-stricken at his father's death, Edmond took stock of his position in the world. He was thirty and already one of Europe's most successful bankers. But he was clearly dissatisfied. True success, he felt, still eluded him. He left Geneva and decided to use the money from the sale of his Brazilian holdings to finance his boldest venture—a bank in New York City, the world's financial capital.

It's not clear why Edmond chose the Knox Hat Company townhouse in midtown Manhattan to house the Republic National Bank of New York. The ten-story beaux-arts building on Fifth Avenue, across from the New York Public Library, was far from the banking hub of Wall Street and surrounded by retail stores. But there was something about the building that appealed to him. "He went there to buy a hat, liked the building and bought it," recalled one of his aides.

But perhaps Edmond was familiar with the history of the Knox Hat Company, which, like the Safra empire, had started out as a nineteenth-century family business.

Charles Knox initially established the hat company on Fulton

Street in lower Manhattan in 1838, but the company fell on hard times following damage from a nearby fire and protracted litigation over a dispute over trademarks. Following the Civil War, the business was taken over by his son Edward, a war hero who was wounded at the battle of Gettysburg. After a long rest cure in Geneva, Edward returned to New York "with the intention of making his name known wherever a hat was sold." With this in mind, he purchased the land on the southwest corner of Fifth Avenue and Fortieth Street, across from the site of the recently vacated reservoir where the New York Public Library was under construction. He hired John Duncan, one of the city's finest architects, and commissioned him to design the building, which was built between 1901 and 1902 and soon became the showplace for New York's finest hats.

It's hard to believe that a man as superstitious as Safra *didn't* know the history of the building and the Knox family's similarities to his own before he began the process of transforming the townhouse into his showpiece bank in Manhattan. Here was the site where Edward Knox, recently arrived from Geneva, was determined to become successful. And here was Edmond, the displaced Lebanese-Brazilian Genevois, some six decades later, determined to conquer the financial world.

"He knew more about the history of the Knox building than I did," said Eli Attia, the architect who would later be commissioned to design an addition to the building. "There were no banks in that area, but Edmond was more intelligent than most developers and he had a vision."

Whatever his reasons for buying the Knox Hat Company building, the townhouse at 452 Fifth Avenue was a perfect fit for him. Nevertheless, he spent $2.5 million converting the retail space for a bank, removing the mezzanine, installing plate glass windows and wood paneling, and decorating the lobby with Louis XIV antiques, of which he had become an avid collector. The Republic's refurbished lobby was without a doubt the most opulent of any bank in New York at the time. On the ninth floor, Attia created a small apartment with space for separate quarters for Edmond's valet. Later, when he became even more successful and his thriving business outgrew the confines of the ten-story structure, Edmond commissioned Attia to add a gleaming glass tower to the original building, and a palatial 13,000-square-foot apartment for himself on the twenty-ninth floor.

His formula for success was little changed from his days in Geneva. He still extolled the conservative banking formula he had learned from his father: "security, seriousness, hard work, careful lending, and controlling expenses."

"You can take a chance in life, but not with a bank," Edmond was fond of telling his aides. "A bank is not a playground. Banking is conservatism. And it has been the same for a few thousand years."

In New York, as in Geneva, he offered discretion to a client base of wealthy Sephardic refugees and royal families from Saudi Arabia and the Persian Gulf, many of whom had banked with Safra Frères for generations.

But doing business in America was markedly different from doing business anywhere else in the world. For one thing, the media-shy Edmond felt he needed to be much more public if he was going to be as successful as he wanted to be. This is why he needed to open with a splash. He told his friends that a relatively unknown swarthy Lebanese banker with thick eyebrows was not going to pass muster among New York's elite, with their Harvard pedigrees and their connections to the Kennedy clan.

So, at the bank's grand opening on a frigid morning in January 1966, Safra made sure he had all the elements that would make New Yorkers sit up and take notice. Robert Kennedy, New York's junior senator, cut the yellow ribbon officially opening the city's newest bank and mingled with the new officers and organizers—themselves a who's who of New York business and legal circles. There was the prominent lawyer Theodore W. Kheel, the mediator of many New York labor disputes who had strong ties to the city's Democratic political machine. Kheel, who was extremely well connected in New

York power circles, was Republic's new chairman, although his authority was nominal. Peter White, a former senior vice president of the Manufacturers Hanover Trust Company and Republic's new president and chief executive officer, was also on hand at the ribbon cutting. In the *New York Times* article that chronicled the opening, Edmond was mentioned almost as an afterthought and was described as "a Lebanese banker whose family controls 36 per cent of the new bank."

Of course, Edmond, who hated publicity, didn't mind receiving only a fleeting mention in the third paragraph of the *New York Times* story, which went on to marvel that the bank's initial capital—$11 million—was the largest of any other private commercial bank in U.S. history.

Still, the newspaper was skeptical about the bank's chances at success: "Republic, of course, will be a pygmy among New York City's banking giants," noted the *New York Times* reporter, adding that the largest, Chase Manhattan Bank, had assets at the end of 1965 of $15.3 billion.

With his obsessive attention to every detail of his new business, Safra set out to prove them all wrong. By 1969, he had come up with an ingenious way to lure more depositors. He offered account holders who brought in new depositors free color television sets and Singer sewing machines for every three-year deposit of $10,000 or more. U.S. commercial banking rules limit the use of gifts as a way to attract new depositors, but the rules do not apply to account holders bringing in a new customer. "If someone brings a friend to the bank to open a deposit, the sponsor gets a color TV," noted the *Wall Street Journal*. Soon depositors crowded Republic's lobby to open accounts.

"Stockholders of Republic National Bank of New York, trooping in for the annual meeting, had to weave their way through throngs of customers shoveling money into the bank," reported the *Wall Street Journal*. "Crowds of customers milled around temporary work tables set up to handle the overflow from tellers' positions, and bank clerks were opening new accounts as fast as they could type up the forms."

It didn't seem to matter that they were locking themselves into long-term deposits that offered extremely low interest rates or that they could have probably gotten a better rate elsewhere. But even as the free sixteen-inch Zenith sets were drawing hundreds of new account holders, some of the bank's own stockholders were urging Edmond to undertake a more aggressive public relations campaign. "As it is," quipped one stockholder, "all anyone knows about us is that we sell more TV sets than anyone else in New York." The giveaways soon earned the bank the derisive moniker "TV bank" in New York business circles.

But attracting new depositors would only prove part of the Republic's success. Like the other Safra banks, Republic was also involved in the trade of precious metals. It was the first bank in the U.S. to be granted a license to sell gold for industry, and eventually it became the largest seller of gold bullion after the U.S. government stopped selling gold in 1968. Safra, whose name means "yellow" in Arabic, set about buying gold coins and industrial gold around the world. After the U.S. Department of Treasury lifted the forty-one-year-old ban on private ownership of gold, the bank became the leading importer of gold coins. By 1980, the bank controlled one-third of the U.S. market for gold used by dentists and jewelers. Its gold holdings eventually became so vast that Edmond ordered the construction of special vaults in the sub-basement of the bank's headquarters to store blocks of gold and silver. The vaults were among the most modern precious metals warehouses in North America, with a loading dock capable of handling four armored trucks and two tractor trailers at the same time.

Even though U.S. tax laws forced Edmond, a nonresident for tax purposes, to take on the title of honorary chairman, everyone at Republic knew he was firmly in charge. Nothing escaped his watchful eye; all loans had to be approved by him. When he faced a particularly difficult decision, Safra would lock himself in a boardroom with only his most trusted Sephardic aides, who included Jacques Tawil, who had accompanied him to Milan in 1948; Cyril Dwek, a fellow Halabim whose family had known the Safras for generations; and, later, Walter Weiner, a New York lawyer who would earn his stripes dealing with Lily's sticky legal issues over the Monteverde estate on two continents. Edmond was so impressed with Weiner's dedication and intelligence that he later made him Republic president, and then chairman.

Edmond was a man obsessed with his banks, which he often referred to as "my children, my life." In the early days of Republic, he lived in his small suite of rooms on the ninth floor, rarely leaving the building until it was time for him to jet off to Geneva to take care of affairs at the TDB. He conducted intercontinental business in the mornings while shaving. Later, after he bought a magnificent villa on the Riviera, he regularly received his clients at home. Peter Cohen, a former board member and chair of Republic, recalled that the reception areas of the grand château often resembled a lavish doctor's waiting room, with elegantly dressed clients awaiting their turn to speak to Edmond.

"His is one of the few banks in the world where the proprietor is at home—the service is that close and personal," said Cohen.

On the rare occasions that he did take time off, he loved to put on a pair of jeans and ride a bicycle through Central Park.

But Edmond's obsession with banking eventually paid off in a big way. In the first month of its history, Republic opened 20,000 accounts—a record for a commercial bank in New York City. From that single townhouse on Fifth Avenue, Edmond transformed Republic into the twentieth largest bank in the U.S. Republic had sixty-nine branches in New York, Florida, and California, and 300,000 depositors in the heyday of its success in the mid–1990s.

"I'm now competing with the big boys in their own country," Edmond told the *New York Times*, six years after the founding of

Republic National Bank of New York. "I must say the Americans have been more than fair to me. Doing business in America is beautiful."

A little more than a decade later, Edmond's fascination with America soured as he became enmeshed in a war that nearly cost him his "children" and, even more important to him, his reputation.

EDMOND WAS USED to getting what he wanted in business. But his romantic life was another matter. His single-minded dedication to his banks, especially when he was building his empire in the 1950s and 1960s, left the young banker, who was growing prematurely bald, little time to socialize, although he did have something of the jet-set playboy in him. He kept a fully staffed and equipped 100-foot yacht named *Aley* after the hillside village in Beirut where he was born and where he operated his first successful venture with the family chauffeur. The yacht was anchored off the coast of Cannes. Friends from Brazil recalled lavish parties and endless backgammon games—which Edmond loved to play—aboard the yacht.

But even as his mother and sisters offered to set him up with marriageable young women from the Levant—Syrian Jewish virgins whose families they knew personally—Safra rarely expressed any interest in marriage. Everything changed, of course, when he saw the blonde in the green satin dress at his brother Joseph's wedding in São Paulo in the late 1960s.

"Who is that beautiful woman?" he whispered to his friend Nasser.

"Don't you see, Edmond?" Nasser replied. "She's with Fred, her husband."

Although Edmond had done business with Alfredo for years, he may have been only vaguely aware of his wives and affairs. After 1957 his Swiss bank kept him away from Rio de Janeiro, where Alfredo's own company was based.

But by August 1969, when Alfredo died under bizarre circumstances at his home in Rio de Janeiro, Edmond's and Lily's fortunes seemed inextricably linked.

Immediately following Alfredo's death, the surviving Monteverde family members were extremely puzzled by his will, although their first instincts seem to have been to trust his widow. At one point, Regina Monteverde, who was promised her Copacabana apartment, which Alfredo owned, and a monthly living allowance from a separate legacy to the will, even signed an agreement with Lily agreeing to the split in assets. But in the months after his death, as they examined Alfredo's business affairs more closely, they questioned why certain assets had not been disclosed. The Monteverdes decided they needed to take action.

They feared that Lily was working closely with Edmond and decided to take their battle for Alfredo's estate to a level that would force them both to come to account. Immediately following Alfredo's death, they feared that Edmond was orchestrating Lily's financial and legal affairs.

A legal challenge in Brazil was simply not an option because of the ease with which judicial officials could be bribed. Besides, Lily and Edmond had too many friends among Rio de Janeiro's power elite—people who could be easily bought and persuaded to falsify an important document or lie under oath. The Monteverdes decided it would be in Britain, in Her Majesty's courts, that the battle over the estate would be fought. At the time, Lily was living in London, where Edmond's Trade Development Bank also had a branch office.

As one of their British attorneys noted in court, the Monteverdes "instituted proceedings so that a British court may establish whether or not there were assets in the possession or under the management or control of Alfredo, and, if so, whether any such assets have been concealed to the English or Brazilian authorities by the defendant."

The Monteverdes, who had all lived in England before the Second World War, had unshakable faith in British justice. But, as they were to find out years later, even British justice proved no match for Edmond Safra.

Still, in the beginning the Monteverdes (Rosy and her mother Regina) were full of hope that justice would prevail. They filed suit against Lily and Edmond's Swiss bank in a British court, convinced that Lily and Edmond had colluded to secure Alfredo's estate.

"The relationship between the bank and the first-named defendant Lily Monteverde is not, as the Bank has sought to suggest, merely the normal relationship between a bank and its client (or a bank and the widow of a former client)," noted the court filing against Lily and the Trade Development Bank. At the time, lawyers for the Trade Development Bank tried to dismiss the Monteverde family suit against the bank, arguing that it had nothing to do with Alfredo's estate.

"On the contrary, it is clear from the information about the Bank and its officers which I have been able to obtain that the bank is directly interested and involved in the matters which are the subject of these proceedings," said Rosy.

Lily, who now controlled Alfredo's vast empire, allowed Safra to oversee all financial and legal decisions. One of her main attorneys at the time, Jayme Bastian Pinto, was a director of the Safra Group in Brazil. Shortly after Alfredo's death, Lily had also appointed Bastian Pinto to head up one of Alfredo's old firms in Brazil, the Universal Company, which she now controlled.

"In October 1970, a meeting at which I was present was held to discuss a possible settlement of the matters at issue in these proceedings," noted Rosy in one of her court filings. "At the request of Lily Monteverde's advisers this meeting was held in Geneva. I obtained the clear impression that Mr. Bastian Pinto was acting on the direct instructions of Mr. Safra and that Geneva was chosen for negotiations in order that Mr. Safra should be able to instruct Mr. Bastian Pinto."

A year later another meeting was held in Geneva to try to come to an out-of-court settlement. "Immediately after [the meeting] . . . Mr. Safra flew to London to join Lily Monteverde."

It didn't take long for the Monteverde family to find out that Lily and Edmond were extremely close. As Rosy noted in court filings, "From my own knowledge and from what I have been told by my friends in Brazil, I can say that since my brother's death by gunshot wounds, Mr. Safra has become extensively involved (either personally or through his agents such as Mr. Bastian Pinto) in the running of the Brazilian companies comprised in the partnership which is subject of these proceedings and that he now has a personal interest in these companies."

One of many exhibits that the Monteverdes entered as evidence to link Lily and Edmond was a letter on Trade Development Bank letterhead in which the widow of Alfredo Monteverde "renounces all rights, title and interest in or arising from the above policy of assurance issued by your company [Abbey Life Assurance Co. Ltd.] on 9th July 1968." The date on the letter renouncing Lily's rights on Alfredo's £750 policy ("It was too little money to bother with," said a lawyer who was familiar with the Monteverde estate) is December 5, 1969, which proved that Edmond's bank was indeed looking after Lily's interests shortly after Alfredo's death on August 25, 1969.

And well he should, for the court challenges against Lily would prove the first major threat to his own Swiss bank as the TDB was directly implicated in the lawsuit. While Edmond, no doubt, assured Lily that he would fix everything, it would take hundreds of thousands in legal fees and years of worry and frustration to repair the fallout from what turned into a legal quagmire on two continents. In the end, Edmond would make the resolution of Lily's legal issues a matter of the most urgent concern, and, in addition to the very capable Bastian Pinto, he would dispatch Walter Weiner, his most trusted attorney, to ensure that everything was taken care of.

The most serious claim in the suit was the accusation that Lily and Edmond, through his TDB, were hiding Alfredo's assets from the surviving family, and, most important, from his son, Carlos, the other heir to the Monteverde fortune. Among the inventory that they alleged had not been noted on a list of Alfredo's assets prepared by Lily's lawyers, were properties, including the house on Rua Icatu, shares in various Brazilian companies, and jewels—diamonds, emeralds, sapphires, and platinum. Also missing from the inventory were important paintings, including two works by Paul Klee (*Helldunkel Studie* and *Côtes de Provence*), *Le Clown* by Fernand Léger, *La Promenade des Jeunes Ecolières* by Pierre Bonnard, *Papier Colle* by Georges Braque, Pablo Picasso's *Le Peintre Colle*, and Vincent van Gogh's *Après l'Orage*. Like the jewels, the paintings had all been insured in London. Lily did declare the Van Gogh and some other paintings of lesser value by Brazilian artists in the inventory of the estate.

"The widow will neither account to us nor even disclose to us the assets which are in question, . . . and the mother and the daughter are seeking relief from this position which I describe as unconscionable," argued Charles Sparrow, the lawyer for the Monteverde family in Britain's High Court of Justice.

For her part, Lily argued that she did not need to disclose the gifts that she had received during her marriage to Alfredo, which included the Icatu house that was transferred into her name in August 1968.

Regina and Rosy demanded nothing less than two-thirds of Alfredo's assets, arguing that they had operated Ponto Frio with Alfredo as a family company, and that the capital for the start-up in 1946 came from the gold and other assets that they took to Brazil from Romania, via England.

In court proceedings that would drag on for more than three years, the Monteverde family claimed that Alfredo's 1966 will was not valid since he was not of sound mind when it was drafted. In October 1966, when the will was signed, Alfredo was going through a particularly bad bout of the "spring disease." He was undergoing intense psychiatric treatment and was on medication that clouded his judgment, the family argued. Alfredo's prescriptions for that period were entered as evidence in court. From 1955, when he was first diagnosed with manic depression, or bipolar disorder as it's known today, Alfredo was, at

various times, put on a combination of antidepressants such as Nardil
(phenelzine sulfate), lithium carbonate, and Tryptizol (amitriptyline
hydrochloride). All of these medications, taken in conjunction with
each other or alone, could have slowed his intellectual functions and
caused confusion, among other side effects.

In an affidavit, Dr. Giacomo Landau, one of Alfredo's physicians
who had treated him since 1955, noted that at the time he drafted
his 1966 will, "Alfredo João Monteverde was under my treatment at
various occasions. It is no doubt about it [sic] that this patient suffered
from a serious maniac [sic] depressive illness and he was so ill that he
was not responsible for any decision that he might have made. He was
all the time on heavy drugs which could cloud his memory." Another
Rio de Janeiro psychiatrist, Dr. C. Magalhães de Freitas, also noted
under oath that Alfredo had been particularly ill in the fall of 1966,
and that he had been interned twice that year at the exclusive São Vicente Clinic in Rio de Janeiro to treat his depression.

It was mainly for these reasons that Rosy and her mother questioned the validity of the 1966 will. "On my brother's death, his
widow the defendant Lily Monteverde obtained a grant of probate to
an alleged will of my brother (the validity of which is not admitted
by my mother or myself) and obtained possession and control of all
the family assets formerly in the possession or control of my brother,"
said Rosy in papers filed with the court in London.

The Monteverdes also said that it was completely out of character
for Alfredo to have excluded his mother, sister, and beloved niece,
Christina, from the will. Both Rosy and her mother had worked as
important consultants and had invested their own portions of the family fortune in Globex, the parent company of Ponto Frio. To prove
this, hand-scrawled letters by Alfredo written to his mother and sister
regarding the family business were introduced as evidence, as were
the powers of attorney that he had drafted for his mother and sister to
act on his behalf in all personal and business matters in the event of
his illness or death.

The court proceedings were particularly ugly, with both sides accusing each other of greed. At one point, Charles Sparrow, the lawyer representing Regina and Rosy, caused some consternation when he declared in open court that his clients did not accept that Alfredo had committed suicide.

Inextricably tied to the English proceedings was a suit brought by Regina against Lily in Brazilian court, demanding the guardianship of Carlos Monteverde, her grandson, who was nine years old when Alfredo died. (Carlos had been adopted from an orphanage in Rio in 1959 while Alfredo was still married to his second wife, Scarlett.)

Under the 1966 will, Alfredo had named Lily as the guardian of his adopted son. Under Brazilian law, this is the standard legal course of action provided that the child is the natural-born offspring of the deceased. But as nearly everyone in Rio knew, a case of mumps as an adult had rendered Alfredo sterile. So it was with much surprise that lawyers found a registry document dated October 17, 1964, allegedly signed by Alfredo and declaring that he was the natural father of the child and that his mother was Silvia Maria Monteverde, a woman no one had ever heard of. The Monteverde family was skeptical about this document and thought it was made by Alfredo when he was in the fog of a depression. Court records indicate that the 1964 registration was used by Lily to prove that her rights to Carlos and his share of the Monteverde fortune were ironclad.

Lily left Brazil with the children almost immediately after Alfredo's death. After all, Carlos didn't need to hear the gossip that was building in Rio social circles. Why did Alfredo Monteverde commit suicide? asked the ladies as they picked through their salads at the Gavea Golf and Country Club and the Rio de Janeiro Yacht Club. Why did Lily leave so suddenly? others wondered. She didn't even pack any of her clothes! She didn't say goodbye!

"On September 15, 1969, she [Lily] escaped with [Alfredo's] son to

London without saying goodbye to me," said Regina in an affidavit. "I never saw the child again, and never received news of him, not even at Christmas or New Year's."

Previously, Carlos had been in fourth grade at the Instituto Souza Leão, an upscale day school near the Icatu house in Rio. The decision to cut Carlos off from his family and friends in Brazil so quickly after the death of his father was also questioned by many of Lily and Alfredo's friends in Rio. Lily's rather cavalier treatment of the boy also became fodder for Regina's lawsuit seeking guardianship.

"The defendant in order to better attend to her interests removed her ward from Brazil, by taking him to a foreign land, where he is being educated in a form different from the Brazilian way, far away from the social contact with his relatives and with his environment," argued Regina in Brazilian court filings.

Lily vigorously denied the accusation, brushing aside the fact that she did enroll the grieving Carlos in boarding school shortly after Alfredo's death, and she did begin living in a flat near Kensington Palace, rented for her by a corporation controlled by Edmond. She defended her decision to go to England by arguing that it was "to safeguard the interests of the minor child Carlos Monteverde, above all in order to prevent him becoming directly involved in this sordid type of defamation, while taking advantage of the deceased's wish to have his son brought up in England, as he himself had been."

Furthermore, Lily noted that Regina had taken little interest in her own grandson when he was in Brazil. "Regina, as her name indicates, has always shown herself to be a willful and dominating person, imposing her wishes and desires, often in an arbitrary manner."

In court papers filed in both Brazil and England, Lily's lawyers did their utmost to present her as the devoted mother, worried for the well-being of her son. "She has given her son all her love and devotion," said Lily's attorney. "If she was already lavishing special affection on [Carlos], she has given him far more since the death of his father, when she redoubled her tenderness in an endeavor to make good that sad loss."

To complicate matters even further, Alfredo's second wife, Scarlett Delebois Monteverde, also demanded the guardianship of Carlos. In court papers filed in Rio de Janeiro, she claimed that she had adopted Carlos jointly with Alfredo after the boy had been abandoned as an infant at the reception room of the judicial authority for orphans in Rio de Janeiro in early 1960.

In her initial arguments to win guardianship, Scarlett made the argument that there was "a collision of interests between the present guardian [Lily] appointed by testament and the minor, and further emphasized that there exists a concealment of property" on Lily's part which was jeopardizing Carlos's interests under the will.

Like Regina and Rosy before her, Scarlett accused Lily of hiding Alfredo's assets and only declaring a small fraction of what they believed to be an immense fortune. For instance, at one point Lily declared that at the time of his death Alfredo owned only 1,479,200 shares of a total of 23 million in Globex. The figure made up just over 5 percent of shares in a company that he had founded and controlled his entire adult life. Moreover, Lily stated in initial court proceedings that Carlos owned only 7,663,165 shares or roughly 25 percent of the company—half of what should have been his entitlement under the 1966 will.

"Where are the remaining 15,396,835 shares of Globex capital?" asked the attorney for the Monteverde family. "If the defendant had any real interest in defending the rights of her ward, it is obvious that the defendant would make, or would be making, every effort to find the whereabouts of such shares 'mysteriously' disappeared. However, it appears that the defendant is simply not interested in finding these shares."

Scarlett's initial challenge to the probate court (known formally as the Court of Orphans and Successions) in Brazil was thrown out by the judge, who upheld Lily's rights over Carlos. Undeterred, Scarlett appealed. When Lily learned that Scarlett had arrived on the scene, she immediately accused the Monteverde family of co-opting her for their own cause. Initially, at least, this was not true. Stelio Bastos Belchior, the Brazilian attorney for Regina, denied that there was any collusion with Scarlett on his client's part, and actually petitioned the court on behalf of Regina to halt Scarlett's initial proceedings.

But Regina must have regretted such a hasty decision, for prior to the appeal, the two women did join forces. Regina and Scarlett signed a joint statement that they would both look after Carlos and consult one another on the management of his assets should Scarlett win the guardianship of the boy.

The team effort enraged Lily. "One sees that the plaintiff, after the death of her son, did not accept his will, scheming and elaborating a plan and a strategy, directly or indirectly to circumvent the will of the deceased, either by trying to obtain the guardianship of the minor by means of the application of Marie Paule Delebois Monteverde, or upon that attempt failing, to sue (as she has done in England) for his share in the fortune of the deceased," said Lily in her testimony.

Lily was relentless in her attacks on her former mother-in-law, whom she characterized as "an elderly lady with an imposing capacity for dissimulation and no moral qualities befitting her age." When she found out about her son's death, Regina grieved with her daughter-in-law and promised to help her, Lily told the court. But "from the moment she learned of the contents of his will like a stroke of magic, all consideration, affection and trust which the plaintiff lavished on the defendant disappeared."

At one point, Lily cautioned Regina "to hold her venom in check so as not to harm the son of Alfredo."

But Rosy and her mother claimed they were only protecting the interests of Carlos and were not after the money for themselves.

As Regina's lawyer made clear, "if as a result of this action Mrs.

Regina Monteverde should obtain any benefit by way of property or assets, she now formally declares that she will take all the legal steps required for the purpose of assigning that benefit to the minor Carlos."

But after accusing the Monteverde family of trying to co-opt Scarlett to their cause, Lily seemed to turn around and do the same thing. It is not clear whether Edmond's legal advisers paid Scarlett to withdraw her claim in Brazilian court, but it is clear that in the end Scarlett abruptly changed sides.

On August 26, 1973, João Augusto de Miranda Jordão, Rosy's attorney in Rio de Janeiro, sent an urgent telegram to Rosy's home in Chiasso. "Scarlett in Rio with Lily's American lawyer asking to stop the legal action, and saying she has come to agreement with Lily STOP."

Walter Weiner was "Lily's American lawyer" who traveled to Rio to take control of the situation. But while Weiner was used to the wheeling and dealing that took place in American boardrooms and courts, the legal complexities of Rio de Janeiro proved a challenge even for him.

Although Scarlett informed her Brazilian attorney that she did not wish to continue with the appeal, she did not have the authority to call it off. Her lawyer, Theodoro Arthou, had been retained by Regina, and he refused her request. Scarlett and Weiner then went from law office to law office in Rio trying to find a lawyer who would take her power of attorney and present a motion to the court to withdraw the appeal. They finally found a lawyer who was willing to take on the case. But it doesn't appear as if he terminated the proceedings.

"I learned only a few days ago that my instructions to terminate the proceeding had not been followed," noted Scarlett in a June 1973 affidavit. "While I believed initially that the lawsuit instituted by me could benefit the minor, I realized finally the motives of Mrs. Regina Monteverde and Rosy Fanto were otherwise. In view of the aforementioned facts, I have decided to bring to a definite end the lawsuit which I initiated and which is now pending before the Federal Supreme Court."

Scarlett's statement to the court withdrawing her action to adopt Carlos is worth noting in some detail because it so completely and utterly contradicts her previous statements.

In her sworn deposition seeking the termination of her petition to adopt Carlos, she says that Carlos Monteverde is Alfredo's "natural son." Yet in a previous deposition, made in 1970, three years earlier, she admits that she and Alfredo adopted two children—Carlos and Alexandra—because they couldn't have children of their own. Alexandra was never mentioned in the 1966 will because Scarlett had retained sole custody of the girl when she split from Alfredo in 1962.

She also contradicted herself with respect to her former mother-in-law Regina. In 1970, she had signed a contract with Regina promising to honor each other's wishes in the care of Carlos, arguing that this would be in the best interests of the child. But less than three years later, she viciously attacked Regina when she sought to have the entire case closed. "The thought of Regina Rebecca Monteverde being appointed as the tutoress of Carlos is absolutely appalling to me. Given the combination of the unstable temperament and advanced age of this woman, her appointment as tutoress would be most detrimental to the best interests of the minor."

Her petition to withdraw the legal action in Brazil appears to have been drafted to benefit Lily's own claim to the boy, and to discredit the Monteverde family's claims against Lily and the Trade Development Bank.

"I am now firmly convinced that Lily Monteverde has fully and faithfully discharged her duties as turoress of the minor and administratrix of the estate and has acted in accordance with the wishes of Alfredo João Monteverde. I am of the firm conviction that the welfare of the minor Carlos Monteverde will best be served by the continued guardianship of Lily Monteverde. I am also convinced that Lily

Monteverde is devoting all of her efforts to carrying out the wishes of Alfredo João Monteverde with respect to Carlos."

In the end, Scarlett's testimony proved a key factor in Lily's legal battle to adopt Carlos. Edmond had indeed fixed everything, and on February 8, 1973, the Brazilian courts cleared the way for her to adopt Carlos. As for the legal case against Lily and the Trade Development Bank in Britain, it was settled out of court, but the terms of the settlement were never made public.

The protracted legal battles in London and Rio de Janeiro left Lily a nervous wreck. According to those who knew her at the time, she lost weight and had trouble sleeping.

But while the battles must have caused both Lily and Edmond much anxiety, they also drew them closer together. Although they were forced to keep their personal relationship under wraps while the legal actions were playing themselves out in court, they clearly found time to be together. Edmond visited Lily on his regular trips to London to oversee the London branch of the Trade Development Bank. Lily frequently traveled to Geneva where Edmond convened meetings with the new principals of Alfredo's companies—many of them Halabim business associates, who reported directly to Edmond. While Lily and Carlos were now the majority shareholders in Globex and Ponto Frio, Edmond was clearly in charge.

Although they were trying to be discreet, many of their friends said that Lily and Edmond frequently went on holiday together. Their favorite destination was the French Riviera, with its fine restaurants and azure waters. In Antibes they could relax on a yacht moored off Millionaires Quay in the shadow of Fort Carré, the sixteenth-century fort where Napoleon Bonaparte was once imprisoned. In the evenings they headed to Juan-les-Pins, the picturesque village that had been the seaside haunt of F. Scott Fitzgerald, Ernest Hemingway, Pablo Picasso, and other luminaries in the 1920s and 1930s.

In the summer of 1970, Lily rented a yacht called the *Blue Finn*. Ever cautious, Edmond told her to rent the boat under a third-party name. The boat, rented under the name Dr. Iperti from Milan, was later traced to Lily Monteverde.

Their friend Marcelo Steinfeld recalls visiting the two lovers and spending a few days with them aboard the yacht. In a black-and-white photograph he took of their boat trip on the Riviera, a relaxed, balding Edmond appears in bathing trunks sitting next to Lily, who is wearing a terry-wrap over her bathing suit, her wet hair pulled back from her suntanned face. They are on the sun-splashed deck of the boat, digging into a late lunch.

"They really knew how to enjoy themselves," said Steinfeld.

Soon after arriving in London, Lily bought herself a full-length sable coat. She became such a good customer at the couture houses in Paris that she was soon on friendly terms with the legendary designers Valentino and Givenchy, later inviting them to her sumptuous balls and intimate dinners. Like a princess in a fairy tale, Lily was finally living her grandest dream, but in order to gain even greater entry into the grandest salons of Europe, she needed to be even more fabulously wealthy. That would surely come when she married one of the world's most distinguished bankers.

But although Edmond was in love with Lily, he wasn't ready for marriage. For one thing, his family did not approve of her. Not only was she divorced and quickly approaching middle age, she had four children from previous marriages and she was an Ashkenazi Jew—an outsider. Joseph had made his family proud when he had married Vicki, a fellow Halabim. Most of his sisters—Eveline, Gabi, and Huguette—would go on to marry within the Sephardic community in South America. The exception was Arlette, who had insisted on a "mixed" marriage to an Ashkenazi Jew. Edmond, who, despite geographic distance was still extremely close to his siblings, knew the grief it would cause his family in São Paulo if he married Lily against their will. At her age, how would she produce heirs to take over the banking empire that he was building?

The free-love hippie movement may have taken hold in Europe and

North America, but in the Halabim communities of São Paulo many clans lived much as they had done in the nineteenth century. In São Paulo, a Halabim man was supposed to marry within the community. If he couldn't find a mate at the synagogue or through family connections, there were ways of finding suitable young women among their extended families still in Syria or the ones who had settled in Brooklyn and New Jersey. There had to be thousands of young, good-looking, eligible women whose families would literally jump at the chance to have a rich man like Edmond as a son-in-law.

"The Safras put a lot of pressure on Edmond not to marry Lily," recalled Steinfeld. "They thought no good could come of the marriage, and they wanted nothing to do with her."

At first, Edmond might have made excuses about the legal obstacles they both faced with the Monteverdes breathing down their necks in the British and Brazilian lawsuits. Furthermore, they couldn't possibly get married so soon after Alfredo's death. That would invite gossip—something Edmond clearly abhorred. Lily had to think of the children and her own reputation. No, it was better to wait. They could simply go on as before.

But Lily wanted to be married, and she wanted to conquer high society. She did wait for a few years, but then she grew tired of waiting.

Edmond, who had been taught to size up a person by looking them straight in the eye, clearly slipped when it came to his lover. For all his intelligence and street smarts honed in the souks of Beirut, he never foresaw the emotional tidal wave that was about to wash over him.

FIVE

Two Weddings

L ILY WATKINS MONTEVERDE, as she now called herself, couldn't have picked a more unromantic spot for the beginning of a torrid affair, but unlike almost everything in her life since Alfredo's death, some things eluded even her control.

On September 28, 1971, more than two years after arriving in London, Lily sat slightly slumped in a dentist's chair at a private clinic in Devonshire Place waiting for her dentist, Brian Kanarek, to examine her days before he was scheduled to extract her impacted wisdom teeth. Lily sat gossiping with Dora Cohen, a former sister-in-law who was married to her first husband's brother, and who had accompanied her to the dental clinic. Although Lily had long since divorced Mario Cohen, she still maintained a relationship with the family. Friends say that Lily and Mario did not get along, but were forced to speak frequently to arrange the children's visits between two continents.

Deep in conversation with Dora, she barely noticed when Kanarek finally arrived, striding into the clinic with the handsome stranger who would shortly change her life.

Or rather, she would change his.

The year had not been a particularly good one for Lily Watkins Monteverde. The lawsuit brought by her former in-laws, who were alleging that she was hiding Alfredo's fortune, continued with no end in sight; her son Eduardo had left yet another school; and Adriana, now a teenager, was challenging her mother's authority and getting into frequent arguments with Lily. Claudio remained her "perfect son" and was a big help to Carlos, who was lonely and full of self-doubt after the death of his father. Then, on July 25, her mother, Annita Watkins, a diabetic, died quite suddenly of a heart attack at seventy-one in Rio de Janeiro. On top of everything, Edmond was still insisting that they hide their relationship, at least until the end of the court cases in Brazil and England. But she knew he wasn't serious about marriage, and that his conservative family in Brazil would never accept her.

So perhaps on the day she went to see her dentist in London, she wasn't thinking very clearly. Perhaps she needed a diversion—something to dull the pain of her mother's sudden passing and Edmond's tacit rejection.

She instinctively sat up when the diversion walked through the door. At the time, Samuel Bendahan was Kanarek's best friend, and a patient. To Lily, he seemed perfect—one of the sexiest men she had ever seen. And after two years of widowhood and a frustrating affair with Safra that seemed to be leading nowhere, she was eager for a new conquest. She raised a hand to her hair to make sure it was perfectly coiffed. She would no doubt have loved to freshen her lipstick and touch up her makeup, but she couldn't very well dig into her purse and reach for her compact, not after the handsome stranger walked into the room.

"I caught a very quick glimpse of her looking bored but the instant that she saw me, she was sitting up and her hand went up to check her hair," recalled Bendahan, years after that first meeting with Lily at the clinic. "This became a shorthand piece of intimacy between us. If subsequently I put my hand up to my hair and went through exaggerated motions of checking my coiffure, you could be sure that this would elicit a broad grin from her. She would do the same to me if, for example, we were in company and she wanted to convey to me that she was impatient for us to be 'alone' (and all that implies!)."

At thirty-five, Bendahan was tall, dark, and exotic, with black hair and brooding brown eyes. Born in Marrakech, educated in England, he seemed the perfect combination of cosmopolitan businessman, charming gentleman, and witty intellectual.

The way Bendahan tells the story, it was clearly love, or rather lust, at first sight, at least on Lily's part. But while he may have instantly seen through her intentions, nothing prepared Bendahan for the dizzying whirlwind of the next few months.

If he could have fast-forwarded his life at that moment—standing in an antiseptic London clinic, politely shaking this woman's hand, making small talk—he never could have imagined the bizarre and dangerous twist his life would take.

AT THAT FIRST meeting, Lily didn't waste any time. Less than twenty minutes after being introduced to him, she asked him on a date. Bendahan claims that he demurred, slightly put off by her aggressive behavior. Had Kanarek purposely set up the meeting between his handsome single friend and the wealthy widow?

But whether it was accidental or by design, that first meeting between Lily and Bendahan must have surprised them both. For in the course of their first conversation, they discovered that they had much in common. Not only did they share the same dental surgeon, but they frequented the same high-powered supper clubs in London, and they both banked at the same Swiss bank—the extremely understated Trade Development Bank in Geneva. As luck would have it, they would both be in Geneva on business the following week. Lily would be passing through with Dora Cohen. Later, the two friends planned to travel to Paris and Tel Aviv.

Perhaps they could all meet for a drink, say, at the Hotel President Wilson, suggested Lily.

Bendahan agreed to stay in touch with Lily, but he didn't commit to anything, still wary of the pushy blonde with the continental accent. Where was she from? He couldn't tell, nor did he care, at least at that moment. He was preoccupied with his own import-export business, with redecorating his new flat. There were also repairs on his father's flat to organize before embarking on a business trip to Switzerland and Belgium.

The following week, in Geneva, Bendahan went about his affairs and didn't think much about the encounter in Kanarek's clinic. Then, on October 5, as he packed his suitcase and prepared to leave for more business meetings in Brussels, the phone rang in his room at the Hotel du Rhône, an art-deco hotel favored by European businessmen on the right bank of the Rhône River.

"Much to my surprise Mrs. Monteverde telephoned me to inform me that they were already in Geneva and that she very much hoped that I would delay my departure to Brussels until the following day," Bendahan recalled. As his presence in Brussels was in no way urgently required and "as frankly her insistence to meet me again touched me," he agreed to her request.

The two met hours later at the bar of the Hotel President Wilson with its fabled view of Mont Blanc. Lily arrived without her traveling companion, telling Bendahan that "Mrs. Cohen had preferred to let us be alone for the evening," recalled Bendahan later. "This from a total stranger!"

After dinner and a few drinks at a nearby club, Bendahan found himself drawn to the cultivated Brazilian widow. He even confided in her a secret ambition: He was ready to give up his business and pursue his dream of enrolling in law school. Lily "seemed impressed with this" and after dinner she invited him up to her suite for another drink. Bendahan politely declined and bid her good night.

Lily was clearly infatuated with Bendahan, who continued to keep his distance. Perhaps he wanted to see how far it would go. In any case, he was enjoying the game. As Bendahan recalled years later, the widow was persistent. She showed up at the Geneva airport the next morning as Bendahan prepared to board his flight to Brussels. "Much to my stupefaction, Mrs. Monteverde asked me to cancel my trip to Brussels," he said. "I naturally refused to do this as elegantly as I could."

Undeterred, she telephoned hotels in Brussels in an effort to find Bendahan after she arrived in Paris. Lily was unsuccessful but she was used to getting her way and refused to give up. She wrote him a letter from the plane en route to Tel Aviv and several postcards—one for every day of her stay in Israel. Bendahan found the notes at his flat when he returned to London on October 20. In fact, barely twenty minutes after he entered his apartment, the telephone rang. It was Lily inviting him for dinner at her home that evening. It was to be a small gathering of friends, she said. Bendahan initially declined, but after some prodding, agreed to join her and her guests for coffee after dinner at her flat at 6 Hyde Park Gardens.

Bendahan remembers few details of that evening with Lily and her chattering guests, all of them well-heeled European and South American couples. Marcelo Steinfeld, who had traveled to London from Rio de Janeiro on business and to deliver the remainder of Lily's shares in Alfredo's company, attended the dinner that night, and recalled meeting Lily's latest conquest. Later, he shared a good laugh with his wife, dismissing Bendahan out of hand as "Lily's latest gigolo"—a description that would haunt Bendahan for the rest of his life. Steinfeld was so unimpressed with Bendahan that he could not even recall his name.

"She was only using the guy to make Edmond jealous," said Steinfeld in his home in Rio de Janeiro years later. "Everyone could see that."

It was a view that was repeated by a number of Lily's friends, and surely there must have been some desire on Lily's part to teach Edmond a lesson after he had refused to marry her. But it's not entirely true. As her intimate letters to Bendahan and his own recollection of their courtship and marriage suggest, the thirty-seven-year-old Brazilian widow fell hard for Bendahan, calling him five or six times a day and writing him anguished, heartfelt letters when he was away from her.

On that mild October night in London, as she saw the last guest to the door, Lily playfully grabbed Bendahan's arm and begged him to stay on for more coffee and brandy. Bendahan effectively moved in some weeks later.

It's not clear when Bendahan became fully aware of Lily's extraordinary wealth. There were hints early in their courtship, of course— the Mercedes convertible she stowed in a nearby garage, the exquisite clothes, the obsequious servants, the chauffeur-driven Rolls-Royce. Although he was a successful businessman who ran his own small company, Bendahan's income fell far short of his new lover's staggering net worth.

Bendahan, who had never had servants of his own, loved spending time at Lily's Hyde Park Gardens flat. "The real comfort came from the (mostly) excellent staff that she employed." Lily had brought Djanira, her maid from Brazil, and along with the chauffeur, she employed a butler, cook, laundress, and housekeeper. Bendahan also loved "the delightful view onto the private gardens and the terrace overlooking these."

It's a testament to how enamored Lily was of Bendahan that she found herself confiding in him some of the most intimate details of her life in Brazil. She told him that she had inherited her wealth from her second husband, an appliance store magnate whose real wealth— the "black money," as she called it—had come from smuggling gold in and out of Brazil.

Bendahan, who considered it in bad taste to ask too many probing questions, didn't pursue the topic. It made him extremely uncomfortable, as did the rather "dour and funereal" photos of "poor darling Freddy" scattered throughout Lily's flat. "As all this was beyond my life's experience, I treated it as though it were a scene from some B movie and gave no credence to the rumors that she had just imparted to me."

There were many things that Bendahan would simply choose to ignore. He didn't probe too deeply when Lily received the calls— sometimes several times a day—from Geneva that sometimes left her shaking and in tears. And he looked the other way when he saw Lily accepting the thick packages of pound notes that arrived every week by personal courier from the Trade Development Bank.

In the end, it was Bendahan's naivete, his reluctance to dig deeply into Lily's past, that would end up ruining his own life. Why didn't he ask about her life in Brazil, her fortune, the strange ironclad hold that Safra had on her financial affairs? To this day, he confessed that there is so little about her past that he knew. Was she really born Jewish, or did she convert to marry her first husband? Why was her maiden name –Watkins—Welsh? Where was her mother born? What had really taken place in Brazil?

But it never occurred to him to ask such questions when he was with her. Bendahan says he was being a gentleman, and gentlemen simply don't ask embarrassing questions. From a young age, he says, his father explained to him "that it was rude to ask personal questions for fear that these might sadden the person questioned. This, coupled with a distinct lack of 'nosiness' on my part, resulted in my asking very, very few direct questions at any period in my life."

But could there have been other reasons for his willful blindness? As he tells it, he was in love for the first time in his life. But perhaps he was also in love with the comforts of this new fairy-tale existence— the servants, the Rolls-Royce, the exquisite caviar at Annabel's several times a week. Perhaps he didn't ask questions because he would have too much to lose if he didn't like the answers. Too many questions might annoy Lily, who could easily get rid of him.

The widow did indeed have a mysterious past and present, but why tempt fate now? In those early days of their romance, Bendahan simply couldn't believe his luck.

SAMUEL HAIM BENDAHAN was born in Marrakech on April 1, 1936, in what was then the French part of Morocco. Following the sudden death of his mother less than two years after he was born, he was raised by his father, Judah Meir Bendahan, a pillar of the Jewish community. Bendahan père, who was known as Merito to observant Jews throughout the country, was a fifth-generation mohel, religious teacher, and founder of several synagogues in Marrakech and Casablanca. He prepared a generation of Jewish boys for their bar mitzvahs, led the choirs in several synagogues, and by most accounts was singularly devoted to his only son, who was later educated at Jewish boarding schools in Brighton and Oxfordshire after the Second World War. To this day, Bendahan, who is in his seventies, idealizes his father, who at a time when it was unheard of for a man to raise a child on his own did just that. Judah Bendahan never remarried.

Bendahan was equally devoted to his father until his father's death in London in 1993. When Bendahan launched himself in business, he insisted upon supporting his father financially, renting a flat for him in London within walking distance of his own so that he could dine with him on the Jewish Sabbath. Although Bendahan is not as observant as his father was, he takes great pride in his heritage. He bought burial plots, side by side, for his father and himself on Mount Herzl in Jerusalem, where Judah Bendahan is buried.

"I come from a proudly and ancient Orthodox family," Bendahan said. "My mother, too, was a Sunday school teacher and came from an Orthodox family. I have not kept up their strict religious code but am proud of my ancestry and our religion."

This family pride explains why he bristles whenever he sees himself depicted in the media as the gigolo third husband of Lily Safra, and why he has never consented to speak until now. In several interviews conducted over the course of a few months, Bendahan spoke of his family's noble Jewish lineage, and was eager to relate the "truth" about his relationship with Lily, and, by extension, Edmond Safra. In addition to Bendahan's father, there was his great-grandfather Judah Bendahan, a headmaster of the English School in the Moroccan city of Mogador. When he died in 1907, an obituary in London's *Jewish Chronicle* noted his "piety, humility, simplicity of manner and gentleness of disposition."

These were all qualities that were passed on to his grandfather and father, said Bendahan. Before his father's death, Bendahan helped him compile a history of every circumcision that generations of their family had performed throughout Morocco and in Paris. In all, he chronicled a total of 2,257 circumcisions, spanning nearly a century, that his father, grandfather, and great-grandfather had performed. The records are now part of the Anglo-Jewish Historical Society and the Spanish and Portuguese Jews' Congregation in London.

As Bendahan proudly pointed out, "our ancestors chose to be expelled from Spain rather than to submit to the demands of the Inquisition, and, to this day, on all our *ketubot* [Jewish marriage contracts] we are entitled to state we are 'of the Expelled,' a title of some significance."

This may explain why Samuel Bendahan, a self-confessed playboy and bon vivant, did not take marriage lightly. He idealized it and fantasized about the perfect woman—"the nice Jewish girl" who would be virtuous enough to present to his dear father.

Was Lily good enough to marry Samuel Bendahan? During those early days, he wasn't sure, which might explain why Lily never met Bendahan's father.

Still, in London, they acted like a wealthy married couple. They dined out several nights a week at ultra-exclusive clubs such as dell'Aretusa and Les Ambassadeurs. As Bendahan recalls, Lily was elegant in Valentino black tails and a smoldering Eve cigarette in hand. He said she turned heads, resembling a rather thin and petite version of Marlene Dietrich.

In late October 1971, as Lily and Bendahan arrived for dinner at Annabel's, they were stopped at the door by Louis, the maître d'hôtel. Lily had clearly dined there often with her former lover Safra, and as she breezed in with her latest conquest, Louis "whispered conspiratorially that we might not want to come in as '*monsieur Safra est ici.*' I could not care less one way or another but Lily refused to be dictated by her past and asked Louis to take us to his table," recalled Bendahan. Perhaps it was also Lily's way of showing off her new lover to Edmond, who had bowed to his own family's pressure in refusing to marry her.

Lily touched up her makeup before taking Bendahan's arm and steering her trophy lover—this younger, much more attractive man—to the legendary banker's table. Edmond, who was dining with a group of dark-suited business associates, glanced up at his former lover in some surprise. It was a momentary look of disgust, recalled Bendahan. But in the end Edmond's Old World breeding won the day, and he extended his hand to Lily's new lover. Still, "his smile was somewhat frozen." For the rest of the evening, the happy couple ignored the Lebanese banker and continued their intimate dinner "as if nothing had happened."

Life with Lily seemed blissful in those early days. They lingered over coffee and newspapers in the mornings. In her love letters to Bendahan at the time, Lily writes about her delight at the routine that quickly became their morning ritual. She would wash his hair in the bathtub. At breakfast, she poured his coffee and buttered his croissants. There are also the racier notes in which she refers to herself as Madame Claude, the infamous Parisian brothelkeeper who provided women for France's power elite in the 1960s and 1970s. She also compared herself to Elizabeth Taylor and pretended Bendahan was Richard Burton, sometimes addressing the little love notes, inscribed in English on elegant little cream cards with the initials *LWM*, to "Richard."

In those early letters, many of them written when Bendahan was on a series of business trips abroad, she refers to herself as his wife. In one letter, she calls him "My adorable husband (oh! How nice)." In other notes, she begs him not to drink too much alcohol because he needs to be in good health in order to have children with her ("lots of them!").

Lily seemed so comfortable with her new lover that she felt it perfectly respectable to take him to visit Carlos and Claudio at the Millfield School in Somerset. In the photographs Bendahan took of that visit in November 1971, there is one of Lily gazing lovingly at Bendahan, fixing her coiffure *("with all that implies!")* and vamping for the camera beside Adriana.

There are also similar photographs of the happy couple taken on a trip to Villars, in the Swiss Alps, to visit Carlos, who had fractured his leg while skiing with his classmates.

In those early weeks, Bendahan recalled that the two never argued and their sex life was "excellent." Lily had "introduced me to *One Hundred Years of Solitude*, she had introduced me to the Lanvin mode of dressing, [and] she had a superb sense of humor."

In letter after letter, Lily expressed her intense longing for him. Writing "from our home" in London, Lily writes of her happiness at having found true love. In another letter, the second written on the same day, Lily refers to Bendahan as "my love, my darling, my beloved, my husband, my man, my everything."

Still, there were strains, especially as Bendahan prepared to embark on an annual month-long business trip that would take him from Bangkok to Mexico, with several stops in between. Bendahan would be accompanied by Kanarek on a trip that he admitted was "partly for business, and mostly to clear my mind in regard to, what to her and to me, seemed to have become a serious relationship." Kanarek, at the time, was also "suffering from nervous exhaustion" and needed to get away from London.

The truth is that Bendahan was looking forward to being away from this all-consuming relationship with Lily. In mid-December, approximately two months after moving in with Lily, Bendahan announced that he would leave for Bangkok in a few weeks' time. The news did not go over well with a woman who had grown accustomed to wielding absolute control over the people around her.

"Mrs. Monteverde was of course incensed that I should appear to be giving someone else priority over her, however much I explained how loyal and affectionate Mr. and Mrs. Kanarek had been to me over the years," he later told his lawyer. Nevertheless, on January 2, 1972, Bendahan and Kanarek left for Paris in order to catch an early flight the next morning for Bangkok.

Perhaps Lily's protestations of love were a little too stifling to a bachelor used to his freedom. Despite the geographic distance between them as he traveled to Bangkok, Hong Kong, and Tahiti, Bendahan simply couldn't get rid of her. Lily pursued him. She wrote to him every day about how she suffered in his absence, how intensely she missed him, how she dreamed of making love with him. Her first letter, written several days before his departure, was already waiting for him in Bangkok when he arrived. And she called incessantly—this in the days when making overseas calls was truly a chore, requiring her to stay glued to the telephone for up to five hours, "to which inconvenience must be added the time differential between London and those places," said Bendahan.

In the course of some of those long-distance conversations, Lily suggested that she fly to meet him. But her life was so filled with luncheons, shopping, and meetings with interior designers—she had undertaken to supervise the work on Bendahan's new flat and his father's flat—that he didn't take her very seriously. Then at the end of his trip, as he was waiting for his luggage at the Acapulco airport, "I suddenly caught sight of Lily bouncing up and down like a four-year-old." Without any warning, Lily had jumped on a plane to surprise him.

The reunion was passionate, and during the first few days they spent most of their time in their suite at the luxurious Regency Hyatt hotel. Judging from the notes that she wrote on hotel stationery and left for Bendahan, Lily was ecstatic with the man she called her "Red Indian" lover. In one note, she tells Bendahan to put on his "beautiful Alain Delon's [sic] hat and come down and kill all the women!"

It was the same straw hat that Lily would borrow to wear on their wedding day at the local registry office in Acapulco. While their marriage may have had the air of spontaneity to an outside observer, there was nothing extemporaneous about it. Lily had planned everything. When Bendahan and Lily went to visit the British consul in Acapulco to discuss the documentation they needed to marry in Mexico, he told them that as it appeared the wedding had not been pre-planned, it would be impossible to marry without Lily producing proof of her divorce from her first husband and the death certificate of her second husband. Of course, Lily was prepared. "She had traveled with these!" recalled Bendahan years later.

Although everything seemed to be in place, Bendahan still urged caution. He was still unsure about Lily. "As a very last precaution I did insist that we wait just one more week so as to be sure yet again that our enthusiasm to marry was not merely a result of the euphoria that we felt at being reunited," he said.

In the days before their wedding, Bendahan was nervous. What did he really know about this woman he had met at a dental clinic? He was also a little embarrassed. "I would be number three in an age when even having a number two was frowned upon." He also said that he was "very concerned about the disparity in our bank accounts. After much insistence *on my part*, she finally agreed that I would pay for the staff at her London residence"—a large amount for Bendahan, who was also paying his and his father's expenses in London. In order to prove to both himself and the world that he was not marrying Lily for her money, he insisted that they marry under "separation of assets"—a fact that is clearly reflected on their marriage license.

As Bendahan later pointed out, this is not the course that a "dedicated fortune hunter" would have chosen. "Please remember that she had just flown halfway across the world to be with me and for the first time in a long time, she felt truly happy," he said. "Thus, modesty aside, she could have been putty in my hands. If I had had an ounce of the Rubirosa in me, she would have agreed to any demand that I made at that time. But the fruit never falls far from the tree and such a thought never entered my mind."

But there was another issue: How would Lily pass muster with his father? Was she really the woman for him—was this to be his *wife*? "She [Lily] was well aware of the fact that my mother had died when I was one year old and that my father had never remarried," he said. "I therefore, perhaps wrongly, held an idealistic view of marriage and would enter into such a union only upon being certain that it would be a permanent union of love, of affection, of tenderness and of loyalty, and most important that it should at all times be based on Truth. All these things she professed to admire and to agree to."

In hindsight, of course, there was little of the Truth that Bendahan so craved in what was about to become the most important relationship of his life.

Despite the bachelor's nagging doubts, Samuel Haim Bendahan entered the municipal registry office with its white-washed stucco walls and dusty wooden floors. Sweating from the heat, he handed over the three-peso fee to the clerk, who duly typed up the marriage license on a manual typewriter. With no fanfare, the presiding judge, Israel Hernandez, married Samuel Bendahan and Lily Watkins (there is no Monteverde on the marriage license) at 11:15 a.m. on January 31, 1972. Their witnesses were Brian Kanarek, the dentist; Humberto Morales, the taxi driver who drove them to the registry office; Graciela Roman, a clerk from the registry office; and Margarita Ramos, an eighteen-year-old maid. They would have a religious ceremony when they were back in London, Bendahan said.

Strangely, only Bendahan thought to wear white for his wedding. In a photograph snapped by Kanarek after the ceremony, Bendahan is smiling, resplendent in white trousers and a long-sleeved white shirt, the first few buttons casually undone. Lily wears a patterned skirt and dark silk blouse, her expression hidden behind her large sunglasses and the Alain Delon straw hat.

AFTER THE LOW-KEY ceremony, they returned to the hotel and called their friends and family. Bendahan wrote a long letter to his father introducing Lily, whom he described as "blonde, blue-eyed and Jewish." Although he didn't mention the civil ceremony, he promised that they would have a traditional Jewish wedding at the Lauderdale Road Synagogue in London upon their return. "Knowing my dad, the two words *synagogue* and *Jewish* would be sufficient to make him deliriously happy, although he had never met her."

Bendahan remembers the days immediately following the wedding ceremony as the happiest of his life. "When I woke up after my first night as a married man, I felt totally cleansed and the fear of not having access to my regular harem came, surprisingly to me, as a huge relief. It was practically a spiritual experience and my cup was overflowing."

Lily broke the news to her children. Adriana, who was then fifteen, promptly hung up on her mother, although she later called her back to congratulate the happy couple. Eduardo was still in South America living with his father, and Lily would speak to him "after a year of total breakdown" when she and Bendahan arrived in Rio de Janeiro on an extended honeymoon.

Carlos, Alfredo's adopted son, who would have been the most vulnerable because he had lost his father two years before, seemed thrilled to have a new father. He even addressed two letters from boarding school to Mr. and Mrs. Bendahan, starting them "Dear mum and dad." The gesture brought tears to Bendahan's eyes. "Perhaps it was his total and innocent trust in the stranger— But now I was determined to be a real father to him." Later, Lily would tease him relentlessly about the letters. "What do mummy and daddy want to do this evening?" she would say when the two found themselves alone.

It was eighteen-year-old Claudio, Lily's eldest son, who would put it best: "Welcome home," he told Bendahan, offering his hearty congratulations when he spoke to them on the phone from Somerset. "How does it feel to be part of a mad family?"

How indeed? But if the comment gave him even the slightest pause, Bendahan shrugged off any doubt. He embarked on his honeymoon a very happy man, convinced that he had been accepted with open arms into a wonderful new family.

To add to his joy, Lily, who was then thirty-seven, announced that she had stopped using birth control while they were in Mexico and desperately wanted to have his children. As they left on the grand tour that would take them to New York, Rio de Janeiro, and the French Riviera, Bendahan saw his life in a new light—the doting husband and father, leading the Passover seder, taking the children for their Hebrew lessons with their grandfather. Life would be glorious! he thought as the couple sailed to South America.

"We arrived in Rio where again all her friends and all her family without exception expressed unqualified joy and commented how well Lily looked after several years of looking drawn." Indeed, the photographs seem to say it all: A bikini-clad Lily running after a soccer ball on the lawn of her brother Daniel's home in Petropolis, in the mountains outside Rio; Lily sitting on the floor of a friend's living room, smiling and eating lunch with a group of her old friends in the elegant beachfront neighborhood of Leblon.

"She was so happy on that trip that while we were having lunch, she saw a Carnaval band passing on the street, and ran out to dance with them," recalled her friend Elza Gruenbaum years after Lily's honeymoon in Rio. "Can you imagine! We all had such a great time with her."

After nine days in Rio, the happy couple left by ship en route to Cannes. It was while they were nearing the port of Lisbon that Lily told Bendahan that she was now convinced that she was pregnant. "Back in London we even discussed the best place for us to be for the birth of our child and I think that we agreed that it might be best for him or her to have dual nationality and that the U.S. might be best . . . the Cold War still being very much daily fare."

Like Bendahan, Lily may have also convinced herself that she had embarked on a new life, and when they arrived in Cannes, they checked in to the luxe Carlton hotel, where Lily made arrangements for Adriana and Eduardo to join them. Almost immediately after arriving in France, they went in search of the perfect home. The previous summer Lily had rented a house in nearby Vallauris, a picturesque suburb of Antibes in the Alpes Maritimes that was home to Picasso for a decade after the Second World War. She knew the house was for sale and she was determined that it would be in Vallauris, with its breathtaking views of the Bay of Cannes, that "we could make our home and have our first child," she told Bendahan. Although the house was no longer available, Lily found an even grander stone villa, known as Mas Notre Dame, near Golfe Juan. The imposing structure boasted four principal bedrooms and four bathrooms, three staff bedrooms with two bathrooms, a kitchen, and laundry area. There was also a two-bedroom beach house, a sizable garage, and a swimming pool and outdoor bar on the property. Lily agreed on the spot to purchase the villa, and the couple returned to the Carlton hotel to draw up their plans for renovating the property on hotel stationery. She sent orders to her bank in Geneva to wire her 3.5 million francs for the purchase. She also demanded that a Geneva-based attorney, a man known to Bendahan only as Zucker, should draw up the paperwork immediately.

Willard Zucker, an American banker who lived in Switzerland and would make international headlines for setting up the complex web of shell companies used to move funds in the Iran-Contra scandal more than a decade later, set out the terms of purchase in a letter to the owner of the house on March 6, 1972. "It is the desire of our client to conclude the transaction at the earliest possible date," he wrote.

Lily was clearly in a hurry. But the haste was not so much to begin her new life in France. It became clear to Bendahan that she was in a hurry to get her hands on the money for the purchase before Edmond found out what she had done.

"Edmond will kill me when he finds out," she told Bendahan, in a moment of utter fear and paranoia that should have given Bendahan some pause. "He'll never let me transfer the money to buy us a house!" Lily had constantly complained to Bendahan that Edmond kept her on an extremely tight financial leash. The only time that she had disobeyed Safra was when she insisted on leasing the Rolls-Royce, which she did shortly after moving to London in 1969. He was furious at her extravagance. So this was simply her banker being cheap, thought Bendahan. Foolishly, he did not read anything ominous into Edmond's potential disapproval.

The newlyweds blithely continued with plans to purchase the French property, with Bendahan insisting upon paying half the purchase price (he would take out a loan from Lily), and Lily instructing Zucker to draw up a contract. She also told Zucker to set up a Panamanian company to purchase the property, with the shares being held in equal parts by herself and Bendahan. Zucker suggested a Swiss company instead, and busied himself with the paperwork.

But Bendahan should have been extremely disturbed by the course of events in France. He was well aware that Safra controlled Lily's assets through his bank in Switzerland. "It would seem that Safra had an unassailable grip on the Freddy fortune," he said. "And this continued well into my day, with Lily expressing great nervousness about what Safra would do to her money when he learned of our marriage." Knowing this, how could Bendahan ever have imagined that he and Lily would be allowed to live happily ever after?

Of course, where Edmond was involved, Bendahan was destined to learn his lesson the hard way. For Edmond controlled more than Bendahan could have imagined. In addition to dispatching, via personal courier, several thousand in cash every week for Lily's expenses in London, he also took care of the leases on her flat, the Rolls-Royce, and the Mercedes convertible. For tax and legal reasons, she still had no assets in her name in London, and no credit card. Both Lily and the Trade Development Bank were still in the thick of Rosy and Regina's lawsuit against them, both in London and in Rio de Janeiro. Furthermore, Lily had not yet obtained probate on Carlos's English assets. Edmond's control was so complete that Lily still routinely used his Geneva address, 56 Moillebeau, on her hotel bills.

Despite Lily's worries about Edmond, Bendahan seems to have deluded himself into thinking that everything was going smoothly. In fact, he was so sure that he would soon be the co-owner of the stone villa that he left $500 with the gardener, telling him to buy new plants and clean the pool. Lily also suggested that they unpack their summer clothes and leave them at the house, since they wouldn't need the clothes upon their return to London. In the evenings, they continued to dine out with Lily's friends on the Riviera (the Abitbols were in town from Rio de Janeiro) and draw up their renovation plans for the property on hotel stationery. "We were excited to be together but, also, totally at peace with each other," recalled Bendahan.

But after Adriana and Eduardo arrived in Cannes, Bendahan couldn't help but notice "a dramatic decline" in his new wife. Days later, Lily informed him that Werner, her London chauffeur, was also flying down to Cannes to meet her.

Why was Werner flying down?

"Oh, he is bringing down a pair of shoes that I particularly like for walking," she told Bendahan, who immediately became suspicious. Since they had been together, Lily had never gone out walking. And while they were staying in Cannes, she never put on those shoes. "I can only assume that Werner was carrying a letter from Safra, either containing threats and/or promises. Probably both."

Bendahan began to press Lily for details of her financial arrangements with Edmond, and the reasons for her sudden anxiety. After Werner's visit, "the pressure became intense," recalled Bendahan. Lily began receiving "endless telephone calls during which I chose not to be present." The calls were clearly from Safra. But again, this was nothing new. Since Lily had begun dating Bendahan, "there was pressure from the day that Safra found out that she was no longer spending her evenings at home in the event that he might phone or visit."

Safra seems to have found out about the marriage during the negotiations to purchase the house at Golfe Juan. Did Zucker inform him? Or perhaps Lily broke the news to him herself. Perhaps this was her little bit of revenge on the Lebanese banker who had refused to make her his wife.

Regardless of how he found out, Lily began to receive a "fusillade" of calls from Edmond. Those calls clearly unnerved her, although it was unclear to Bendahan what they were discussing. Yet during one of those calls from Geneva, Lily passed the receiver to Bendahan. It was Edmond, straining to sound cheery. "He offered me his warmest congratulations on getting married to Lily."

Still, Lily was clearly dreading her imminent return to London. In Cannes, "she was subjected to a barrage of telephone calls which had a discernible effect on her. I was concerned about this and she told me that she was under very great pressure as 'he never thought I would marry you.'"

Despite the tension, Bendahan was still hopeful about their relationship. "On the airplane to London I asked Lily if she wanted to sit next to her [daughter] as they [Lily and Adriana] had after all been separated for over a month," he said. "Lily thought it a ridiculous suggestion and we held hands for the whole of the flight from Nice to London."

However, things deteriorated almost as soon as they arrived in London. Within minutes of entering the Hyde Park Gardens flat, Lily showed signs of tension again, and went around inspecting every lampshade "as she claimed that burnt-out bulbs were never changed in her absence." Suddenly, she had trouble sleeping.

"I now no longer had to press her to speak for she quite calmly told me that she was wondering if we had not made a mistake in marrying so hastily and that she was no longer even sure whether she loved me." Lily told her new husband that she wanted to be alone for a few days, and even helped a dazed Bendahan pack a suitcase.

Bendahan was devastated, but agreed to give his new wife her own space. Surely Safra was putting pressure on her, but what else was driving this bizarre behavior? Perhaps it was the lawsuit that was scheduled to go to trial shortly in London. For weeks, Lily had repeatedly spoken about how much she hated her former sister-in-law Rosy and how Rosy was making her life miserable. On one occasion, she became so distraught about the upcoming trial that she begged Bendahan to hide a painting that she claimed was a Van Gogh that Rosy was alleging belonged to her family. Bendahan readily obliged and hid the painting, which was "dark and ugly" and belonged to the period before the artist discovered the French countryside. In more innocent days, it was the same painting that Alfredo had convinced his friend to cart from the Rio airport in a Volkswagen van years before. Lily had the painting professionally crated and shipped to Bendahan's office. That night, in a coincidence that he is hard-pressed to explain, thieves broke into his office, overturning his desk drawers, ransacking filing cabinets. They were clearly in search of valuables, but, curiously, they did not steal the Van Gogh, even though they had punched several holes in the crate. The incident left him shaken, and he immediately called Lily to have the painting removed.

"That evening, she told everybody about the event and could not stop laughing about it and teasing me," recalled Bendahan. "I wonder what her reaction would have been had it been stolen. I do not know what happened to the painting after she had it collected."

Perhaps now the stress of the upcoming legal battle with Rosy was simply too much for her, thought Bendahan as he returned to the cold comfort of his messy flat, which was still in the process of being re-decorated by Lily's interior designer. The old fabric had been torn off the walls, which were now bare, and the sitting room was littered with fabric swatches and paint samples. Later, he would be stuck with more than £10,000 in unpaid decorating bills.

Two days passed without word from Lily. Alone and completely bewildered, Bendahan grew frantic, dialing her number several times a day. There was no response from his wife. The servants had obvi-ously been instructed not to forward his calls. On the one occasion when he was able to get through to her, he encountered a cold re-sponse: "When I thought that I would not be able to live through another minute I telephoned again and my wife calmly informed me that upon further consideration she had thought that it would be wiser not to call me back after all."

When he couldn't stand to be away from her anymore, he showed up at her flat, sick with worry and completely sleep-deprived. Lily fell into his arms, clearly relieved to see him again. In that moment, life seemed to return to some sense of normalcy. They traded heartfelt apologies and made plans to have dinner later in the evening. Lily was scheduled to meet with Felix Klein, Alfredo's former business associate who had been so useful to her in the days after Alfredo died. Klein had been dispatched to Switzerland to remove Rosy's power of attorney from Alfredo's Swiss holdings at the Union Bank of Switzer-land. He had also allegedly threatened Rosy when she tried to launch an investigation into Alfredo's death. Bendahan had met Klein in Rio during their honeymoon. Klein, who now handled Lily's business affairs in Brazil, had met with the couple in the bar of the beachfront Leme Palace hotel in Rio where they had discussed Lily's finances. It was the only time he had seen Lily in a vicious mood. Where was the $15 million that was supposed to have been transferred to her in Europe? she had demanded of Klein. What had her "thief-director" done with her money? she demanded. Unbeknownst to Bendahan, Lily was speaking about Geraldo Mattos, Ponto Frio's chief director, who had been so indispensable to her when she was dealing with the arrangements for Alfredo's funeral and the annoying police investigation in Rio.

Still, days after the heated exchange, all seemed to be well again. Klein showed up for the good-bye party aboard their ship before it sailed to Europe. Lily sat chatting and chain-smoking Eve cigarettes as Klein expressed his good wishes for the happy couple.

Now, during this terrible crisis in their marriage, Klein had again appeared on the scene in London. He probably had urgent news of the Brazilian business, or perhaps he was bringing Lily the cash she had demanded. At that moment, Bendahan didn't stop to think about why Klein was in London; he simply agreed to drive her to the nearby Mayfair Hotel where Klein was staying. Lily kissed him and promised that she would return within the hour, in time for a late dinner.

But as the hours passed, Bendahan grew distraught. He called the Mayfair repeatedly and had Klein paged. For nearly four hours, there was no answer. Then Bendahan grew completely desperate and called his nemesis Edmond Safra, who he knew was in London on business and staying at the Dorchester hotel. "I felt that with the court case to be heard in London shortly that it was possible that my wife and Mr. Klein had gone to see Mr. Safra." It was ten to midnight on March 11, 1972, when the hotel operator connected Bendahan to Edmond's suite.

"Mr. Safra informed me that he had not seen my wife and not unnaturally seemed a little surprised that I should be unaware of her whereabouts after six weeks of marriage," Bendahan said.

At about half past midnight, Bendahan heard a knock on the door. Finally, she had returned! But why wasn't she using her key? Bendahan rushed to the door, ready to greet his wife, but stopped dead in his tracks when he saw Klein and the man he knew only as Raymond, an executive from Edmond's bank who was in charge of delivering Lily's weekly packages of cash. Both had dour expressions, and immediately Bendahan knew that the nightmare of the previous week was about to begin again in terrible earnest.

In measured tones the two businessmen took turns explaining that Lily was very confused and needed a few days on her own to recover from an unspecified ailment. They explained to him that such things happened occasionally with Lily, that she was inclined to behave irrationally. But they assured him that the best chance for her recovery and their marriage would be for Bendahan to respect her wishes and leave the flat immediately.

At first, Bendahan stood his ground. *But I am her husband*, he argued. *Lily is my wife*. Klein and the other man were unmoved, and repeated that Lily wanted him out of the flat immediately. How could this be happening? How could these two strangers kick him out of the matrimonial home?

"I asked to speak to Lily but they told me that she was under great stress and that a doctor had had to be called and that she was under sedation," recalled Bendahan years after the event that would result in the end of his marriage.

"So I left to their repeated assurances that everything would be all right the next day. By then, I clearly remember, my heart was beating so hard that I could hardly hear them and my mouth was so dry as to hardly be able to speak."

Bendahan says he spent the next month in a cloud. For the first time in his life, he began to take sleeping pills every night in order to rest.

Bewildered by the bizarre turn of events, he sought out a lawyer, writing out the whole story of his and Lily's meeting and courtship as if to affirm to himself and the world that it really had happened, and that as recently as a few weeks before the dreadful meeting with Klein and his accomplice at the London flat, they had both been deliriously happy. He made repeated and rather pathetic efforts to contact his wife.

"I have tried to reach my wife at the Plaza Athenée in Paris, at the President Hotel in Geneva, at the Palace hotel in St. Moritz, at the Hotel du Rhône in Geneva, at the Dorchester in London," he told his lawyer.

But there was no response. Lily seemed to have disappeared without a trace.

"This is in effect how our marriage broke up," he later wrote. "With no more prelude than I have described."

IN THE SPRING of 1972, Edmond Safra was a busy man. In addition to preparing his defense in the lawsuit that was threatening his beloved Trade Development Bank in London, he was in the process of acquiring another bank—the Kings Lafayette Bank in Brooklyn—and preparing to meet with U.S. regulators.

But clearly Lily's marriage was the most pressing item on his agenda. After all, she must have represented one of the single biggest depositors at his bank. Of course, he was also desperately in love with her, and underneath his hard-nosed business exterior, he was extremely hurt by her behavior and must have been insanely jealous of Bendahan, who was younger and far more handsome than himself.

"Edmond told me that he couldn't sleep at night thinking of Lily, that she had gotten married, that she was living with someone else," said his friend Albert Nasser.

The escapades of the previous few months simply couldn't be allowed to continue. He had to put an end to her marriage and regain control of Lily, even if it meant going public with their own relationship and eventually marrying her against his family's wishes.

He summoned his various aides and top executives from around the world, beginning with Simon Alouan, the able Lebanese mathematics professor he had put in charge of Alfredo's old company. "He called Alouan and asked him to go to London to tell Lily that if she divorces, Edmond will marry her, even against the wishes of his family," said Nasser. But Bendahan needed to be eliminated first.

For weeks, he plotted. Paying off the man who had become Lily's husband must have turned Edmond's stomach.

But what to do?

First, he needed to put Lily in her place. At the Geneva headquarters of the Trade Development Bank, Edmond asked his secretary to get him on the next flight to London. He called Alouan, who hated Lily and didn't want to travel to London, so he settled on Felix Klein, ordering him to get on the first flight from Rio de Janeiro to London.

We have an emergency.

Klein, a chain-smoking Romanian émigré who was fond of dark suits and Brylcreem, knew better than most how to deal with emergencies. He had arranged everything in Rio after his former employer Alfredo died.

Now Edmond was entrusting him with a far more sensitive mission as he realized the huge threat that Bendahan represented to his future. If he were to lose Lily, he might also eventually lose Alfredo's fortune—a situation that could prove catastrophic for his growing banking empire.

The night that Lily left Bendahan alone at Hyde Park Gardens, Klein escorted her to Edmond's hotel. It's not clear what was said behind closed doors, but Edmond, who had repeatedly asked her to put an end to her foolish marriage to Bendahan, must have resolved to do it himself—by any means necessary.

"I CAN ONLY think that my wife is either very sick or very evil and with much regret I can't but feel that the latter is true," wrote Bendahan in a letter to his attorney eight days after Klein and his assistant ordered him to leave Lily's flat.

But the signs had been everywhere during their relationship. And in the dark days after his ouster, as he struggled to come to grips with what had happened to his marriage, he searched through the letters and notes in an effort to understand what had just befallen him.

In a chatty letter she wrote to Bendahan during the first glorious weeks of their life together describing the progress of decorators at his new flat and professing her undying love for him, Lily also confessed to a terrible premonition. She wrote that she was very afraid for their future together. It was January 5, 1972, and she was off to Geneva and then on to St. Moritz for undisclosed business. Bendahan had just begun his round-the-world tour, and the letter must have reached him in Bangkok or Tahiti.

Bendahan dismissed the sentence, as he did all of the other troubling little insights into her character. What did he make of a subsequent letter, dated only three days later? On Saturday, January 8, 1972, Lily wrote to her beloved from the train en route to Gatwick airport to pick up her daughter Adriana. The previous evening she had heard from an ex-brother-in-law in Buenos Aires that her son Eduardo had come down with an illness and suffered hallucinations. A maid at the penthouse apartment where he was staying called his uncle, who took him to a local hospital.

Lily went on to describe how she felt about her son's condition. She informed Bendahan that her eldest son, Claudio, whom she referred to as her "Jesus Christ, Esquire," had offered to bring his brother to London. But if she couldn't convince him to travel, Lily was prepared to "see to it" that Eduardo would be sedated and brought to London, accompanied by a doctor. The letter ended with Lily pleading with Bendahan to find a solution to be with her because she could no longer cope on her own. In a separate letter to Bendahan, written on the evening of the same day, Eduardo's problems seemed entirely forgotten and she spent much of the letter writing about her feelings for Bendahan.

Was Bendahan at all perturbed by this response to Eduardo's situation? Bendahan said he advised Lily not to bring her son to London by force. In the end, Lily seemed to forget about her son's state of mind since she was able to hop on a plane to meet her lover in Acapulco.

Lily later met up with Eduardo in Rio de Janeiro. After a year of being apart from him, she didn't seem very happy to see him in Rio, recalled Bendahan. "It is clear that she is uncomfortable with him and he with her," said Bendahan, referring to a photograph he took of mother and son on their honeymoon in Rio. "To be fair to her, pretty well everybody was uncomfortable in his presence. I went out with him a few times in Cannes and although he was friendly I was always conscious of an undercurrent of some demon that he was wrestling with." Later, there was a reconciliation of sorts, and Lily convinced Eduardo to join his brothers and sister in London, no doubt so she could keep a watchful eye on him.

But on occasion, Lily's behavior did give Bendahan some pause. For one thing, she discarded friends with seemingly little feeling. When he asked her if she was going to keep in touch with Carmen Sirotsky, a woman she described as her "best friend" in Rio, Lily said she simply didn't have time. She also tossed off her friendship with Jo Kanarek, the dentist's wife, when she was no longer useful to her, Bendahan said.

But if Bendahan was concerned at her flip-flopping emotional state, it was only in hindsight. "For the first time in a letter there is an indication of her mental makeup, the significance of which unfortunately escaped me at the time," Bendahan later confessed, referring to the letter she wrote to him on January 8, 1972, outlining Eduardo's emotional problems. Bendahan added that her anguish and depression at being away from him was extremely short-lived.

Later, the callous treatment of the man to whom she had professed her undying love should have come as little surprise to Bendahan.

Still, for weeks after he left Lily's Hyde Park Gardens flat, Bendahan tried to contact her. But in the end, it was Lily who contacted him through her lawyers. She was demanding a divorce, and her lawyers wanted him to sign the legal papers quickly, releasing her from any financial responsibilities. Bendahan refused. Years later, he claimed that he was not after money so much as a final meeting with Lily. He even suggested the tea room at Claridge's Hotel in London. Or, if her advisers suspected that he might have the press or police present, he was prepared for them to pick him up and take him to a meeting place of their choosing without giving him any kind of advance knowledge of where that would be. But Lily's lawyers "were persistent and categorical in refusing to let Lily spend a minute in my presence, even under close supervision."

In the final negotiations leading up to the divorce Bendahan demanded payment for the decorating work Lily had commissioned on his flat—a figure roughly equivalent to $35,000, which she agreed to pay. He also demanded compensation for his suffering. The strain had left his business "in tatters" and he would need the next two years to bring it back up to speed. Lily refused to negotiate. The final indignity came when her lawyers invited him to go to New York to negotiate his divorce settlement in person. Bendahan's father, who was only ever told a small part of the story of his son's marriage and untimely separation, told him not to go.

"He advised me against this and recommended that I let lawyers take care of that unpleasantness," recalled Bendahan.

Bendahan should have heeded that advice, for almost as soon as he stepped off his plane at John F. Kennedy International Airport, he was arrested by a plainclothes policeman. Bendahan spent a terrifying night at the Rikers Island jail, charged with "attempted extortion." He was charged with trying to extort $250,000 in a final divorce settlement from Lily. One Brazilian newspaper erroneously reported that he tried to extort more than $6 million from her. Benda-han would later settle for what he claims amounted to a pittance.

According to press accounts, Bendahan had threatened to conduct an investigation into Lily's business interests in New York and in Bra-zil unless the money was paid to him. Among other things, he ac-cused her of transferring funds illegally from Brazil to Switzerland.

During his brief stay at Rikers Island, Bendahan claims that he shared a cell with a self-confessed murderer and saw a man throw himself off an upper floor. "You can well imagine the impact this had on me," he recalled. "One minute married to the woman of my life who adored me, and the next, incarcerated with murderers, rapists, etc."

Bendahan's lawyers obtained his release the following day after pay-ing $50,000 in bail, although he was forbidden to leave the country. In the weeks of arduous divorce negotiations that followed, he claims he was bullied and threatened by Lily's lawyers, who told him that if he did not do exactly what they wanted they would arrange for him to be sent to prison for a much longer period of time in the United States.

"Imagine how popular a good-looking boy like you would be with all those violent Negro criminals," said one of the lawyers, who worked with Edmond.

Lily's lawyers were anxious that Bendahan sign off on any rights to Lily's estate. The legal proceedings dragged on for the next two years, during which time Bendahan nearly declared bankruptcy.

For Lily, life went on swimmingly. Despite protracted legal pro-ceedings against her and Edmond in London and the messy separa-tion from Bendahan, Lily emerged triumphant. That year, she was named one of the best-dressed women in London society.

Bendahan demanded the payment of the decorating bills. But Ed-mond wanted revenge and insisted upon proceeding, even as his law-yers must have told him he had a weak case against Bendahan, trying to nail him for attempted extortion. When Edmond finally did lose the case, he went on to appeal. The case was eventually dismissed by a panel of five judges.

In the meantime, Lily applied for a divorce in Reno, Nevada. During the proceedings, she made a request to the presiding judge that she not be present in the courtroom with her soon-to-be ex-husband.

Lily and her third husband appeared separately, although their paths briefly crossed in the corridors of the Second Judicial District Court of the State of Nevada. Ever the gentleman, Bendahan stepped aside when he saw her approach. As she passed him, she instinctively raised her hand to her head.

And all that implies!

But this time she wasn't checking her coiffure. The gesture was no longer meant to impress or to seduce. In his last sighting of his wife, Bendahan was certain that she was raising her hand to cover her face in shame.

LILY AND EDMOND didn't formally extricate themselves from *l'affaire* Bendahan until three years after Lily's divorce, when the appeal in New York State Supreme Court was thrown out in July 1976 because it was wasting valuable court time.

"There is no reason for the State of New York to be concerned with protecting the property interests that were threatened," noted Justice James J. Leff, the appeals judge. "Those interests are in Brazil and Britain. If carried to a conclusion this case will continue to pre-empt valuable court time, utilize the limited staff of the prosecutor's office and impose a burden on criminal justice facilities."

Although Edmond would have loved to have put Bendahan in his place, the matter was now clearly out of his hands. Edmond and Lily traveled back and forth between New York and London, where Lily finally established her residency, and vacationed on Edmond's yacht in the Riviera. Edmond took Lily's children under his wing, helping Carlos to study for his bar mitzvah when he turned thirteen in 1972. Later, he would put him to work at his banks. Eventually, Edmond also gave Claudio a plum position at Ponto Frio in Rio de Janeiro. Ed-

uardo was pretty much left to his father's care in Argentina. Like her
mother, Adriana was being prepared for marriage when she reached
her late teens. Edmond would help find her a suitable mate in the Sephardic community—a Lebanese businessman named Michel Elia.

But despite what appeared to be a happy family life, he refused to
marry Lily until all legal actions against them were firmly settled.
Edmond still lived in mortal fear that the Monteverde family might
find some excuse to go after them, even though the actions against
Lily and the Trade Development Bank had been neatly settled out-of-
court in Brazil and in England.

Edmond was also mortified that Lily had caused him so much unwanted gossip. What if Bendahan decided to go to the press? Not that
Bendahan would dare go public after all the legal threats Edmond had
made against him. Edmond and his boys had done a good job of putting
Lily's third husband firmly in his place. But even the powerful Edmond
Safra must have realized that certain types of human behavior were
beyond his control, and Bendahan, whether he knew it or not, had the
power to deeply embarrass the international financier and philanthropist.

But Bendahan also preferred to put the whole matter out of his life.
When the appeal ended in his favor, he tried to recapture his old life
in London. He returned to his "old harem," and Shabbat dinners with
his father. He bought himself a condominium in southern Spain, and
he even helped his father compile an historical account of his family's
services to the Jewish communities in Morocco and England.

Following the unsuccessful appeal in July 1976, Edmond finally
decided that it was the right time to marry his mistress, even though
the Safra clan was still very much against the union. Now more than
ever, they looked upon Lily with a great deal of distrust. How could
Edmond marry such a woman who had embarrassed him with this
English gigolo? Would she also drag the worthy Safra family name
through the mud?

But Edmond had had enough of his family's interference in his personal life. Although he agreed to marry Lily, he insisted that it be a low-key affair in Geneva, but he made sure that no one less than Rabbi Ovadia Yosef, then Sephardic chief rabbi of Israel, presided at the traditional ceremony.

Lily, who loved ostentation, was no doubt deeply disappointed that her fourth wedding—by far her most brilliant accomplishment—had not generated more publicity. She would have loved at least one bold-face mention in *Women's Wear Daily*, but it was not to be. Nothing she could do or say would sway Edmond Safra, and she knew better than to press her luck on this point.

Deeply disappointed at the low-key nuptials, to which only a handful of their friends were invited, Lily made sure that the next marriage in her life would make headlines.

SIX

"The Billionaires' Club"

THE HEAD OFFICE of a media conglomerate in Rio de Janeiro's historic but down-at-the-heels Gloria neighborhood may not have been the most elegant venue for an important society wedding. But by the time Lily Safra got her hands on the guest list and the preparations for the 1983 marriage of her son Claudio Carlos Cohen to Evelyne Bloch Sigelmann, the nuptials would go down in the city's history as the most luxurious and stunning society soiree of all time.

When Claudio announced that he was determined to marry Evelyne, Lily threw herself into the wedding planning with great gusto—much to the annoyance of her son and future daughter-in-law, who would have preferred that she not interfere. But it wasn't to be. Lily was determined to create a magnificent party.

Clearly, Lily wanted to make up for her own understated wedding to Edmond by turning her eldest son's nuptials into a day no one in Rio high society would soon forget. As most of those who were close to Lily knew, she simply adored Claudio—the tall and handsome boy she had once referred to as "Jesus Christ, Esquire." Claudio was her first-born, beloved son. "As a mother she was totally besotted with her eldest son, Claudio," said Samuel Bendahan.

Perhaps Lily threw herself so diligently into the planning and execution of the wedding because she also had something to prove to her old friends in the city where *tout le* fashionable *monde* still whispered about the Monteverde family tragedy. Not that Mrs. Edmond Safra cared what anyone said in Rio, which in the spring of 1983 must have appeared to her a quaint provincial backwater compared to the places that she now called home. Now that she was an international socialite and beginning to become a well-regarded philanthropist with her important banker husband she had little time for old friends in Rio, many of whom were too afraid to approach her after she and Edmond became part of what one old friend respectfully called "the billionaires' club."

Indeed, Lily now moved in more rarefied circles. The Safras lived between homes in London, New York, and Geneva, and they threw fabulous parties for their friends, who included the wealthiest Wall Street financiers as well as designers like Hubert de Givenchy, Valentino, and Karl Lagerfeld. They also made a splash with their philanthropy. A year after their marriage, Edmond, Lily, and their friend Nina Weiner, who was married to Edmond's lawyer and Republic Bank chief Walter Weiner, founded the International Sephardic Education Foundation, which provided scholarships for needy Sephardic students to study at universities in Israel.

Despite his annoyance with high-profile social affairs, Edmond must also have been in a celebratory frame of mind when he arrived in Rio for his beloved stepson's wedding. Three months earlier, in January 1983, he had made a huge splash in international finance when he sold the Trade Development Bank to American Express. The deal, which saw him sell TDB for $520 million to the American company, still had a few snags in it. For one thing, tax issues prevented him from moving to the United States for a year to take up his new position as chairman and chief executive of the company's International Banking Corporation. So until the following year, at least, Edmond would be able to remain happily anonymous, cooling his heels in Geneva, far away from the hordes of journalists who had announced the American Express purchase on the front pages of the world's newspapers—a state of affairs that must have made the very private financier cringe with annoyance.

But Lily paid little attention to American Express in 1983. All her efforts were focused on Claudio's wedding. But if she thought she would dominate the event, she would meet her match in Adolfo Bloch, the Ukrainian Jewish immigrant who was the great-uncle of her future daughter-in-law. Bloch, who had turned a small graphic design business into a mighty media empire, insisted on holding the ceremony and the reception at his magnificent twelve-story company headquarters in Rio with its panoramic views of Sugarloaf Mountain and the Atlantic Ocean. Indeed, the building that housed Bloch Editores on the seafront Rua do Russel near the historic center of Rio was an architectural showpiece designed by modernist architect Oscar Niemeyer in 1968. Bloch, who had founded *Manchete* magazine in 1952 as a glossy, large-format, celebrity-studded weekly that took its inspiration from *Paris Match*, had been a faithful friend to a host of Brazilian leaders. He made sure that they received favorable attention in his magazines, and even provided a sumptuous office for Juscelino Kubitschek, the Brazilian president who presided over the building of the country's futuristic capital Brasília when he was president from 1956 to 1961. When Kubitschek died in an automobile accident in 1976, Bloch insisted that the public viewing of the corpse be held at his cherished building.

On the occasion of his niece's wedding into the mighty Safra clan, Bloch was determined not to be outdone. Besides, he had another great cause to celebrate. He had just brokered a deal to add five television stations to his empire, and no doubt wanted to use his niece's wedding to show the world what a scrappy immigrant could do. On top of that, he adored Edmond and Lily, which was one reason why he insisted upon paying for the wedding reception himself.

In 1922, Bloch had arrived in Rio de Janeiro at the age of fourteen with his destitute parents who were escaping anti-Jewish pogroms in the Ukraine. Now, six decades later, he was dining with important politicians, European royalty, and celebrities. "For years, every ambassador who made his way to Brazil presented his credentials to the Brazilian president and to Adolfo Bloch," said his widow, Ana Bentes Bloch, who had gone to school in Rio with Lily.

On the penthouse floor of Bloch Editores with its stunning views of the ocean, Bloch had also entertained U.S. actor Jack Nicholson, feminist Betty Friedan, and Michael Jackson, who had recently visited Rio de Janeiro to promote his wildly successful "Beat It," which had just topped the Billboard music charts. Moreover, few successful businessmen in status-obsessed social circles could boast that they had shared a *cafezinho* with the American astronaut Neil Armstrong shortly after his historic landing on the moon in 1969.

There was no arguing with Bloch about the venue for his niece's wedding. There was also no denying that the Bloch Editores building was a spectacular work of modernism. Bloch had spared no expense. The foyer leading to the auditorium where the wedding would take place was decorated with sculptures by Frans Krajcberg and paintings by such important Brazilian artists as Emiliano di Cavalcanti and Candido Portinari. The chairs in the twelfth-floor restaurant with its breathtaking views of Guanabara Bay were cut from rare jacaranda wood and designed by the country's best furniture maker, Silvio Rodrigues; the round tabletops were made of the finest Carrara marble.

In the battle to win control over who could organize the most memorable party, Lily set about to complete her own redecorating efforts. Upon inspection of Le Méridien, a five-star, thirty-seven-story seafront hotel next to Copacabana Beach that would accommodate her guests, Lily decided that some of the fixtures were shabby, some of the rooms too small. She happily agreed to pay for the upgrades needed on the hotel floors that the Safras rented for their out-of-town guests. Months before the wedding, a construction crew set about reconfiguring rooms at the Méridien for Lily's wedding guests, most of whom would not stay beyond a few days. The night before the wedding, Lily hosted a lavish supper for her guests at Le Saint Honoré, Rio's finest French restaurant, on the top floor of the Meridien, where the floor-to-ceiling windows offered tremendous views of the Atlantic Ocean and the twinkling lights of Copacabana below.

Although she was eager to show off her grandiose efforts, she knew that Edmond would not appreciate too much publicity. Which is why she told Claudio to make "absolutely certain" that no one in the Brazilian press commented on her jewelry, particularly a rather large diamond ring that had been a present from Edmond. Claudio was extremely well connected in Brazilian media circles, largely because Edmond had installed him as the director of marketing for Ponto Frio, the company founded by Alfredo, his late stepfather. Although he duly informed one of his associates of his mother's wishes, he was, as usual, annoyed by yet another one of her ludicrous requests.

"I told her that if she didn't want anyone to gossip about the ring, then she should just leave it at home!" said Claudio to his friend Guilherme Castello Branco, who worked in advertising in Rio.

"I called every gossip columnist in the city and told them that under no circumstances were they to mention Lily Safra's ring," recalled Castello Branco, adding that he did not have to pay any of the journalists he contacted to do Claudio's bidding because just about every media outlet received advertising from Ponto Frio. To go against the wishes of the son of Lily Safra would have been to sacrifice millions in advertising revenues.

"Claudio was my friend, and he was a great guy, but he couldn't stand his mother meddling in his life," Castello Branco said. "He was really nervous when his mother came to visit because she wanted to control everything."

In fact, before his marriage to Evelyne, Lily did control everything. Claudio had been married to an Argentine dancer named Mimi. The marriage was short-lived because Lily was furious with his choice.

"Lily didn't think she was a good match for her son, and it was Lily, not Claudio, who ended the marriage," Castello Branco said.

Although Claudio divorced Mimi at his mother's behest, he continued to support her financially for years, said Guilherme, who was charged with sending regular wire transfers of cash to Mimi, who went to live in Chile after the divorce.

"Claudio was very solitary and very timid," recalled Castello Branco. "It was difficult for him to find women because he always distrusted them. He never knew if they wanted him or his money."

According to other friends in Rio, Claudio was so awkward with women that when it came to sending flowers to Evelyne—the first time he had sent flowers to a woman in his life—he needed to consult an associate at Ponto Frio because he didn't know how to go about it.

Evelyne was neither beautiful nor royal, and her parents did not belong to the rarefied "billionaires' club." Before her marriage, she was a lanky brunette fond of parties and exercise classes. Like many well-to-do women in Rio, she had a personal trainer to help her with her daily exercise routine—a priority for many women in a city where their bodies are regularly exposed on the city's beaches. Evelyne grew up in an upper-middle-class home in Rio de Janeiro with important family connections through her uncle. Still, "there was a distinct separation between Lily and the bride's family," recalled one observer. "Evelyne's parents were not extravagant people, and at first they just didn't know how to handle Lily. They were a quite normal Jewish family from Rio."

Lily had once been part of a similarly "normal" Jewish family from Rio, but that was years ago now, before she became an international jet-setter and shunned her past and stopped communicating with her old friends from the city. It's not clear how Lily felt about her future daughter-in-law, but she whole-heartedly dove into the preparations for the wedding.

Lily's efforts paid off, and the event was considered a success. At the Bloch Editores building, the auditorium was filled to beyond capacity, with some guests standing in the aisles. The chuppah, or traditional Jewish wedding tent, was set up on stage, and the marriage took place under the auditorium's spotlights. "An event like Rio has never seen and will never see again," read the headline in *O Globo*, which devoted two entire broadsheet pages to the ceremony and the sumptuous reception where nine hundred guests dined haute kosher on imported smoked salmon, Norwegian salted cod, and Chilean sea bass. The Veuve Clicquot "was poured like water from a faucet" while the waiters and ushers were all flown in from the Plaza Athenée in Paris to take care of the guests, who included everyone from European and Pakistani royalty to politicians and Wall Street financiers.

The guest list featured the usual Brazilian luminaries—socialites like Carmen Mayrink Veiga and Regina Marcondes Ferraz, the former caught wearing the same black-and-white Givenchy gown that she had worn to a previous society dinner in Rio. Roberto Marinho, the owner of the Globo media empire and one of Brazil's richest men, was photographed wearing a white skullcap and tuxedo. The media baron and Brazilian kingmaker to generations of Brazilian politicians arrived late, and was forced to stand for much of the nearly two-hour ceremony conducted in Aramaic by three rabbis, including the chief rabbi of Paris and Rio's Sephardic rabbi Abraham Anidjar, "the most Orthodox of rabbis," noted one of the society columnists for Rio's newspaper *O Globo*. In addition to the São Paulo branch of the Safra clan, who all attended the wedding, Roberto de Oliveira Campos, a leading Brazilian economist and one of Edmond's best friends, was also one of the high profile guests, along with the Israeli consul general in Rio, a parade of federal ministers from the military government of the day, and the presidents of all the big Brazilian banks.

But the far more impressive lineup was the group of guests with jet-set pedigrees—friends of Lily's from haute society circles in New York and the French Riviera. Not to be outdone by Bloch, who insisted upon hosting the event, Lily chartered a jet to make sure that her own friends showed up. The Turkish-American record producer Ahmet Ertegun arrived from New York with his wife Mica, the interior designer, who wore the family rubies. New York society hostess Susan Gutfreund, a glamorous former Pan-Am stewardess, was photographed chatting with Italian-Brazilian businessman Ermelino Matarazzo. The wife of John Gutfreund, who was then CEO of Salomon Brothers Inc. and the most powerful man on Wall Street, must have been miffed that the Rio society columnist covering the event clearly had no idea who she was. In the caption underneath the photograph that shows her in a lacy-sleeved gown, her blonde hair in a discreet chignon, she is referred to as "Suzan Goodfriend," which covered the pronunciation but not the spelling of her last name.

The Gutfreunds were probably on a par with Lily when it came to unbridled extravagance. They thought nothing of renting an industrial crane to lift an enormous Christmas tree into their duplex apartment along the East River in the days shortly after their 1981 marriage, and before they moved to their massive sixteen-room apartment on Fifth Avenue. Years later, when they wanted to impress the Safras, they rented Blenheim Castle, the Churchill family's ancestral home in Oxford, to throw a party for them and several hundred other invited guests.

The statuesque Begum Aga Khan, the elderly widow of Aga Khan III and for decades a high-society fixture in the south of France, towered over Edmond in a photograph that appeared in *O Globo*'s society section a week after the wedding. Edmond, who was a few months away from celebrating his fifty-first birthday, is almost completely bald, and appears stiff and ill at ease posing for an unseen photographer in his tuxedo. Maybe the ostentation of the event proved a little bit too much for Edmond. He would probably have much preferred a smaller gathering of close friends and family.

Lily would have none of it. The budding socialite, who was nearly forty-nine, looked resplendent, although extremely thin, in a cream-colored gown with a sheer back. Her blonde hair was discreetly pulled back into a conservative but very tasteful bun. Friends say she positively glowed when the cameras were pointed in her direction.

"There were moments of great emotion, and such great luxury," noted Perla Sigaud, one of *O Globo*'s society columnists, who attended the wedding.

Even those used to the excesses of the Brazilian upper classes were impressed. "The wedding was truly spectacular," recalled Ricardo Stambowsky, a leading wedding planner for Rio's high society. "The entire theater in the *Manchete* building was turned into a huge synagogue. A bridge was built over the pool. People talked about that wedding for years afterwards." And to make sure nobody forgot about the event, Bloch ordered his editors to devote eight pages of photographs to the ceremony and the reception in the next issue of *Manchete*.

On stage, Claudio, who was just shy of his thirtieth birthday, stood stock still and somewhat ill at ease in front of so many important guests. In a newspaper photograph of the ceremony, Claudio is shown clasping his bride's hand. The caption says he is surrounded by family, but curiously Edmond is the only family member who is visible in the photograph. Lily, who is standing at attention next to her husband, is obscured in the photograph by a white piece of paper from which the rabbi is reading.

Switching from Aramaic to Portuguese towards the end of the ceremony, the rabbis blessed the bride and groom. "A couple with such good roots will quickly bear good fruit," said the rabbi from Rio. Later, Claudio awkwardly moved to kiss the bride after removing her veil.

The auditorium echoed with applause as the bejeweled and black-tied guests began to form themselves into a long line to wish the happy couple well. On the penthouse level of the Bloch Editores building, waiters polished crystal goblets, popped champagne corks, and readied hors d'oeuvres for the throngs of designer-clad luminaries who began to make their way up to the top floor. Dinner would be served later, in the restaurant, which was several floors below. In the wee hours of the morning, as the partygoers began to file into their chauffeur-driven black cars, they congratulated Adolfo Bloch and Lily Safra for putting on a great party.

None of the revelers could have imagined that they would all meet again, hours later, to attend a funeral.

THE WINDING ROAD that circles the Pontifical Catholic University in Rio de Janeiro's upscale Gavea neighborhood on a lush mountain overlooking the city is difficult to negotiate at the best of times—on a sunny day with almost no traffic. There are large yellow warning signs proclaiming "Dangerous Curve" in Portuguese, and most experienced drivers know to proceed with caution.

Claudia Bloch Sigelmann, Evelyne's twenty-two-year-old sister, must have rounded that curve in her tiny Fiat dozens of times as she made her way from Claudio's sprawling house, where she frequently escaped with her boyfriend when no one was around to use the pool and smoke pot. On the night of Evelyne's wedding, Claudia left the party at her uncle Oscar's building in Gloria and drove with her boyfriend to Claudio's house on the Gavea mountainside. Claudia's boyfriend was so drunk that the bartenders at the wedding reception refused to serve him. At one point, the chef, Severino Dias, asked him to leave at once. Determined to have a few more drinks before heading to the Gavea house, Claudia and her boyfriend headed to the Hippopotamus bar. But they were eventually kicked out when the boyfriend became unruly.

Once they arrived at Claudio's home, they went for a moonlight dip and smoked a few joints. The drugs mixed with the alcohol that was already in her system from the party must have clouded Claudia's judgment. The next thing she did was to get in the passenger seat of the Fiat with a man in the driver's seat who was not only drunk, but now stoned. They were heading to an all-night club in Baixo Gavea, a bohemian neighborhood at the bottom of Gavea mountain that was a frequent haunt of university students and artists.

In the pitch dark, Claudia's boyfriend drove recklessly down the cobblestone streets that wound their way past the dense tropical vegetation with its bursts of colorful hibiscus flowers that hid the gated mansions and exclusive private schools nestled in the elite hillside neighborhood. By the time the driver could make out the myriad lights of the city down below, he was driving much too fast to negotiate the infamous curve that circled the university, which locals refer to by its acronym, PUC. Claudia may have tried to take the steering wheel when he lost control of the car. But it was too late. The Fiat crashed into a wall. Claudia was pronounced dead when the paramedics arrived. The boyfriend miraculously survived, with only a sprained ankle and a few scratches.

It was dawn when Guilherme Castello Branco got the call. He had just drifted off to sleep after spending most of the night at Claudio's wedding when the telephone jerked him awake.

"It was Magna, Claudio's secretary, on the other end, and her voice sounded terrible," recalled Castello Branco. "She told me to call all the newspapers, radios, television stations, and anyone else I could think of to block the story. Claudio did not want the story in the press."

But the bleary-eyed Castello Branco had no idea what she was talking about. "What story?" he asked. After being told of the tragedy, he hung up the telephone and, for the second time in a week, called every media outlet in Rio to keep a story from reaching the press. Again, he claims he paid no money to censor the news. A simple phone call was enough to halt any bad publicity.

The censorship seemed to have worked because while just about every media outlet in the city gushed about the wedding, there were only fleeting references to the terrible accident and the funeral, and they only appeared a week after the events.

According to an editor who was close to both the Bloch and Safra families, they went out of their way to make sure that the story did not end up in the press, partly because Claudia "was either drunk or on drugs or both."

"The whole thing was simply too embarrassing for the families, and really too tragic," said the editor, who did not want to be identified. "Can you imagine? On Saturday night you have the wedding, and then on Sunday morning the funeral?"

The families clearly did not want bad publicity to upstage what had been a very glamorous and important "happening" in Rio high society. On top of that, in a Catholic country under a military dictatorship, it would simply not do to reveal that the niece of one of Brazil's most important tycoons had died because she had been under the influence of drugs and alcohol.

Edmond and Lily heard the news as they made their way to their luxurious suite at the Méridien in the early hours of Sunday morning. Edmond, still in black tie from the wedding, immediately called his chauffeur and drove to the morgue to offer his support to the Bloch-Sigelmann families. He also took it upon himself to make the funeral arrangements. After the body was released from the morgue, the funeral was immediately scheduled for that morning. Many of the guests who had attended the wedding now found themselves at a wind-swept Jewish cemetery on the industrial outskirts of Rio de Janeiro, presiding at the burial of a young woman whose sister had just celebrated what should have been one of the happiest days of her life.

Inês Sigelmann, the mother of the bride, her tear-stained face hidden behind large sunglasses, had worn a flowing gown the color of pink hydrangeas for her eldest daughter's wedding but was now dressed in a sober suit to bury her younger daughter. Most of the mourners were dumbstruck: They shook their heads in disbelief; they had no explanation for such a senseless tragedy.

"Life sometimes sends us difficult times, and I know that none of

the well-wishers at the wedding had the words to express their sadness for what happened right after," wrote Perla Sigaud in her society
column on the Cohen-Bloch wedding, which appeared the following
week. "I was hesitating over whether in the face of so much pain I
should write about the happiness that occurred on the eve of so much
tragedy. It was climax and anticlimax; euphoria and extreme sorrow.
Life sometimes forces us to deal with the most dramatic contrasts.
And we must learn to take from every difficult experience an important lesson in humility."

But Sigaud's rather poetic musings seem to have fallen on deaf
ears, at least when it came to exercising humility. Here were two extremely wealthy families whose single-minded pursuit of wealth and
status had been, and continued to be, ruthless and overreaching. At
least that proved to be the case with Bloch. The media baron would
famously overextend his reach after making his bold move into television on the eve of the wedding in 1983, and see his whole empire
collapse a little more than a decade later. His beloved sparkling glass
office building in Gloria where he had pulled out all the stops for
the wedding of a lifetime, and where he had entertained some of the
most important figures in recent history, would fall into disrepair. In
due course, it became the property of the Brazilian courts and was
auctioned off to pay the tens of millions in salaries that the company
owed to its former employees.

"Everyone said that the death of Evelyne's sister on the heels of the
wedding was a terrible omen," said one of the wedding guests, who
also attended the funeral the following day.

It was a curse, others said—a warning of some unimaginable tragedy that would surely befall those families in the future.

For the Safra family at least, that was exactly what it turned out
to be.

———————

MONTHS BEFORE THE wedding and the funeral, Joseph Safra warned his brother not to sell the bank. He had even flown from São Paulo to Montreal, in the midst of a January deep freeze, to tell his brother in person that he was making a huge mistake by selling the Trade Development Bank to American Express. The final negotiations were underway at the Four Seasons Hotel in the frigid Canadian city, and Joseph needed to try to convince Edmond that what he was doing was sheer madness.

"You don't even know these people," pleaded his younger brother, who must have found it hard to believe that Edmond was breaking with family tradition by entrusting one of his beloved "children" to strangers who did not understand the Safra way of doing business.

But Edmond could be stubborn. Despite their heated discussions about the suitability of Lily as a wife seven years before, Edmond had gone ahead and married her anyway, even after the public shame of *l'affaire* Bendahan. Joseph had also pleaded with him not to marry Lily. But in the end, Edmond refused, and for years after their 1976 wedding, the Brazilian Safras had frosty relations at best with Lily, whom they considered an opportunist and an arriviste.

But in many ways, the imminent sale of the bank was far more important than any woman. It must have bothered Joseph and the rest of the Safra clan that for the first time since the death of their father in 1963 Edmond had not consulted them over one of the most important business decisions of his life.

John Gutfreund, chair of Salomon Brothers investment firm, agreed that Edmond was making a terrible move. Gutfreund also took an intercontinental flight—from New York to São Paulo where Edmond was attending a bar mitzvah—shortly before the negotiations with American Express were scheduled to begin. Gutfreund tried to convince his friend to reconsider. A hard-nosed veteran of Wall Street, he knew that Edmond's aristocratic banking methods would be mocked in a huge American company like American Express. American executives at the company simply wouldn't take him seriously; they would find a way to subvert his power. The experience, Gutfreund warned, would be disastrous.

But Edmond had made up his mind, partly because he had developed the niche market in European private banking so well that he felt there was no longer any space to expand. "It was an economic decision to join American Express because he felt that the private banking market in Europe was going into a downturn," said one observer familiar with the negotiations. "And here was American Express under Jim Robinson III wanting to develop the private banking market and turn itself into a financial services supermarket. At the time, it seemed like a good fit."

Edmond also worried about the worsening Latin American debt crisis and the exposure that his Swiss bank faced as country after country in the region showed signs of defaulting on their loans to international creditors and commercial banks. Between 1975 and 1982, Latin American debt to commercial banks skyrocketed, and the region saw its external debt grow from $75 billion in 1975 to more than $315 billion in 1982—a figure that then represented 50 percent of the region's gross domestic product. If Argentina and Brazil—two of the largest economies in the region—began to default as Mexico had done in August 1982, what would become of his own bank, which had made large loans to Brazil and other Latin American economies?

Edmond also offered up the usual excuses for wanting to get rid of the bank—he was tired of the pace, he wanted to spend more time with Lily and the grandchildren. These would all have been quite normal reasons for wanting to lighten his business load, but Edmond was not a normal businessman. From the age of eight, when he followed his father into the souks of Beirut, banking had been his life. Besides, what would his clients say? Many of these people banked with him because they trusted his family. Now he was selling the crucial Swiss arm of his business *and* his loyal clientele to a huge American company that did not understand the old ways, that would not provide the same kind of personal attention to their needs that Edmond had done over the years. Of course, Edmond did try to reassure them, reminding his best clients that he would still be their point of reference as chief of American Express's international banking division. No, everything would work out fine, he had said. There was nothing to worry about.

In the end, it was Jeffrey Keil, the keen young treasurer at the Republic National Bank of New York, who helped persuade Edmond to sign on with American Express. Keil, along with former Republic executive Peter Cohen, now himself part of the American Express group, felt that incorporating Trade Development Bank within the massive American Express structure would boost the declining fortunes of the company's own bank—the American Express Bank—and offer the TDB a safe haven.

After weeks of discussions with Keil and Cohen, Edmond seemed convinced by their arguments and signed the deal. He waited until the stroke of midnight on January 18, 1983, because 18—the numerological value of the *chai*, the Hebrew symbol for life—was considered good luck among some Jews. The TDB sale hit the front pages of business papers around the world with American Express executives gushing in print that they had added one of the most brilliant banking minds to their team.

Although they listed his accomplishments and his banking lineage, many of the reporters covering the story also noted that Edmond would not be taking up his new appointment as chief of American Express's International Banking Corporation for at least a year, citing unspecified "complications," a reference to his delicate tax situation. Although none of his aides voiced this openly at the time, there was some concern that an absent new chief executive might not get the respect he deserved.

A year later, when his U.S. tax issues were resolved, the *New York Times* formally announced Edmond's appointment, noting that he would be taking over his new duties in New York on March 1, 1984. Jim Robinson III, the chairman and CEO of American Express, was quick to point out that Edmond had not been idle since the deal was signed in January 1983. He had been doing a lot of work, integrating TDB into the larger company's framework.

"Over the course of last year, since we completed the combination of American Express International Banking Corporation and Trade Development Bank, Edmond Safra has worked very closely with senior management of the bank and the entire American Express Company," he said. "Clearly we are fortunate to have a business leader with his banking experience and stature."

But Robinson's statements to the press couldn't have been further from the truth. In the year that Edmond was forced to stay in Europe, relations between American Express and the TDB deteriorated rapidly. As Gutfreund and others predicted, American executives did not appreciate Edmond's Old World banking style, which clashed with the massive American Express bureaucracy. Even before Edmond formally took over the post, American Express executives assigned to review the day-to-day operations of Trade Development Bank shook their heads in disbelief—they simply could not figure out how it functioned.

"TDB ran like nothing we'd ever seen," said one American Express official. "It ran like an extended family. The management style was just Edmond, who knew everyone. It was very loose, there was no documentation, and only Edmond knew the structure. If someone wanted to talk to him, they simply picked up a phone and called him. It was about as different from a McKinsey model as you could find. Our attitude was, well, we'll show these guys how to run a company."

Another executive who was close to the company noted, "Safra's a brilliant guy, but he needs to do everything himself. He's not used to a bureaucracy. He insisted on approving every loan. It began to grate on both sides."

But while American Express executives shook their heads in frustration at having spent so much money on a bank whose methods

seemed a throwback to the nineteenth century, Edmond was growing increasingly frustrated with the way he was being treated by the
company hierarchy. Used to being in firm control at his banks, he
was finding out about American Express business ventures and losses
after the fact. After the sale of TDB to the company, Edmond was
its biggest shareholder, and he considered it a huge slap in the face
every time he found out about the company's dealings in the press.
Shouldn't Robinson and his associates be consulting *him* about what
was going on in the company? For instance, Edmond learned from a
Dow Jones wire story about American Express's plans to pay $1 bil-
lion for a Minneapolis-based financial services company. He was also
stunned when he learned from news reports just before Christmas
1983 that the Fireman's Fund, the company's California-based insurance company, would post a pretax loss of $242 million, dragging
down American Express's total earnings for the year.

Edmond was livid. To make matters worse, American Express was
now reaching out to its newly acquired private banking customers in
Europe—the TDB clients—and they were sent all sorts of promo-
tions for other services that the company offered in the mail. For this
select group of deposit holders to suddenly be receiving a barrage
of mail and promotional material was too much for Edmond. These
were people who had banked with him out of a need for utter discretion; now they were on the American Express mailing list!

He worried; he lost sleep; he couldn't relax. How could they treat
him and his customers like this? In retaliation, Edmond decided to
dump almost all of his American Express stock—a slap in the face to
his new bosses that ended up costing him more than $100 million in
losses. Now, Edmond openly threatened to resign; he even offered to
buy back the Trade Development Bank. American Express refused,
saying his offering price was too low.

But Edmond simply couldn't continue to feel like a hostage of the
global conglomerate, and in October 1984 American Express formally
announced that Edmond would be resigning as the head of interna-

tional banking, although he would be made a director on the company's board. The deal allowed him to buy back several foreign banking operations that he had sold to American Express the previous year. As an article in the *Wall Street Journal* noted, "Mr. Safra, a private sometimes eccentric 52-year-old billionaire whose holdings include Republic National Bank in New York, apparently didn't fit well into American Express's more bureaucratic style of management." But a year later, the break became final when Edmond simply could no longer abide the American way of doing business at the company.

After he decided to rid himself of the American Express albatross, Edmond felt like a different man. He threw a party for Lily's fiftieth birthday at Annabel's in London, inviting the Gutfreunds, the Erteguns, and many of the others who had attended Claudio's wedding. Edmond arranged for the restaurant to be decorated in "pillars of white and pink tuberoses," and the menu featured eggs with caviar and Becheyelle '70 at intimate tables of eight and ten. The party earned Lily one of her first mentions in *Women's Wear Daily*, which described Edmond, Lily, and their guests as "the international camera-shy money-doesn't-talk set." Later, on a whim, Edmond and Lily flew from New York to Rio de Janeiro for a much-needed vacation. "For the first time in my life I left New York without telling my secretary where I will be," said Edmond to his friend Albert Nasser as the two men settled into a backgammon game at Nasser's luxurious beachfront Ipanema apartment. "I feel as free as a bird and I am very happy to be this way."

As soon as he had broken ties with American Express, Edmond set about building another bank—a Swiss extension of his Republic National Bank of New York. But as per his original and very complex contract with American Express, Edmond was forbidden from luring away his former employees, and had to agree that he would not start a competing bank for three years—until March 1, 1988—after his final departure from the company in 1985. However, Edmond was anxious to save face and recoup his losses, and demanded that his lawyers find a loophole in his original contract with American Express to allow him to get away with it. The loophole came in the form of a small clause that stated that his relationship with the company would not affect his dealings with Republic National Bank of New York, his other "child."

"Nothing in this agreement shall impose any restriction on the conduct of the business and affairs of Republic or any of [its] subsidiaries," noted the contract, which Edmond's lawyers quickly interpreted as carte blanche to hire back their top TDB people for the new Republic Bank that they were planning to open in Geneva.

It was a bit of a legal ruse, to be sure, and it disingenuously assumed that American Express's senior executives simply wouldn't notice when all of Edmond's top people started leaving TDB in droves. American Express executives saw their chance to get even with Edmond when they suspected one of his old TDB employees of stealing irreplaceable internal bank information system information, known as IBIS files, which contain a bank's entire administrative system. American Express rapidly launched a criminal probe of Edmond in Geneva. The March 1987 complaint, which was kept secret as per Swiss law, also accused Edmond of unfair competition and raiding American Express employees.

Edmond was a wreck when he found out about the Swiss investigation, which one of his aides discovered quite by chance. To make matters even worse, American Express then tried to block Republic's application for a Swiss banking license that would allow the new entity to accept deposits in Switzerland. American Express asked the Swiss federal banking authority to turn down Edmond's request and demanded a full inquiry.

Soon there would be no way to avoid media scrutiny. Edmond and his aides knew that American Express had a huge publicity machine, and they braced themselves for the terrible months ahead.

The American Express smear campaign against Edmond Safra began quietly enough with small articles appearing in relatively unknown newspapers in Europe and Latin America, beginning in the late summer of 1988. Sporadic articles about Edmond and his banking empire began to appear in the right-wing Parisian newspaper *Minute*, the Peruvian paper *Hoy*, the Mexican *Uno Más Uno*, and Toulouse's *Dépêche de Midi*. The tone of all the articles was the same: They tried to portray Edmond as a shadowy financier who had links to organized crime, the Medellín cocaine cartel, and the Iran-Contra scandal. The articles were also anti-Semitic in tone, noting at every opportunity that Edmond was "a Lebanese Jew" who wielded formidable power.

For Edmond and his brothers in Brazil, the articles could prove devastating for business. What if the wealthy Halabim and other clients started to ask about the articles? What if they started to get nervous about the prospects of looming investigations of their banks? Edmond knew he had to act, but in the early days he and his aides didn't quite know how to go about it.

In August 1988, *Minute* published an article linking Edmond with Willard Zucker, the Geneva-based American lawyer whose specialty was setting up shell companies in tax havens such as Panama and the Cayman Islands. In April 1987, a U.S. congressional committee investigating the Iran-Contra affair had named Zucker as the financier who had helped set up some of the shell companies involved in the Reagan administration's secret transfers of funds from the clandestine sale of arms to Iran. The proceeds were geared towards encouraging the release of U.S. hostages in the Middle East and the financing of the Nicaraguan Contra rebels who were trying to overthrow the democratically elected Marxist government of Daniel Ortega. Zucker had set up shell companies for his client Albert Hakim, an Iranian-born middleman who was, in turn, working with a retired U.S. Air Force major general named Richard Secord and Lt. Colonel Oliver North—both of them major figures at the center of the scandal. Hakim, who had important contacts in the Iranian military, sold weapons at inflated prices to Iran and funneled the profits into secret government deals. Zucker was his man in Switzerland—"a discreet, efficient and rapid channel for moving money." Later, when he was named in the investigation, Zucker agreed to cooperate with American prosecutors in exchange for immunity from prosecution.

In the past, of course, both Edmond and Lily had sought out Zucker's valuable expertise in setting up offshore companies to protect their own assets. Zucker, who in the 1970s headed up the Compagnie de Services Fiduciaires S.A. on the rue Charles-Bonnet in Geneva, had set up the shell company through which Lily bought her home in Vallauris with Samuel Bendahan in 1972. A year earlier, Zucker worked with Jayme Bastian Pinto, Lily's Brazilian lawyer, to help sort out the various legal and tax issues that dogged her after Alfredo's death. In a letter dated December 13, 1971, Zucker wrote to Lily's British attorney seeking advice on "Mrs. L. Monteverde's potential liability for income tax in certain jurisdictions." In the letter, Zucker suggested that Lily avoid declaring income in Britain and "carefully segregate her accounts abroad." This way, if she were served in conjunction with the Monteverde lawsuit or questioned in a British court she could truthfully say that she was not a resident of the United Kingdom. With a fortune valued at nearly $300 million it was of paramount importance to Lily that she avoid paying high taxes in the UK. At the same time, she didn't want to jeopardize her long-term ability to gain residency in the UK. The country is a tax haven for UK residents of "foreign domicile" who pay a nominal levy on their non-UK income.

Edmond had also used Zucker's services in the past to set up Republic Air Transport Services, the offshore company that incorporated a small jet that Edmond had purchased in 1988.

Edmond was furious that the newspaper accounts seemed to suggest that his business connections to Zucker also linked him by default to the Iran-Contra scandal, and to all sorts of other unsavory activities such as money laundering for various mafiosi. Some of the stories even dredged up his stake in the Kings Lafayette Bank, which was linked to organized crime in Brooklyn in the 1960s and 1970s.

Edmond did buy up the bank in the early 1970s although his methods generated a great deal of unwanted publicity in New York.

In 1971, the publicity-shy banker and his aides decided to take advantage of an obscure securities loophole that allowed him to accumulate shares in the Kings Lafayette Bank as an individual rather than as a corporation. But when these secret maneuvers led to protracted negotiations with state banking authorities in New York, the negotiations just happened to take place at the same time as the arrest by federal authorities of eight members of New York-based crime families who had sought loans under false pretenses from Kings Lafayette in the past. One of those arrested was mobster Joe Gallo, a major suspect in the shooting of rival mob leader Joseph Colombo, who was attacked at an Italian Day rally in 1971. Colombo, who died after spending seven years in a coma, had forged strong alliances with the Jewish Defense League, and for years the Colombo family supplied arms to the organization that in turn armed Jewish militant groups in Israel and the U.S., according to press reports.

It's unclear whether Edmond was aware of any of the mob connections when he bought the bank, which expanded the Republic's reach throughout Brooklyn and Queens.

Still, the mob connections would come back to haunt him seventeen years later, as his purchase of a bank that had been caught loaning money to New York crime bosses formed the basis of innuendo-laden articles in newspapers in Latin America and Europe. In an effort to try to stop the negative publicity, Edmond launched a series of lawsuits in France against *Minute*, which proved victorious and helped to restore his reputation.

But despite these small legal victories, the larger smear campaign continued unabated. The question of just who was behind the spread of these unsubstantiated rumors dogged Edmond's advisers for months. Of course, they immediately suspected American Express's mighty publicity machine, but they needed to prove that the global conglomerate was behind the attacks. Edmond and his aides soon be-

gan their own counteroffensive, hiring a crack team of private investigators and publicity experts to fight back.

"Safra . . . exhorted his aides to rehash everything they knew, everything they could do, to root out the source of the articles and prove
once and for all that American Express was behind them," writes in-
vestigative journalist Bryan Burrough, whose 1992 book *Vendetta*
provides an exhaustive retelling of the massive smear campaign engineered by a handful of American Express executives against Edmond. "For Safra it was time to strike back at American Express for
what it had done to him."

With his team of private investigators working around the world,
Edmond was able to link the complex and highly developed media
disinformation campaign back to American Express. While he prepared his own legal attack on the conglomerate, the Swiss authorities
finally granted him a banking license, and on March 1, 1988—three
years following his resignation from American Express—he opened
the Republic National Bank of New York (Suisse) in Geneva.

Although the battle with American Express wasn't quite over, Lily
had had enough of the stress and trauma. She was tired of the pressure, of the sleepless nights and Edmond's mood swings. So when the
official permission came through for the bank, and the case against
the nasty American executives seemed almost over, she decided to do
what she did best: She would throw the most lavish and extravagant
party that European and New York society had ever seen. Lily convinced her husband that it was finally time to throw open the doors
of their recently acquired estate in the south of France and attract a
different kind of media coverage—the boldface mentions in the most
fashionable society columns.

Women's Wear Daily, the haute-society bible for the international
jet set, couldn't resist giving Lily's soiree advance notice in one of its
June 1988 society columns. "The biggest—and most anticipated—

ball of the summer season in Europe is actually two balls," wrote the reporter for the magazine, noting that "Lily and Edmond Safra's doubleheader" was scheduled for the following August sixth and eighth at their palatial new home in the south of France. The article explained that the couple simply could not accommodate all of their friends and business associates at one party.

It wasn't that their new villa on verdant, terraced hills overlooking the azure waters of the Mediterranean in Villefranche-sur-Mer was small. The villa was a sprawling, majestic home set among tall cypress trees and orange and lemon groves that had been first owned by King Leopold II of Belgium.

Like the new owners of the villa, King Leopold II was known for his extravagance. But it was his rapacious greed in the African Free State of Congo that became his real legacy. King Leopold II ran the Belgian Congo as a private fiefdom, and he was condemned for the brutal colonization and gross human-rights abuses that were committed by his forces against the native population, who were forced into slavery in the extraction of rubber and precious metals for the Belgian crown. An estimated ten to fifteen million people died as the result of mutilation and illness spread by Belgian colonial masters. Children regularly had their hands amputated if they didn't meet the labor demands of the Belgians. Atrocities practiced by the Belgian colonists in the Congo were so horrible that they became the inspiration for Joseph Conrad's novella *Heart of Darkness*.

Still, with part of the proceeds from his business ventures in the Congo, Leopold II was determined to live well. On a visit to the Riviera, he bought a tract of land overlooking the Mediterranean and ordered construction crews to begin work on Domaine La Leopolda, as it was then called. The villa was a gift to his mistress, Blanche Zelia Josephine Delacroix, a Romanian-born prostitute who bore him two sons out of wedlock. Blanche, who was also known as Caroline Lacroix, married the ailing king on his deathbed, in December 1909, five days before he died. But the Belgian courts refused to recognize the marriage, nor did they recognize the legitimacy of Blanche and her sons, who had been given royal titles before Leopold's death. Blanche and the children were cast out of the royal court and La Leopolda was taken over by Leopold's nephew and successor, King Albert I, who donated the land to a hospital for Belgian soldiers wounded during the First World War.

Twenty years after Leopold's death the land was purchased by Ogden Codman Jr., an American architect and interior designer who had designed some of the greatest homes on the American east coast. He redecorated the novelist Edith Wharton's home in Newport, Rhode Island, and went on to design homes for Cornelius Vanderbilt II and John D. Rockefeller Jr. before leaving for France in 1920.

Codman envisioned La Leopolda as a grand château, with formal, manicured gardens, inspired by the Château Borelli in Marseilles and the Villa Belgiojoso in Milan. Although he painstakingly designed the villa for himself, by the time the construction was completed the place was so grand that he could no longer afford to keep it.

Later, Gianni Agnelli, the powerful industrialist and head of the Italian car company Fiat, bought La Leopolda as his summer home. Alfred Hitchcock used the property as a set in his 1955 film *To Catch a Thief*, which starred Cary Grant and Grace Kelly.

Nearly a century after Leopold bought the land for the villa, it was Lily and Edmond who would do the Belgian king proud. The Safras commissioned Renzo Mongiardino, the éminence grise of interior design, who had also designed theater sets for director Franco Zeffirelli and opera singer Maria Callas. Mongiardino had done work for La Leopolda's previous owner, and he set about blending the Safras' eighteenth-century European furniture into a grand, formal setting that would have definitely pleased the Belgian king. The second-floor bedrooms were decorated by the Safras' friend Mica Ertegun. Lily spent $2 million in decorator fees just on her own bedroom, although the bill did not include the eighteenth-century furniture (which she later sold at a Sotheby's auction in 2005).

"La Leopolda was surely never this grand when Belgium's King Leopold II summered there," noted *Women's Wear Daily*, making an erroneous reference to the Belgian king, who died before he could begin construction on the property. "Nor was it nearly as royal when Gianni Agnelli kept it as his Riviera retreat. But for Lily and Edmond J. Safra, the current owners of this immense mansion overlooking the Mediterranean, near excess is not enough." In addition to the interiors, the Safras expanded the swimming pool and nearly doubled its size.

The first ball, on August 6, featured three hundred of Lily's closest friends—the A-list crowd, according to *Women's Wear Daily*—to fete Edmond's fifty-sixth birthday. Lily, who had honed her hostess skills preparing children's parties and feeding the hungry businessmen who participated in Alfredo's all-night poker games, and had outdone herself at his funeral luncheon in Rio—like the "undersecretary of state" as her former sister-in-law had noted at the time—was now showing the world what a meticulous and generous hostess she could be. No expense was spared. Flowers were flown in from Holland, and Sergio Mendes and his entire orchestra were flown in from California. A rumor that Liza Minnelli might show up at the party with Frank Sinatra proved false, but the party was a huge success without them. The menu—*soupe de poisson, feuilleté aux asperges*, and *saumon aux truffes*—was prepared by star chef Roger Vergé of the Moulin de Mougins, one of the finest restaurants on the Riviera. The dinner was served outdoors under huge white hurricane-proof tents and "decorated Pompeii style." For those who did not get enough of the magnificent feast, the Safra chefs laid out a spaghetti dinner at 4:00 a.m. for the remaining guests. As a parting gift, the hostess presented each of the women guests with an enamel box featuring a picture of La Leopolda.

Security was tight. A French SWAT team was hired for the event, and there was "half a man per guest—to protect the glorious three hundred who were arriving." Princess Caroline and her father, Prince Rainier, insisted that all the guests be in place before they made their grand entrance. In addition to the Grimaldis, other security-conscious royal guests included Princess Firyal of Jordan and the Amyn Aga Khan. As a correspondent for *Women's Wear Daily* noted, "the grounds were guarded as heavily as the White House, and security almost outnumbered the guests. Even the day before the fete, passersby who strayed off the Moyenne Corniche [the picturesque highway from nearby Nice] to steal a glimpse of the imposing place would be chased by hulks on motorcycles."

Valentino, the designer of choice for "at least two dozen" of the women at the first party and a Safra banking client, arrived on his new 152-foot yacht, the *TM Blue One*, with his business partner Giancarlo Giammetti and dancer Mikhail Baryshnikov. The Niarchos clan also arrived in their giant yacht, the *Atlantis II*, which was equipped with a helicopter. The Countess Isabelle d'Ornano, one of Europe's most elegant women, was resplendent in a taffeta gown designed by Jean-Louis Scherrer to match the villa's ocher and green tones.

John and Susan Gutfreund, who had flown to Rio for Claudio and Evelyne's wedding, also attended the grand opening of the Safra estate. Like her friend Lily, Susan was also a fan of excess, but on this occasion she wore an understated white Chanel mousseline dress. "With the opening of a place like this, the home and the hostess should be the stars," she said. "I wanted to dress to disappear like a rat in the woodwork."

Lily wore a pink mousseline gown designed by Valentino with exquisite butterfly earrings designed by the world's most exclusive artist-jeweler, JAR, the acronym for Joel Arthur Rosenthal, the New York-born Parisian jeweler whose shop on the place Vendôme has no display window and no regular hours. JAR only designs one-of-a-kind creations for an elite clientele.

Lily's friend Lynn Wyatt, the wife of Texas billionaire Oscar Wyatt, wore a striking black, white, and pink satin gown, also by Valentino. The Wyatts, who owned a spectacular home near La Leopolda on the Riviera, would almost always be mentioned in society columns alongside the Safras, whom they considered among their best friends.

The second party, which included many of Edmond's business associates, did not warrant much mention in the society press, largely because it was a more private affair. At both parties, Edmond and Lily also invited their children and their beloved grandchildren, whom Edmond referred to as *mes amours*. In addition to Claudio's two boys, Adriana now had three children of her own.

The *grand vernissage* of the Safra mansion would cost the Safras more than $2 million, but it was a huge success. It was a small price to pay for their grand entry into high society. For with the La Leopolda parties, Lily became the consummate society hostess on an international scale. As *Women's Wear Daily* publisher John Fairchild himself noted, "The Safra event itself . . . marked the culmination of the Safras' meteoric rise to social power; they have taken over the Riviera, Southampton, New York, the Metropolitan Opera, Geneva—all in the space of five years. What's next?"

As the air-kisses flew on that muggy night in August and the Safras greeted everyone from Karl Lagerfeld to Barbara Walters and Betsy Bloomingdale, Lily was living her dream as the grand society hostess of the world's glitterati and movers and shakers. Here was Felix Rohatyn, an investment banker who had restructured New York City's debt in the 1970s and resolved a huge fiscal crisis, arriving with his wife Elizabeth and stepdaughter, the New York socialite Nina Griscom. Across the lawn stood the brooding Christina Onassis, heiress to one of the most fabled fortunes in Europe. Like Lily, Christina had married four times, and had recently broken up with her fourth husband, Thierry Roussel, the father of her only daughter, Athina. As it turned out, Lily's fabulous party was one of the last social events she would attend, for three months later Christina would be found dead of an apparent drug overdose at a country club in Buenos Aires.

If they believed in omens—and Edmond certainly did—maybe the Onassis death might have given the Safras a few moments of pause. Were they not tempting the evil eye with such a grandiose celebration—so monumental, so costly, and so *public*!

But 1988 had dawned with such hope. After years of sleepless nights and the agony over his ill-fated decision to sell TDB to American Express, they were back on the society track, attending openings, galas, and fundraisers around the world. Edmond was rebuilding what would turn into a stronger, more lucrative empire on the ashes of a costly mistake; he was reclaiming his most valued employees from TDB and he had started a new bank. He was also building a good case against his former employer—a case he knew he would eventually win. So after the parties, and after a few business meetings with old Halabim clients he had invited to La Leopolda, Edmond looked forward to a few days off in his palatial new home with Lily's six grandchildren.

But their newfound happiness and relief were extremely short-lived.

THE ARGUMENT THAT escalated into a screaming match between Claudio and Evelyne on the morning of Friday, February 17, 1989, had actually begun at their house on the Gavea mountain in Rio de Janeiro the night before. As usual, Claudio had had a particularly grueling day at work. Simon Alouan, a former professor of mathematics from Beirut who had been appointed by Edmond to head up Alfredo's old company in 1973, was not known for his manners. He could be rough and obnoxious at times, and he was generally feared by everyone in upper management at the appliance chain. Everybody knew that Alouan hated Claudio—hated him with a passion. After all, Claudio was everything he was not—a well-educated, well-mannered member of the Brazilian elite, and certainly a mama's boy, who had been parachuted into his job as head of marketing because of his mother's influence at the company. Although Lily, as majority shareholder, was technically Alouan's boss, Alouan openly despised her as well. When it came to discussing business matters and the future of the company, he spoke only to Edmond, a fellow Halabim and his most important benefactor. It was Edmond who had brought Alouan to São Paulo to help run one of the Safra family's investment houses in the early days. Alouan, who hailed from an impoverished Halabim family, was eternally grateful to Edmond, who had financed his education in Lebanon.

"Edmond brought Alouan to Brazil and gave him something like 20 percent of the Ponto Frio business," recalled Albert Nasser. "He always reported to Edmond and refused to take Lily seriously. Every time that she said she was coming to Rio, Alouan would make sure he was on a plane to Europe. With Claudio, he used to put him down all the time and let everyone at the company know that he was good for nothing."

Claudio's friend Guilherme Castello Branco also recalled the disputes between Claudio and Alouan at the company. "Alouan was very rough, and it was clear that he really despised Claudio," he said.

Usually by the end of a workday at Ponto Frio Claudio was a nervous wreck. He yelled at Evelyne over the slightest problem and lost his temper with his two young sons—four-year-old Raphael and fifteen-month-old Gabriel. He was looking forward to taking a few days off on this summer long weekend and was glad that they had decided to go with their friends Rubem and Ana Maria Andreazza to their summerhouse in Angra dos Reis.

On that muggy Friday morning, as the nanny and the housekeeper readied the children for the two-and-a-half-hour drive to Angra, a beach town southwest of Rio where the coastline is dotted with hundreds of small islands, Claudio and Evelyne picked up their argument of the night before.

"Evelyne was truly an annoying person," said one of the couple's friends. "Claudio, who was a wonderful person, was a henpecked husband. After Claudio married her, a lot of his friends stopped going to the house in Gavea. They were always at each other's throats."

The fight got so ugly that Claudio suggested they drive to Angra in separate cars. He stormed out of the house with Raphael, who had begged Claudio to take him in the car with him. Claudio and Raphael piled into his jeep, a Brazilian-made Chevrolet, to pick up his friend Rubem. Raphael, who loved Rubem, wanted to sit in the front with his father and his friend. Claudio reached in the back to pick up his son and placed him gently between the two adult passengers. Evelyne, Ana Maria, and little Gabriel would drive ahead in a Ford Galaxy Ltd Landau, with Mario, the couple's chauffeur. They would all meet in Angra in a few hours.

Claudio drove fast, past the mansions and grand apartment blocks of the chic beachfront neighborhoods of Leblon and Ipanema, past the crowded favelas, or shantytowns, that cling to the mountainsides, and onto the potholed highway that was the only road to Angra dos Reis. Deep in conversation with Rubem, Claudio probably didn't even notice the *policia militar* truck as it barreled into his lane on kilometer 17 of the Rio-Santos Highway near Itaguai, an impoverished municipality of half-finished brick and plywood houses that marks the halfway point from Rio de Janeiro to Angra dos Reis.

Like Claudio, the driver of the police truck was going far too fast after negotiating a particularly difficult curve. Witnesses said the truck literally passed over the jeep, leaving it a mangled mess of metal.

All three passengers in Claudio's car were killed almost instantly; the impact crushed the Chevrolet, which erupted in flames, and ripped human limbs from their sockets. Claudio's body was unrecognizable when a fire crew pulled him from the wreck. Body parts were strewn on the highway along with pieces of smoldering, twisted metal.

Barely an hour after Evelyne and Ana Maria pulled into the summerhouse they started to worry about the jeep. Later, when a carload of their friends arrived, shaking their heads at the terrible accident they had just passed on the road, Evelyne feared the worst. Trembling, she demanded a description of the mangled vehicle that police and firefighters were trying to tow to the side of the road to relieve the snarling traffic of weekend travelers that the accident had caused. When her friends described the car, Evelyne drove back along the Rio-Santos Highway. Before she even saw the mangled vehicle, she saw the body parts strewn along the asphalt. When she recognized her little boy's T-shirt, Evelyne started to scream. She never forgave herself for allowing little Raphael to travel with his father. Before the accident, he had always driven with her.

The news of the accident was the lead item on TV Globo's *Jornal Nacional* nightly news program that evening, largely because Claudio's friend Rubem Andreazza was the son of the former minister of the interior in Brazil's last military government, which had ended four years earlier. In Sunday's *O Globo*, the paid obituaries took up nearly two broadsheet pages. Ponto Frio communicated their "profound sadness at the sudden death of our dear director Claudio Cohen and his son Raphael." The Bloch, Sigelmann, Cohen, and Safra families noted their "great sorrow." But the saddest announcement came from the grieving mother and widow, Evelyne. It was addressed to Fayale and Cloclo, the names that fifteen-month-old Gabriel used for his older brother and father, respectively: "We will love you always."

The funeral was on Sunday because Jews cannot be buried on the Sabbath. The extra day also allowed Edmond and Lily enough time to make the trip to Rio from Geneva, where Edmond was plotting his strategy against American Express. Edmond wept openly when he received the phone call from Rio informing him of the accident; Lily was inconsolable.

The burials of Claudio and Raphael occurred just before noon in Rio's high summer, and the air at the Jewish cemetery in Caju, on a bleak stretch of Avenida Brasil in the city's gritty suburbs, was thick and muggy. The mourners sweated in their suits and watched helplessly as Evelyne threw herself sobbing onto the coffin of Raphael, who was four years and four months old when he died. The impact had fractured his skull. The cause of death, according to the autopsy, was an internal hemorrhage. Claudio, who was thirty-five years old at the time of death, died of a similar injury—the sudden impact dislocated and fractured his cranium. He also suffered massive internal bleeding.

Among the group of dark-suited mourners was Claudio's boss, Simon Alouan. But he only made it to the gates of the cemetery to pay his respects to the family before he was ordered to leave by Claudio's sister, Adriana.

"I want to know why you are here!" she screamed hysterically. "You killed him. You're the cause of this. Please, just leave right now."

Adriana echoed what Lily was also feeling. If Alouan hadn't been such a tough taskmaster, if he hadn't berated Claudio the way he had, perhaps Claudio would not have been under so much stress, perhaps he wouldn't have argued with his wife before getting into his jeep, Lily reasoned. Desperate to lay blame for the death of her beloved son and grandson, Lily also struck out at Alouan. But if she raged against him, she did so quietly. Perhaps she even suggested to Edmond that Alouan could be replaced. The problem with Alouan was that he was doing a good job. Not since Alfredo's day had the company seen such good returns. No, Alouan would stay, ordered Edmond. Lily would have to wait for the best time to strike. It would take fourteen years, but in the end Lily would get her revenge against the man she accused of killing her son.

Although the Cohen and Safra families were devastated by Claudio's death, it was Alfredo's son, Carlos, who went into a deep mourning after the death of his stepbrother. Since their years together at the Millfield School, where Carlos was sent at nine years old immediately following the death of Alfredo, Claudio had embraced the younger Carlos as his little brother. "I was so comfortable with him," said Carlos. "He was an extraordinary person."

Later, it was Claudio who supported Carlos without reservation when he decided to marry a French Muslim woman named Isis. Like his father before him, Alfredo's adopted son would marry his wife not once but three times—twice in Las Vegas and once in Israel, after Isis spent time learning the principles of Judaism on a kibbutz.

Still, despite Isis's best efforts to please Carlos's family after they met in Paris in 1987, relations between Carlos, Lily, and Edmond became somewhat strained. Edmond, whom Carlos would describe as a "second father," had taken Carlos under his wing when the boy was thirteen. Edmond became his religious mentor and oversaw the study for his bar mitzvah. When he married Isis after a whirlwind romance, Carlos feared Edmond's disapproval so much that he preferred to sever family ties rather than risk raising his ire. Relations between the Monteverde newlyweds and the Safra couple remained diplomatic but somewhat frosty. But Claudio embraced Isis with such ease that after his death, the Monteverdes named one of their girls Claudia in his memory.

Of course, it was Lily who took Claudio's death the hardest. She was so distraught that she all but disappeared from high society. "Lily is made of steel," said an aging Copacabana socialite who knew Lily well in Rio. "But she was passionate about her son and grandson. I know that it really hurt her to lose Claudio and Raphael."

BOTH EDMOND AND Lily were in deep mourning for Claudio and their grandson. They returned to New York and disappeared from the social scene. It wasn't until a year later that their social life began to get back to normal. When they returned to La Leopolda, they hosted an intimate dinner for their friend former first lady Nancy Reagan and the designer Karl Lagerfeld.

Edmond spent much of the year after the tragic events in Rio fighting his clandestine battle with American Express. The efforts paid off, as Edmond handily won his legal battles against the company in the summer of 1989. The coup de grâce came when Edmond's lead attorney and investigator, Stanley Arkin, a streetwise legal scrapper, used his column in the *New York Law Journal* to question what kind of criminal fraud charges could befall a hypothetical company that did not cooperate in the investigations into a smear campaign that involved them. Of course, the hypothetical company was American Express. Shortly after the column appeared, the company agreed to settle with Edmond. As part of the settlement, Edmond agreed not to use any of the information that he had uncovered about American Express before any government investigating agencies. The company, which had conducted a campaign of disinformation that led to defamatory articles about Edmond in the press, also paid Edmond $8 million, which went to several charities, including the United Way of America, the Anti-Defamation League of B'nai B'rith, Hospital Cantonal de Geneve, and the International Committee of the Red Cross.

At first, in a pathetic attempt to save face, American Express admitted on July 28, 1989, to the campaign and said that it had paid Edmond $4 million. Three days later, the news emerged that American Express was actually paying $8 million. Company officials hastily explained that the first $4 million was meant as an apology and that the second $4 million was a gesture of good will.

This time, nobody bought the clunky PR move. "More and more it seems that American Express came kicking and screaming to its embarrassing settlement with Edmond Safra, the rival banker who used private detectives to discover that his former employer had mounted a smear campaign against him," noted the *New York Post*. "Amex is determined not to seem any sorrier than it must, insiders say, since its first mea culpa offer was way below $4 million while Safra originally demanded a penance far above $8 million."

On August 4, 1989, Harry L. Freeman, an executive vice president of American Express known for his close ties to Jim Robinson III, resigned from the company after accepting "executive responsibility" for an investigation that led to the smear campaign against Edmond. Although officials at American Express told the *New York Times* that Freeman did not have personal knowledge of the campaign to discredit Edmond, he had ordered an investigation into his background.

"A well-intentioned effort for which I had executive responsibility went awry," said Freeman in his letter of resignation to Robinson. "Mistakes were made on my watch, and accordingly, I believe my decision to retire, while painful, is appropriate."

It's unclear who at American Express knew about the smear campaign, stated the article in the *New York Times*, which questioned whether company employees were in fact "misrepresenting the situation to each other."

But it no longer mattered to Edmond Safra. The worst, he believed, was behind him, and he vowed that the next time he parted with any of his children, it would be over his dead body. A decade later, that was exactly what happened.

SEVEN

"When I Give Lily a Dollar, Lily Spends Two Dollars"

THE EFFORT INVOLVED in drafting a last will and testament in Rio de Janeiro can be a daunting exercise in bureaucracy at the best of times. When you're struck with a terminal illness and in a hurry, as Evelyne Sigelmann Cohen was in the fall of 1992, then it becomes a Herculean effort.

The "public testament," as it is known in Portuguese, is carefully typed by a clerk onto letterhead bearing the emblem of the state of Rio de Janeiro, the pages duly numbered and signed by five witnesses, each of whom must swear that they know the testator and affirm that what they are witnessing is the truth. All of this, including the typing, is conducted in the presence of a notary public, who then places the document—adorned with a seal and myriad stamps—in an official leather-bound folio.

A month before she died, Evelyne, pale, weak and easily fatigued, quite literally dragged herself to a notary's office in downtown Rio, accompanied by five witnesses, to draft her will. It was the last wish of a dying woman, and nobody dared deny her. It wasn't that Evelyne was concerned about what would happen to the Gavea house or the money she had inherited from Claudio, although she did make provisions for all these assets in her will. What ultimately drove Evelyne to a dingy, airless office in downtown Rio, where she took a number and prepared to dictate her postmortem instructions, was her mother-in-law, Lily.

In the year since she had been diagnosed with a rare form of cancer, Evelyne had worried about Lily. It was the anxiety and not the cancer that interrupted her sleep, tore up her insides, she told her friends. Specifically, she worried about what would happen to her five-year-old son, Gabriel, after she died. She had no doubt that Lily loved the little boy as she did her other grandchildren. Perhaps she even had a special fondness for Gabriel because he was the son of her beloved Claudio. But Evelyne fretted about Gabriel's future. She was concerned about Lily's imperious nature, about her need to control everyone around her. She knew that Lily had her own ideas for his upbringing that didn't include allowing the child to stay in Brazil, close to familiar surroundings and the friends and family he had grown to love. Would she send him to an English boarding school as she had done with Alfredo's boy, Carlos, in 1969? And how would Gabriel, an orphan after her death, react to being sent away?

Evelyne couldn't bear what she perceived as Lily's control. Hadn't Lily interfered with Claudio's first marriage to Mimi?

Evelyne had once joked to a friend that she assumed her every move was watched by Monaco.

"It was common knowledge that the house was watched by headquarters in Monaco," said a friend of Evelyne's who did not want to be identified. "When it was clear that Evelyne would die, Lily began to take control of the situation."

There was no doubt she was dying. Less than a year after Claudio's death, Evelyne was diagnosed with pericardial mesothelioma, an extremely rare form of cancer that attacks the membrane around the heart. In the early days of the disease, she had gone to New York for surgery, staying three months to recuperate, and telling herself that the worst was over. But the cancer returned, and by September 1992, she knew she didn't have long to live. And so she set out the terms for Gabriel's upbringing in her last will and testament. Perhaps she knew that the legal document was a feeble gesture, a flimsy weapon in the fight against Lily. But for a young woman who had lost nearly everything in the space of a few short years—a younger sister, a husband, and a son—it was a final accounting, an attempt to order the chaos, a powerful affirmation of her wishes.

With feverish intensity, Evelyne dictated her instructions to the clerk: Parenting duties would be shared between her sister-in-law Adriana and Antonio Negreiros, an often unemployed actor and choreographer who had become her closest companion after Claudio's death. She referred to Antonio, who had once worked as her personal trainer, as Gabriel's "father." Shortly after Claudio's death, Antonio moved into the house in Gavea with Evelyne, and helped her raise her son.

Gabriel would spend his school holidays with Antonio, and at sixteen would be allowed to choose where and with whom he wanted to live. If he was taken away to another country, his maternal grandparents and Antonio would need to be informed. "A separation between Gabriel and Antonio should be gradual," wrote Evelyne. "Always tell Gabriel the truth, never half-truths. When Gabriel feels lonely, act with clarity and compassion, without trying to avoid the topic. After all, he has already had many separations."

The ultimate separation—from his mother—occurred on October 17, 1992, the day Evelyne died. For all her effort and concern, the plans and terms that she had so painstakingly set out for the future of her son effectively died with her.

"Evelyne died on a Friday, and I told Gabriel about the death of his mother on the Saturday morning," recalled Antonio. Gabriel went to sit in Antonio's lap and wrapped his legs tightly around his surrogate father.

Antonio was determined to carry out Evelyne's last wishes. But in hindsight, he says he was naive, and should have predicted what was coming. Lily was not about to allow some minor actor/personal trainer in Rio de Janeiro to have anything to do with her grandson, especially now that Gabriel was sole heir to his father's share of the family fortune.

As Lily began to emerge from a year of deep mourning for her son, she and Edmond continued to travel between homes in New York, the south of France, and Switzerland. Although they busied themselves with their philanthropy, throwing lavish parties for good causes on two continents, they also took great pleasure in their grandchildren, inviting them for summer vacations at La Leopolda. After Claudio's death, Lily redoubled her efforts with Gabriel and Evelyne, encouraging her to visit often with the little boy.

ON THE AFTERNOON of Evelyne's death, Antonio went to help the Bloch and Sigelmann families with the preparations for the funeral. He left Gabriel at the house in Gavea with his nanny, promising him that he would return shortly. When he returned a few hours later, the house was empty.

Later Antonio learned that Mario, the chauffeur, picked up the child and the nanny and drove them to his "Uncle Watkins" home. In this case, Uncle Watkins was Lily's brother Daniel, who always seemed to be charged with the family's most difficult tasks. It's not clear whether Lily ever bothered to read Evelyne's will. No doubt she was convinced that she was looking out for Gabriel's best interests, which clearly did not include the boy being brought up by a perennially unemployed actor. Never mind that these were Evelyne's last wishes. For Lily, Evelyne could not possibly have been of sound mind when she wrote her will, for why would she entrust her only son to this *stranger?*

After Gabriel went to live with his relatives, Antonio tried every means possible to see the little boy. But his efforts were met with icy indifference. Every day for weeks, Antonio waited for Gabriel to emerge from Rio's tony American School in the Gavea neighborhood where he had been enrolled. But the boy had already disappeared from his life. Months after Evelyne's death, Antonio arranged to travel to Florida where Gabriel was going to be vacationing with his cousins at Disney World. Antonio tried to convince Adriana, now Gabriel's legal guardian, that it would be good for Gabriel to meet him again on neutral ground. Like her mother, Adriana had several homes around the world, including a grand apartment in Rio de Janeiro. With some of the money that Evelyne left him in her will, Antonio bought a ticket to Miami and arranged to rent a car for the drive to Orlando. But at the last minute, the trip was canceled by Adriana with no explanation.

It's not clear what excuses were given to Gabriel about Antonio's sudden absence from his life, but it appears that the effort to prevent him from seeing Antonio also had the cooperation of his maternal grandparents in Rio de Janeiro.

Always tell Gabriel the truth, never half-truths.

Antonio wondered about the "half-truths" that the little boy was hearing. Had he been told that his surrogate father had abandoned him? That he had also gone to heaven, like his parents and his older brother Raphael?

Antonio never got the opportunity to ask him. The last time he saw the boy was the day after Evelyne died, which was also the day that Antonio claims Gabriel finally called him daddy.

But despite Antonio and Evelyne's concerns, Gabriel flourished under the care of his aunt and his paternal grandmother. He lived surrounded by a loving family in grand homes on three continents.

Despite his mother's fears, he never forgot his Brazilian roots and had a good relationship with his maternal grandparents in Rio. Perhaps Lily and Adriana refused to allow Gabriel to maintain a relationship with Antonio because they never trusted his motives. Perhaps they feared that he would try to somehow claim the little boy's inheritance.

Although Antonio claimed he was never after money, the Safras were not so sure. Everyone was after money, and they simply couldn't risk opening themselves up to a potential problem, especially when it involved a vulnerable little boy.

THE 1980S AND early 1990s were surely among the most difficult in the lives of Edmond and Lily. In addition to the deaths of Claudio, Raphael, and Evelyne, Edmond wrestled to recoup his financial losses and, perhaps most important for him, his reputation, which had taken a beating after the American Express smear campaign. Following his legal victories over the company, Edmond would no doubt have gladly retreated to his homes around the world and returned to work at his banks where he put in long hours, often dining on a simple meal of cottage cheese and fruit prepared by his personal chef. He would have gladly stayed away from the international party circuit. "I try to remain unknown as much as possible," he had happily told a journalist. But Lily was having none of it. Now that she was part of the social firmament on two continents, she wasn't going to slow down. In many ways, it was in the 1990s that the Safras were the most active socially and philanthropically.

Months before Evelyne died, in April 1992, Edmond had been honored along with Turgut Ozal, the president of Turkey, at a gala dinner at New York's Plaza hotel—a lavish event hosted by Edmond and Lily's friends Ahmet and Mica Ertegun.

The evening honored the arrival of Sephardic Jews in Turkey and the peaceful coexistence of Jews and Muslims in that country, with benefits going to the Quincentennial Foundation USA, a Turkish-American group that fosters understanding between Jews and Muslims. "It is very important that the world know that there have been 500 years of peaceful coexistence in Turkey between the Jews and Muslims," said Ahmet Ertegun, who was a Muslim. "Over the last 500 years, the Sephardic Jewish community has contributed to art, culture and society."

Special guest Elie Wiesel, the Holocaust survivor and Nobel laureate, presented Edmond with a special humanitarian award for his "outstanding leadership in the international Jewish community." Years later, he would find himself honoring Edmond in another way—as one of the speakers at his funeral.

The gala dinner for more than five hundred invited guests included everyone from Henry and Nancy Kissinger to former UN secretary general Javier Pérez de Cuéllar and his wife, Marcela. Even Edmond's brothers Joseph and Moise made the trip from São Paulo to see their brother honored for his philanthropy.

But while Edmond was fêted, it was Lily who was the star of the evening—"the beauty of the night, ravishing in a white top and striped silk skirt by Givenchy, with her blond hair in a halo of tiny braids." The photograph later appeared in *Women's Wear Daily*, signaling that Lily had finally solidified her credentials in New York society.

She was one of the Ladies Who Lunch, and the society press loved her and her exquisite taste in clothes, art, and interiors. A few months after the Turkish gala, at the summer society wedding in Cap Ferrat of Pamela Lawrence, the daughter of advertising legend Mary Wells Lawrence and airline executive Harding Lawrence, it was Lily who seemed to upstage the bride. She made a "big hit" at the wedding, according to columnist Aileen Mehle, who also attended. She wore "pinky red chiffon by Valentino and her silky blonde hair in a long braid woven with ribbons. What a way to go!"

Not to be outdone by anyone, Lily now planned functions on a grand scale. In 1993, she organized a reception for Edmond at the Knesset, the Israeli legislature in Jerusalem. "Joseph Safra had just thrown a huge party for his son's bar mitzvah in São Paulo, and Lily was determined to upstage him," said one of Edmond's business associates who did not want to be identified. "What better way to do this than to have a huge party at the Knesset?"

The party was to honor the International Sephardic Education Foundation (ISEF), which Edmond and Lily had founded with Walter Weiner's wife, Nina, in 1977. The organization gives out university scholarships to needy students in Israel. The planning for the reception was so complex that it required a vote on the floor of the Knesset before it could go forward. But despite her best efforts to impress, Lily was unable to pull it off. Just before the party was to take place, Edmond's eldest brother, Elie, died in Switzerland, and the whole affair was immediately canceled as the Safra clan mobilized for the funeral.

With her pretensions to grandeur, it must have bothered Lily that no matter how extravagant her parties or how elegant her clothes, she would always be considered an arriviste by the old money elite in Europe, and especially in New York. In his memoir, *Chic Savages*, John Fairchild, former publisher of *Women's Wear Daily*, called the Safras the epitome of the Nouvelle Society, "part of the social history of the greedy eighties."

According to Fairchild, Nouvelles, a category in which he included the Safras, the Trumps, the Gettys, the Kravises, and the Taubmans, among others, were fond of "elaborate decorations and period furniture in gargantuan apartments, regal entertaining with flowers flown in from England, travel by private jet or on the Concorde, and couture clothes at prices high enough to build a small summer cottage."

As Edmond himself noted in an exchange with Fairchild, "When I give Lily a dollar, Lily spends two dollars," he said. "That's our one big problem in the world today. We are all spending money we don't really have." In *Chic Savages*, Fairchild describes dining in Rome with the Safras at an elegant dinner hosted by the designer Valentino in his extravagantly decorated palazzo on the Appian Way—itself a prime example of the decadent 1980s with its pool "grand enough for an Esther Williams production number" and its garden "straight out of Ben Hur." Lily had just finished buying her wardrobe for the season from Valentino, and told Fairchild that she was heading back to New York—"my favorite place," she confided. "It is the capital of the world." Or, as Fairchild puts it, "the capital of Nouvelle Society."

Fairchild recalled other Safra soirees in their many homes. "When Nouvelles eat, it's a formal affair," he recalled. "Petrus, one of the most expensive of the French Bordeaux, flows like water, and the caviar is heaped up. Banker Edmond Safra and his wife, Lily, served so much caviar at one of their dinners that a guest—who shall remain nameless—dispensed with the toast points altogether and called for a spoon, to go after double helpings of the 'Iranian gold.' At leave-taking, each guest was presented with an exquisite ivory picture frame."

At another party, Lily, ever generous with her friends, gave each of the women a pair of Manolo Blahnik shoes, which typically retail for more than $500 a pair.

Others recalled absurd conversations between Edmond and Lily.

"Darling, I bought you an airplane today," said Edmond, in a conversation overheard by one of their good friends in Rio. According to the friend, Lily then went on to question whether Edmond had made the right choice in his airplane purchase, enumerating the attributes of the latest model Gulfstream that had just come on the market.

According to Fairchild, the old money families "disparage the Nouvelles behind their backs but never turn down one of their invitations"—especially when the party favors are so luxurious.

But at times the experience of dining with the Safras could be unnerving, especially after Edmond decided that the family needed a small army of bodyguards to protect them. "The number of body-guards probably outnumbers the guests," quipped one Riviera resident when describing a flurry of "intimate" dinners—no more than forty guests at a time—that the couple hosted shortly after buying and renovating La Leopolda.

It's not clear when Edmond made the decision that he and Lily needed a security detail. As early as 1978, when he was consulting with his architect Eli Attia on the plans for the expansion of the Republic National Bank of New York, Edmond insisted on a state-of-the-art security system. Attia put Edmond in touch with an Israeli firm in Geneva that ended up handling his security around the world. At the bank, Safra's twenty-ninth floor residence was inaccessible to visitors. Guests had to get off at the twenty-eighth floor and be escorted one floor up by an armed security guard.

Edmond must have redoubled his security efforts after the kidnapping of his nephew Ezequiel Edmond Nasser in São Paulo in 1994. Ezequiel, the son of Edmond's sister Evelyne, cut his teeth in banking working for his uncles Edmond in New York and Joseph in São Paulo. He was the prosperous owner of Banco Excel in São Paulo at the time of the kidnapping. Nasser spent seventy-five days in the hands of his captors, who kept him confined to a tiny basement room where they blasted loud music and kept the lights on twenty-four hours a day. He was finally released when his family paid an undisclosed ransom. But the experience damaged him. For the next three years, he became a virtual recluse, refusing to leave his home.

The kidnapping spooked the entire Safra clan. In São Paulo, Moise and Joseph increased their security staff and brought in former Mossad agents to train their Brazilian team. They also refused to battle São Paulo traffic, where they would be sitting ducks for well-trained kidnappers. In Brazil, many kidnap victims—most of them well-to-do executives and the children of the rich and famous—have been snatched driving to work. The Safra brothers' solution was to buy helicopters and build helipads at their sprawling homes in the exclusive Morumbi neighborhood of São Paulo. This way they could fly to work every day and avoid the mad rush-hour frenzy on the streets of São Paulo, a city of more than 20 million people.

Although Edmond had long been obsessed with his personal security, he must have felt a heightened sense of paranoia shortly after he was diagnosed with Parkinson's disease in the mid–1990s. In addition to crippling rigidity and uncontrollable shaking, other symptoms associated with Parkinson's include anxiety and a reduction in cognitive function. In other words, Edmond may not have been able to think very clearly, to perceive real dangers as opposed to Parkinson's-fueled paranoia.

In 1996, before he and Lily moved into their new apartment in Monaco—"so glorious and impeccable in every detail that that may well be what heaven looks like"—Safra created a mini-fortress. After he consulted his specialists in Geneva, steel windows and doors were ordered for the 10,000-square-foot apartment where they would be spending most of their winters. As in New York, his residence was on the top floor of the building, which housed the Monaco branch of his Republic National Bank on the avenue d'Ostende.

Samuel Cohen, Edmond's security chief in France and Monaco, helped set up the security system at the Monte Carlo penthouse. "The system of security was based on several things," he said. "The windows were bulletproof, and there were cameras, burglar alarms, and fire alarms. All the systems were connected to Monaco Sécurité. If one system didn't work, there was a backup of a second one. If one system wasn't registering, there was another one that took over." There were fifteen surveillance cameras at the penthouse, ten of them outside, with alarms attached.

The only problem with the elaborate security system was that it could do nothing if a potential attacker was already *inside* the apartment. The reinforced doors and windows also made it difficult for the apartment's inhabitants to leave in an emergency. As Cohen himself noted: "There is no security system if someone from inside decides to do harm. There is nothing you can do. If someone gains the confidence of the people and you are on the inside, there is no limit to the damage you can do."

Edmond's bedroom was the safest part of the twenty-room duplex apartment. The bedroom, fitted with panic buttons and steel doors and shutters, was described by security experts as "a survival cell" that was impregnable.

Cohen trained with the Mossad in Israel. He was "in perfect physical condition, a tough, no-nonsense guy trained in the art of protection," noted *Vanity Fair* journalist Dominick Dunne. Cohen commanded eleven other bodyguards, all of them highly trained former elite members of the Israeli army, and all of them billeted at La Leopolda, a twenty-minute drive from the Monaco penthouse. Cohen, affectionately known to staff as Schmulik, was himself paid $1,000 a day to supervise Edmond's security.

With the onset of Parkinson's, Edmond retreated to the safety of his bunker-like homes around the world. By the time he started to shuffle to get across a room, slur his speech, and drool uncontrollably, Edmond had limited his public appearances and often conducted his business affairs from his bedroom. After Edmond went public with his illness in July 1998, several nurses were added to his staff to provide him with care around the clock. In a statement released to the press at the time, Edmond acknowledged that he suffered from the disease, but reassured his business associates and investors that he would continue to work closely with his brothers Moise and Joseph to oversee his banking empire. At the same time, he also committed $50 million to the launch of a foundation to support research into the disease.

Despite his illness, Edmond's philanthropic good works continued apace, precisely because he was gravely ill and determined to leave a lasting legacy. Like his father, Jacob, who had contributed to many Jewish and non-Jewish causes in Lebanon and Syria, Edmond also focused a great deal on philanthropy. Throughout the world, there are medical research centers, and religious and educational trusts that bear the family name. At Harvard University alone, the Safra

NOME DO ALUNO *Lilly de Castro Watkins*

Data do nascimento: *17 de novembro de 1934*

Natural de: *Porto Alegre - Rio Grande do Sul*

Nome do pai: *Wolf White Watkins*

Nome da mãe: *Annita de Castro Watkins*

Residência: *rua Joaquim Nabuco 50 apt° 101*

Observações: ....

Lily Watkins as a teenager in her school picture. Her birth date is erroneously noted as November 17, 1934. *(Courtesy of Colegio Anglo-Americano, Rio de Janeiro)*

Wolf White Watkins, Lily's father, from his Brazilian identification papers, 1946. *(National Archives, Rio de Janeiro)*

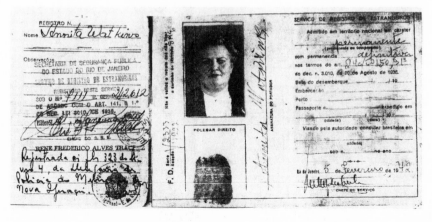

Annita Watkins, Lily's mother, from her Brazilian identification papers, 1942. *(National Archives, Rio de Janeiro)*

ABOVE: Birthday party of Alfredo Grunberg (Monteverde) in Romania, circa 1930. Alfredo is the child sitting in the front. *(Courtesy Monteverde family archives)*

LEFT: Alfredo Monteverde at his summer home in Aguas Lindas, Brazil, undated. *(Courtesy Monteverde family archives)*

Alfredo, Regina, and Rosy in Rio de Janeiro, mid-1940s. *(Courtesy Monteverde family archives)*

One of Ponto Frio's stores in Rio de Janeiro. *(Courtesy Monteverde family archives)*

RIGHT: Alfredo and Lily leaving for their beach house at Aguas Lindas, Brazil. *(Courtesy Monteverde family archives)*

BELOW: Alfredo and companion Silvia Bastos Tigre in an undated photograph. *(Monteverde family archives)*

BOTTOM: Lily and the children in a 1967 portrait. From left to right: Carlos, Adriana, Claudio, Lily, and Eduardo, Rio de Janeiro. *(Courtesy Monteverde family archives)*

Alfredo and Silvia Bastos Tigre (in sunglasses) lunching with friends at the Rio Yacht Club, Rio de Janeiro, where Alfredo kept his boats. *(Courtesy Monteverde family archives)*

The last photo of Alfredo Monteverde taken in Italy in July 1969, a month before his death. Standing in the back: Rosy, Alfredo. In the front, Giuseppe Jermi, Regina Monteverde, Lily. *(Courtesy Monteverde family archives)*

Police photo of the revolver used in the death of Alfredo Monteverde, showing four out of six bullets in the chamber, August 25, 1969, Rio de Janeiro. *(Police Department, Tenth District Precinct, Rio de Janeiro)*

Alfredo Monteverde lying dead on his bed at his home in Rio de Janeiro. *(Police Department, Tenth District Precinct, Rio de Janeiro)*

Lily and her eldest son, Claudio, the boy she called her "Jesus Christ, Esquire" at the Millfield School, Somerset, England, 1971. *(Courtesy Samuel Bendahan)*

Lily and her daughter Adriana, Somerset, England, 1971. *(Courtesy Samuel Bendahan)*

Samuel and Lily in France, 1971, shortly before their marriage. *(Courtesy Samuel Bendahan)*

Lily and Samuel shortly after their marriage at the registry office in Acapulco. Lily is wearing Samuel's "Alain Delon hat," January 31, 1972. *(Courtesy Samuel Bendahan)*

Samuel and Lily dining with friends in Acapulco shortly after their wedding, February 1972. *(Courtesy Samuel Bendahan)*

Samuel Bendahan and Lily Bendahan shortly after their marriage in Acapulco, February 1972. *(Courtesy Samuel Bendahan)*

Lily and Samuel on a yacht in Acapulco, 1972. *(Courtesy Samuel Bendahan)*

Acapulco marriage license of
Samuel Bendahan and Lily Watkins,
January 31, 1972. *(Courtesy
Samuel Bendahan)*

Lily and business associate Felix Klein in Brazil, February 1972. *(Courtesy Samuel Bendahan)*

Lily and her son Eduardo in Rio de Janeiro, February 1972. *(Courtesy Samuel Bendahan)*

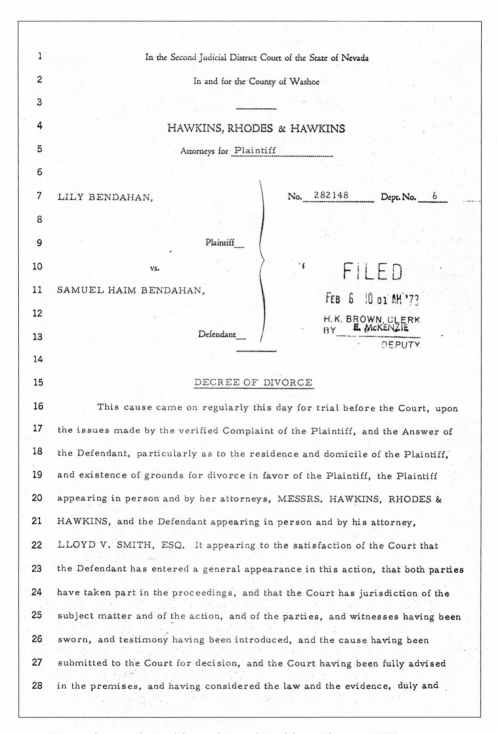

In the Second Judicial District Court of the State of Nevada

In and for the County of Washoe

————

HAWKINS, RHODES & HAWKINS

Attorneys for _Plaintiff_

LILY BENDAHAN,

No. 282148   Dept. No. 6

Plaintiff

vs.

SAMUEL HAIM BENDAHAN,

FILED

FEB 6 10 01 AM '73

H.K. BROWN, CLERK
BY E. McKENZIE
DEPUTY

Defendant

DECREE OF DIVORCE

This cause came on regularly this day for trial before the Court, upon

the issues made by the verified Complaint of the Plaintiff, and the Answer of

the Defendant, particularly as to the residence and domicile of the Plaintiff,

and existence of grounds for divorce in favor of the Plaintiff, the Plaintiff

appearing in person and by her attorneys, MESSRS. HAWKINS, RHODES &

HAWKINS, and the Defendant appearing in person and by his attorney,

LLOYD V. SMITH, ESQ. It appearing to the satisfaction of the Court that

the Defendant has entered a general appearance in this action, that both parties

have taken part in the proceedings, and that the Court has jurisdiction of the

subject matter and of the action, and of the parties, and witnesses having been

sworn, and testimony having been introduced, and the cause having been

submitted to the Court for decision, and the Court having been fully advised

in the premises, and having considered the law and the evidence, duly and

Divorce decree, Lily Bendahan and Samuel Bendahan, February 6, 1973.
(Second Judicial District Court of the State of Nevada, County of Washoe)

ABOVE: Evelyne Bloch
Sigelmann and Claudio Cohen
at their wedding in Rio de
Janeiro in May 1983. Edmond
Safra is pictured on the left.
(Agencia O Globo)

RIGHT: Lily and Edmond Safra
at wedding of Lily's eldest
son, Claudio Cohen, in Rio de
Janeiro, May 1983. *(Agencia O
Globo)*

ABOVE: From left to right: Adolfo Bloch, Inês Bloch (mother of Evelyne Bloch Sigelmann), Mario Cohen (Lily's first husband and Claudio's father, standing behind Inês, to the right), and Oscar Bloch (Evelyne's father) at the wedding of Claudio and Evelyne, May 1983 in Rio de Janeiro. *(Agencia O Globo)*

LEFT: Vicky Safra and her husband, Joseph Safra, at the wedding of Claudio and Evelyne, May 1983, Rio de Janeiro. *(Agencia O Globo)*

Lily and Edmond Safra leave a luncheon at the Metropolitan Club in New York, September 1990. *(Photograph by Marina Garnier)*

Lily and Edmond Safra at an awards dinner at the Pierre Hotel in New York, honoring the king of Spain, hosted by the Elie Wiesel Foundation, October 1991. *(Photograph by Marina Garnier)*

name is particularly prominent. There is the Jacob E. Safra Professor of Jewish History and Sephardic Civilization and the Jacob Safra Courtyard at the Harvard Hillel that Edmond funded to honor his father. In 1986, Edmond and the Republic of New York Corporation also established the Robert F. Kennedy Visiting Professor in Latin American Studies at the college, allowing academics, businesspeople, and artists from Latin America to teach at Harvard for one semester.

At one point, Edmond also decided that he needed his own synagogue and asked Eli Attia, the architect who had worked on the Republic tower, to draw up the plans for a house of worship around the corner from one of his apartments on Fifth Avenue and East Sixty-third Street. The synagogue was also conceived for a group of fellow Upper East Side Sephardim who prayed in a dingy basement on Sixty-second Street. Although the grand Temple Emanu-El is located just three blocks away on East Sixty-fifth Street and Fifth Avenue, it is mainly an Ashkenazi and Reform temple. Edmond and his small group of Sephardic congregants—all of them Orthodox Jews—could never feel welcome in the Temple Emanu-El community.

Edmond probably felt that a synagogue named in memory of his father would round out his philanthropy in New York. Attia found an old townhouse 100 yards from Edmond's Fifth Avenue home and began drafting plans and seeking city building permits for a 25,000-square-foot synagogue, comprising five stories and two basements, with space for nearly four hundred congregants. "As was the case with a number of Attia's projects for Safra, the agreement was consummated with a handshake."

But Edmond's synagogue, which was named Beit Yaakov, in memory of Jacob Safra, proved problematic from the start. Attia, who had worked with Edmond and his brothers since 1978, became exasperated "because Edmond and Lily kept changing their minds about what they wanted."

Work on the project, which had begun in earnest in 1991, dragged on until 1993. But the coup de grâce came when Edmond and Lily refused to pay Attia's bill for work he had done on the synagogue and the renovation of burial plots for two Sephardic rabbis in Israel. The Safras claimed that Attia had completed only a small percentage of the total work, but was charging as if the job was already completed. Attia's bill was estimated at more than $600,000. As a result of the financial shortfall, he was unable to pay his employees. He filed a lawsuit against Edmond in a U.S. district court in New York City after Edmond fired him in 1993. Attia had lost so much money in the stalled synagogue project that midway through court proceedings he could no longer pay his attorneys.

"He [Edmond] told me that the bill was the responsibility of the Beit Yaakov congregation," said Attia in an interview with the *New York Post*. "But he and Lily hired me and to all intents and purposes they *are* the congregation."

In the early days, the Beit Yaakov congregation comprised Edmond's family and employees. One of the trustees was Jacqui Safra, Edmond's nephew, the son of his eldest brother, Elie, and a film producer who worked on several films with Woody Allen. Republic president Dov Schlein and Nathan Hasson, vice chair of Republic, were also among the trustees of the synagogue. Walter Weiner, one of Edmond's most trusted advisers and the chairman of the board and chief operating officer of Republic of New York Corporation, was on the synagogue's executive committee.

But in court papers, Edmond tried to argue that he had no signed contract with Attia and that Attia had done only 10 percent of the job and was demanding more than 70 percent of the payment—an allegation that Attia dismissed outright. Attia alleged that Edmond was putting pressure on him for other reasons. In addition to the synagogue, Attia was involved in a project in Israel at the time. The Shalom Center was the largest real-estate development in the country's history. David Azrieli, the Canadian architect and developer who had hired Attia for the project, wanted to share the design credit with him, and was allegedly withholding Attia's fees until he agreed. Attia initiated arbitration proceedings in Israel to obtain the $1.5 million that he was owed. But what Attia didn't know at the time was that Edmond's bank in Israel, the First International Bank of Israel Ltd. (FIBI), had been competing to finance the Shalom Center. According to legal papers, "In the course of the five month arbitration hearing it became clear that Safra's decision in January 1993 to force Attia to resign from the synagogue project had been an attempt to pressure Attia into dropping his fight with Azrieli, which was impeding the chances for Azrieli (and FIBI) to develop the highly lucrative Shalom Center Project."

Edmond denied the allegations. A furious and disappointed Attia sued Edmond personally. "I have always given you all that I can give—my talent and my time," wrote Attia in a handwritten resignation letter dated January 15, 1993, that was introduced as evidence in court. "The telephone conversation we had last night caused me to realize that you, unfortunately, see our relationship in a different light." For all of his "devotion and sacrifice," Attia says he was left with "financial strangulation, insult and more than anything else, mistrust."

The court dismissed Edmond's petition to have the case thrown out, and the suit was eventually settled out of court in October 1996. But the fissures between the Safras and the Sephardic community had already begun. In many ways, they had always been just under the surface after Edmond married Lily. Not only did Edmond's siblings disapprove of Lily, but many in the Sephardic community who were close to Edmond had little tolerance for his ostentatious wife. For years, Edmond and his brothers supported Sephardic causes and synagogues all over the world. But after his marriage to Lily, she began to divert their giving to other charities. Perhaps Sephardic community leaders were aware of Lily's lack of interest in their causes and so treated her with frosty indifference. Or perhaps she simply was never accepted because she was of Ashkenazi origins.

"We were having dinner with Lily and Edmond at the Pierre hotel in New York when Lily asked me about the Jewish community," recalled Albert Nasser. "She asked me why the Syrian Jews who live in Brooklyn hated her so much. I told her it was because every father in Brooklyn had hoped to marry his daughter to Edmond Safra, and she beat them all to it. Lily laughed hysterically."

Whatever the reason for their dislike of her, Lily didn't pay too much attention, and almost as soon as she married Edmond she began, at first quietly, to redirect their charitable contributions to the arts and education. Gifts to the Sephardic community in Brooklyn just didn't create the high-level buzz that Lily loved. They didn't make the society pages of the *New York Times* Style section, and they had no place in *Women's Wear Daily*.

In September 1996, the Safras threw a magnificent party to honor a generous gift that Edmond and Lily had made to the Israel Museum in Jerusalem. Edmond donated a seventy-two-page manuscript written by Albert Einstein in 1912 in which the scientist laid out his theory of relativity for the first time. The manuscript had been purchased at a Sotheby's auction for an undisclosed price, although the presale estimate was $4 million.

"The ... party was a celebration of a magnificent million dollar gift from the super rich and super generous international banker Edmond Safra of Albert Einstein's manuscript in which, for the first time, he outlines his theory of relativity and its famous $E=MC^2$ formula," noted a columnist for *W*. "Edmond and his beautiful wife Lily flew in with a planeload of friends and *foie gras* and gave one of their opulent dinners in a flower-bedecked tent under the desert sky. Heaven." It was the last time that the entire Safra clan, including brothers Joseph and Moise, would be together with Edmond.

Lily took a break from the couple's philanthropy in the fall of 1998 when she decided that she wanted to simplify her life and get rid of her controlling interest in Ponto Frio in Brazil. But just as she prepared to sell, tragedy struck. Her stepson, Carlos, suffered a horrific crash on the Imola racetrack in Italy. Carlos, a serious collector and racer of antique sports cars, lost control of the vintage Ferrari he was driving on the same racetrack curve that had killed Formula One champion Ayrton Senna in 1994. For Lily, the accident was a blow. Following the accident, Lily, who had had little contact with Carlos after he married Isis in the late 1980s, now frantically called the family to make sure he was all right. Carlos spent several weeks in the hospital recovering from his injuries and thousands of dollars on plastic surgery to repair his mangled body. The accident left his face partly paralyzed, making it impossible for him to chew his food properly.

Lily was distraught after the accident, said one observer who was close to her at the time. She may have also been concerned about how the accident would affect the sale of the company, but clearly it was her stepson who took priority. In the end, it wasn't Carlos's accident that scuttled the deal. The sale did not go through because they simply could not obtain a good price for their shares.

When the Ponto Frio sale failed, Lily refocused her energies on taking the Safra philanthropy in a new direction. In 1999, the year he died, Edmond was honored for his contribution to the arts in the United States. Trustees of the National Gallery of Art in Washington, D.C., presented Edmond and Lily, among others, with the Medal for Distinguished Service. For this occasion, Edmond's banks had financed an exhibit of Italian baroque painter Annibale Carracci's drawings at the museum.

In addition to the arts, the direction of their giving now had a decidedly royal bent. Lily's critics say the new thrust in the couple's philanthropy—mostly charities run by the British royals—was simply an ill-disguised effort to promote her own social advancement. Others simply praised her generosity. Clearly, Lily loved the attention and the opportunity to gain access to Britain's royals.

The royal giving had begun sporadically at first. In May 1985, the couple threw a fund-raising party at their home in Geneva for the World Wildlife Fund, with Prince Philip, a royal patron of the charity, as their guest of honor. But in 1999, Lily attended a flurry of royal events in New York and London. In a burgundy velvet jacket and silk skirt by Yves Saint Laurent, she attended a benefit concert by Zubin Mehta at Buckingham Palace in March along with a reception for the Prince's Trust. In April, she was among a select group that included billionaire Michael Bloomberg and cosmetics executive and philanthropist Evelyn Lauder at a luncheon at the Carlyle hotel in Manhattan for the Foundation Claude Monet Giverny. Princess Michael of Kent was the keynote speaker.

Lily and Edmond were also considered near and dear friends of Prince Charles and Camilla Parker Bowles. They were among a select group of guests at Buckingham Palace in June 1999—the first time that the royal couple hosted a joint event at the official residence of Elizabeth II. The occasion was a reception for the American members of the Prince's Foundation. The next day, the select group was invited to lunch at the Prince of Wales' official residence at Highgrove, and then back to London for a drinks party chez Viscount Linley, the Queen's furniture-designer nephew. Later, they gathered for Pimms at Blenheim Palace, the birthplace of Winston Churchill.

The royal weekend in the summer of 1999 marked the last time that Edmond would appear at a high-society function.

In the months before he died, Edmond was preparing to make a different kind of news. Once again, he was rocking the world's financial markets with the sale of one of his beloved "children."

IN THE WEEKS before Edmond sold his Republic holdings to HSBC in what would be the biggest business deal of his career, the photographs started to disappear. They were the intimate family snapshots—happier moments of the Safra clan at a bar mitzvah or wedding of a favorite nephew in São Paulo. The images of the Safra sisters on the beach in Punta del Este also disappeared, as did the pictures of

Moise and Joseph and the faded black-and-white photos of the family patriarch, Jacob.

It's not clear that Edmond, in his heavily medicated state, noticed that the pictures were gone from the Monaco apartment or La Leopolda, the villa that he no longer had the will or the energy to enjoy. In the months since he had appeared in Washington to receive his award from the National Gallery of Art and had attended the royal parties in London, Edmond had retreated to the beaux-arts apartment in Monaco attended by his small team of nurses, who administered his medications and helped him to eat his food and go to the bathroom.

By most accounts, his health continued to deteriorate and he became increasingly isolated from his family in Brazil. In better days, Edmond used to speak to Joseph or Moise or both on a daily basis. But in the spring of 1999, the intercontinental telephone calls ceased. Sem Almaleh, a bank manager who worked with Edmond for four decades, said that Edmond "called his brothers several times a day, but there was a problem and they had had a rift" just before Edmond died. During the last months of his life in Monaco, Edmond spoke only to a few trusted employees, his nurses, and, of course, Lily, who now wielded tremendous control over every aspect of his life.

Family friend Albert Nasser attributes Edmond's split with his brothers to a family spat over undisclosed financial matters. Perhaps the Safra brothers could not understand why Edmond had decided to sell his Republic holdings to HSBC, especially after the press announcement of the previous year which clearly stated that Edmond, despite his illness, would be working closely with his younger brothers to oversee his banks.

"It was my understanding that Edmond wouldn't speak to his brothers for a year before he died," recalled Nasser.

Joseph seemed to confirm this years later when he told a Monaco court that he had not seen Edmond for a year before his death, and that indeed there had been "a few problems," although he was confident that they would see each other again. A month before Edmond died, he had even spoken to him on the phone, recalled Joseph.

"He was a brother—a real brother—and also a father," said Joseph. "He was the head of the family. I adored him, and I still adore him."

Still, it seemed strange to Nasser and other friends that such a deep split had occurred between Edmond and his brothers. He also couldn't understand why Lily abruptly changed Edmond's most trusted physician. Edmund H. Sonnenblick, a pioneering New York cardiologist, had been one of Edmond's physicians for thirty years, said Nasser, who was also a patient of Sonnenblick until the cardiologist's death in 2007. The Sonnenblicks were so close to the Safra clan that Annie Sonnenblick, the cardiologist's daughter, had worked as an assistant treasurer at Republic National Bank in New York before her death from septicemia in 1984.

"Lily cut him off after thirty years and started parachuting other doctors into Monte Carlo to take care of Edmond," said Nasser. "The doctor [Sonnenblick] was the same person who took care of the Safra brothers in São Paulo. Joseph had him flown to São Paulo when he was not well."

According to those closest to Edmond at the time, Lily was so concerned about Edmond that she kept consulting new doctors. In the spring of 1999 he was so overmedicated with the drugs that each new physician recommended to control his Parkinson's that he started to be seized by violent hallucinations. Edmond was hospitalized in New York for the condition, but when his team of lawyers and accountants informed him that the hospitalization was going to cause tax problems because he would be overstaying his six-month residency limit in the United States, Lily made the decision to go across the border to Canada for medical treatment. The Safras moved with their entourage of aides into Toronto's Four Seasons hotel for a few weeks while Edmond recuperated from the violent seizures and his deep depression.

Whether his depression was brought on by the medications he was

taking—a daily drug chart shows he took drugs to control his cho-
lesterol and Parkinson's—or the estrangement from his brothers and
the imminent sale of his bank, or all of these, is difficult to say. But
by the time he returned to his apartment in Monaco in the fall, Edmond was taking a potent cocktail of antidepressants that included
daily dosages of Xanax, Samyr, Clozaril, and Depakote. While most
of these drugs are administered to Parkinson's patients to keep the
anxiety associated with the disease at bay, physicians who regularly
treat Parkinson's disease were puzzled as to why Edmond was taking
Depakote. The drug, which is used to treat bipolar disorder, has been
known to cause tremors, and could have canceled out the effects of
the other drugs that Edmond was taking. It could have also led to
severe depression.

Similarly, before he died in 1969, Alfredo Monteverde was also taking a potent mix of antipsychotic medications that included lithium
carbonate, which was used to treat schizophrenia, and Tryptizol and
Nardil, both powerful antidepressants that interfered with his cognitive function.

It was during their time in Toronto that the Safras met Bruce Sutton, a local psychiatrist who helped Edmond through his crisis. Sutton would become such an important figure in the Safra universe
that Lily would fly him and his family for a vacation at La Leopolda,
where he helped Edmond deal with his depression.

The Brazilian branch of the Safra family has provided few details
about the rift since Edmond's death. It is also unclear if Edmond ordered the removal of the family photographs from his home, or if they
were removed without his knowledge. Did he make the conscious
decision to stop speaking to his brothers, or was that decision simply
made for him when they called and were told he was indisposed? Was
his judgment so clouded by the medications he was taking that he
had become paranoid about his family in São Paulo? What was their
real intention in helping him to oversee his banks? Were they being
honest with him? Perhaps these were now questions that were going

through Edmond's own mind. Yet it's hard to believe that the Safra brothers had anything but Edmond's best interests at heart. This was their beloved elder brother who had been instrumental in building the Safra banking empire on three continents. Their relationship had always been one of complete trust.

Whatever the reason for the family split, it became irreversible when Edmond, frail and in ill health, began to negotiate the biggest deal of his financial career—to sell Republic New York Corporation to HSBC, a venture valued at over $10.3 billion when it was first announced in May 1999.

"The acquisitions we have announced today will bring together two complementary private banking franchises," said Sir John Bond, HSBC chairman. "At the stroke of a pen, it doubles the size of our consumer-banking operations in the United States, and it doubles the size of our private-banking business around the world."

But while the sale would prove a huge boon to HSBC, it effectively ended Edmond's banking career. As the *New York Times* noted in a front page article, the deal would "mark the end of independence for a banking business founded more than three decades ago by Edmond Safra, a Lebanese-born Jewish businessman who is regarded as an enduring figure in the banking world."

If Joseph and Moise saw traces of Edmond's ill-fated gamble with American Express in the HSBC deal, they were unable to make their protests heard. They had lost the battle when they couldn't even reach him by phone or visit him at his home. The negotiations for the sale of Republic took place without the wise counsel of his brothers. Bond and Republic executive Jeffrey Keil, who had first encouraged Edmond to make his ill-fated deal with American Express years before, conducted the negotiations. Keil was very close to Lily, and in the absence of Edmond's brothers, Keil effectively became one of the ailing banker's closest confidants.

Still, weeks before it was to be signed, the deal hit a snag as accountants from the HSBC Group conducted a financial review of Republic. Ultimately, Martin Armstrong, a major client of Republic's futures brokerage and chairman of Princeton Economics International, a hedge fund, was indicted on charges of defrauding Japanese investors of nearly $1 billion. Armstrong, who has vigorously denied the charges, allegedly sold assets known as Princeton notes, promising his investors that the notes were backed by Republic. At first, Republic was not named in the investigation into Armstrong's alleged fraud scheme. However, Republic did launch its own inquiry into the scandal, which delayed shareholder voting on the HSBC deal.

Later, New York authorities revealed the collusion between some Republic employees and Armstrong, who began by opening thirty-six brokerage accounts and depositing $350 million in the bank in 1995. By the time HSBC began to analyze the bank in the fall of 1999, Armstrong had deposited more than $3 billion in 450 accounts. According to court papers, Armstrong's investors received assurances that he had invested their money in U.S. government securities. But in fact, Armstrong used the investments to speculate in commodities markets, losing millions of dollars in the process. The Ponzi scheme developed as he began losing money in the speculation and allegedly used proceeds from the sale of new Princeton investment notes to pay off old Princeton investors as their accounts came due. When two Republic executives discovered the scheme, they agreed to help Armstrong by issuing fake account statements.

The incident nearly scuttled the HSBC deal until Edmond agreed to take a personal loss of $450 million and cut the price for the sale of Republic from $10.3 billion to $9.85 billion. "I am taking this action because I believe that a swift completion of the transaction will be to the benefit of Republic's clients, shareholders and employees to whom my life's work has been devoted," said Edmond in a statement in November.

Even before the deal was sealed, Edmond unwittingly began the grim preparations for death.

Edmond, who deeply loved his wife of twenty-three years, and had become estranged from his extended family in São Paulo during his final days, signed the bulk of his fortune over to her.

In São Paulo, Edmond's brothers and sisters were unprepared for such a slap in the face. They were even less prepared for his untimely death.

EIGHT

"Not Our Fault"

THEODORE MAURICE MAHER entered the rarefied universe of the Safras one day in the summer of 1999 as he prepared to begin his shift at New York Presbyterian Hospital, where he worked as a nurse. Dressed in surgical scrubs and sneakers, the New England–born Maher made his way through the wide hallways of the hospital towards the neonatal nurses' station, balancing his clipboard and a steaming Styrofoam cup of coffee. Ted, as he was known to his family and colleagues at the hospital, had just driven the seventy-two miles from his home in Stormville, New York—a quaint hamlet in Dutchess County that was about twenty miles from the West Point military academy.

The school's historic cemetery is the final resting place of great American heroes like Major General George Custer, who famously made his last stand against the Indians in the battle of Little Bighorn. The cemetery also contains the remains of General Lucius Clay, who defied Soviet aggression when he repeatedly pierced through the Communist blockade of Berlin to deliver supplies to the city's entrapped population.

The tall, lanky nurse with auburn hair and a steady gaze was also a hero, or at least that was what Ted told himself everyday. Ever since he enlisted in the army in the mid-1970s, Ted had considered himself a misunderstood hero. Ultimately, it was this hubris that would ruin his life.

It's true he had heroic qualities. He was loyal to his wife, Heidi, a fellow nurse he had met in nursing class at Dutchess Community College in 1988 and married five years later. He was a good father to his three children, for whom he happily endured the long commute from Manhattan to Stormville after finishing a grueling twelve-hour shift. He had also gone through a costly and protracted legal battle to gain custody of his eldest son, Christopher, whom he had taken away from his first wife while the boy was still an infant.

He was dedicated to his tiny patients, most of whom were born premature and jaundiced or with other serious problems that threatened their lives. Fellow nurses would marvel at his patience and ability to soothe the screaming babies under his care.

On that breezy morning in the summer of 1999, Ted casually sipped his coffee as he traded notes with Cathy, the night nurse, who briefed him on the condition of the premature infants on the ward. It was after she left that he noticed the camera, next to a set of keys and Cathy's plastic-coated nametag, at the neonatal nursing station. Ted made some inquiries, but nobody on the ward seemed to know who owned it. Which is why Ted put the camera in the pocket of his scrubs and decided to find out for himself. When he returned home to Stormville, he had the film developed at the local WalMart in order to track down the owner through the photographs. There were about five photographs on the camera, and, ever practical so as not to waste the remaining film, Maher took photos of his own children before dropping it off to be developed.

Ted immediately recognized the woman in the photographs—her fraternal twins had been recent patients of the ward—and obtained her address from the hospital's finance department. Ted wrote a note to the new mother and returned the camera to her Manhattan address. Laura and Harry Slatkin, the new parents of twins Alexandra and David, were deeply touched by Maher's gesture. Harry, a New York society figure and designer of bath products and perfumed candles, was completely surprised that Ted would return a camera that was worth well over $400. Shortly after receiving it, he called Ted to offer him a reward. In testimony at his trial in Monaco, Ted says he refused any compensation. "I said it's the right thing to do." If Harry really wanted to show his gratitude, he could make a donation to the hospital, Ted told him.

But Harry Slatkin seems to have had an even better idea, and during that first telephone conversation he made Ted an offer that the neonatal nurse would find hard to refuse. The Slatkins were good friends of Adriana Elia, Edmond Safra's stepdaughter, and knew that Edmond needed to find a responsible nurse to join his team in Monaco. Harry asked Ted if he had ever heard of the Republic National Bank (he hadn't) and whether he would consider working for one of its senior executives who lived in Europe and was suffering from Parkinson's disease. The job paid extremely well and would give Ted the opportunity to live in Europe for a while, said Harry, although he did not offer any specifics. He did offer to set up a job interview for him right away.

At first, Ted didn't know what to think. The legal battle with his first wife over the custody of his eldest son had left him extremely short of cash. There were also rumors of a looming strike at New York Presbyterian, and Ted was worried about providing for his family since both he and Heidi worked there as nurses. It took Ted a week to decide to make the call to set up a meeting with one of Edmond's most trusted aides.

The interview took place at the Fifth Avenue offices of the Republic National Bank. Ted brought along Heidi, who spoke about moving the entire Maher clan to Monaco if Ted was successful. She also wanted to be considered for a nursing position.

On the surface, Ted seemed ideal. Here was a nurse with military training—a former Green Beret who had worked for four years with U.S. Army Special Forces on classified missions. He was also a highly respected and dedicated nurse. George Morelli, who knew Ted in New York, recalled that when an ambulance arrived with a sick infant, Ted was often the first to rush over to the child. "He was a great nurse," said Morelli.

But the great appeal of Ted Maher to someone as security-conscious as Edmond Safra was that he knew how to use a weapon and could easily double as a bodyguard. Ted had a sterling record in the military, graduating third in his class in Special Forces.

For anyone reading his impressive resumé, Ted Maher seemed the kind of man Edmond could respect. His diligence and honesty had already been established when he went out of his way to return the Slatkins' camera. But Edmond's team had serious doubts about the tall, lanky stranger with the piercing blue eyes. Did he seem too eager, too aggressive? Why did he speak so loudly? In the end, Edmond's team was not impressed. Shortly after the interview, one of Edmond's secretaries called Lily to inform her of his decision.

Ted Maher was a man with skeletons in his closet. Did Edmond's team know about the history of schizophrenia in Ted's family? That his biological father had been institutionalized for the disorder when his son was barely two years old, and spent his life in the hospital? Or how about Ted's conviction in Nevada in June 1985? A year earlier, Ted had been arrested for burglary when he removed objects from a home he had helped build in Nevada after the builder refused to pay him. Ted was eventually sentenced to seventy-five hours of community service for what amounted to a misdemeanor offence. Could this man really be trusted with one of the wealthiest bankers in the world?

Edmond's team rejected Ted, yet they were overruled. Ted was interviewed by Bruce Sutton, the psychiatrist who had helped Edmond through his bout with severe depression. After a forty-five minute conversation with Ted, Sutton seems to have pronounced the nurse the perfect candidate for the job, and on August 13, 1999, Ted began a short trial run at La Leopolda, where Sutton had also been invited to spend a holiday.

Lily, who was so careful about everything and everyone who entered her homes, probably assumed that Maher had been thoroughly vetted. After the four-day trial period at La Leopolda, Lily informed the staff that she wanted Ted to start immediately.

The deal with Ted was struck while Edmond's personal secretaries were on vacation, and by the time they returned, it was a fait accompli. In New York, Ted was given his new responsibilities: His salary would be $600 a day, and he would be required to work only four days a week. Ted balked, and negotiated for six days a week, which was initially refused, although eventually a deal was made that he would be paid for six days and work only five so as not to upset the other nurses, who had different arrangements. Like the other nurses employed by the Safras, Ted would be hired by a corporation—Spotless & Brite Inc.—whose address was the same as the Republic National Bank at 452 Fifth Avenue. The arrangement allowed the nurses to enter Monaco as tourists on vacation, not as professionals, to avoid the strict labor laws in the principality. In addition, Ted would have to sign a confidentiality and "nondisparagement" agreement, promising that he would not "engage in any conduct that is injurious to any Safras [sic] reputation and interest (including, without limitation), publicly disparaging or inducing others to disparage any Safra."

Under these conditions, and with the promise of medical coverage for himself and his family, Ted began work in Monaco on October 28. Every week, he faxed his hours to a Safra family aide, and within forty-eight hours Heidi received a wire transfer of his salary in Stormville.

By all accounts Ted loved working in the sun-drenched principality. He could walk to work from his lodgings at the Balmoral, a nineteenth-century hotel where the rooms had stunning views of the port. The three-star hotel, where Ted stayed with the other

nurses, was on the avenue de la Costa, which was located directly
behind the Safra penthouse. On his way to the penthouse, Ted
passed expensive boutiques and elegant cafés where impeccably
dressed patrons sipped café au lait and munched on croissants.
When he wasn't working, he spent a great deal of his time in nearby
Nice, disappearing for days at a time, although no one is quite sure
what drew him to the French beachfront city so frequently. Ted
says he was simply sightseeing, but others have attached darker motives to his sojourns in Nice.

He was also a regular visitor, with some of his fellow nurses, to the
glittering casinos, although he was careful not to gamble too much
of his wages, and balked at what he thought were absurd prices for
drinks.

On November 20, another one of Edmond's aides told Ted he had
been hired full-time. That was when Ted, who was terribly lonely
and homesick, began searching for suitable accommodations for his
family in Nice, which was about ten miles away from Monaco and
much cheaper to live in. At that first interview, Ted and his wife had
also spoken of homeschooling their children on the French Riviera,
and perhaps now here was their chance to move to France.

In many ways, Ted had the greatest job of his life. His salary was
tax-free, his expenses were paid, and the work was relatively stress-
free. But there were problems. From the outset, he didn't get along
with Sonia Casiano Herkrath, the unofficial head nurse who had the
greatest seniority of the ten nurses who looked after Edmond. She had
started work with the Safras in March 1998 and was now in charge of
scheduling and billable hours for the nurses under her watch. It was
on her authority that many of Edmond's previous nurses had been
fired. From the outset, Ted complained to her that he didn't receive
enough hours, and later told the other nurses that he hated her. Behind her back, he called her a "scorpion" or "the snake," and told the
others that Sonia was making his life "hell."

"Ted was strange in some ways," said Sonia at his trial. "He had the tendency to be aggressive. He was so overeager to help Mr. Safra he pushed himself to be the first to him, and even pushed me aside."

Sonia also criticized him for being greedy and extremely jealous, especially of her. For his part, Ted says he was just trying to please his employers.

"I considered it the best job," said Ted. "I had a lot of respect for Mr. Safra. I went out of my way to make his life as comfortable as possible."

In the weeks that he worked for Edmond, Ted massaged his legs when he was struck with paralyzing cramps, helped him go to the bathroom, and administered medications, especially to help him sleep at night. Edmond was in the advanced stages of the disease and suffered a great deal from muscle cramps and vertigo. At least one nurse needed to be present when he went to the bathroom so that he wouldn't fall. Edmond's pain was worse at night and he often needed to take a great deal of medication to help him sleep.

"In the day he [Edmond] moved fairly well," said Lily in her testimony at Ted's trial. "We went out every day walking, sometimes we even went to the swimming pool so he could swim. His life in the day was almost normal. But in the evenings, when he had the strong medication for Parkinson's, he could have some 'off' moments. These were terrible moments, very painful especially in the legs, which became rigid with cramps."

The medication caused him to go to the bathroom frequently. "Two or three times a night, he had to go to the toilet and it was difficult to move around," said Lily. "That is why we had two nurses. When he went to the bathroom, one was always in front of him and he would hold on to that person."

According to the nightly schedule, Edmond's night nurses often had their hands full. "He was heavily medicated," recalled Ted. "He was so screwed up." Safra would have vivid dreams and he hallucinated frequently, said Ted.

In addition to massaging his feet to relieve tremors and accompanying him on frequent trips to the bathroom, nurses had to document what were described as "active vivid dreams" that could be "troublesome." Nurses were repeatedly told to "always be alert during the night so as to respond quickly to Mr. S's needs."

As the nurse's schedule clearly notes, Edmond was an invalid unable to function without the round-the-clock care of a team of professionals who administered everything from laxatives and daily vitamin injections to the Parkinson's and antipsychotic medications that fueled hallucinations and the "troublesome" dreams.

But just before he died, Edmond's health had improved. He had been working out with Ted in his private gym, and getting stronger. "Ironically, he was doing so much better the weeks prior to his death," recalled Sonia. "We were so outraged that this had happened. He could have lived longer."

THE EVENTS OF the early morning of December 3, 1999, still remain confusing more than a decade after they took place. Initially, Ted admitted that he had started the fire in order to alert authorities to the presence of two masked intruders who had entered through a window that had been mysteriously left open in the apartment. The fire was meant to trigger the alarms in the apartment and get immediate help for his boss, he said.

This at any rate was the first version of the story that Ted told the authorities. The second was far more sinister and warped, and it's the one that Monegasque authorities decided to stick with at all costs. In this version of events, an eager Ted set the fire to impress his boss—to create a situation where he would be seen as a savior, like the heroic American military men and women buried at West Point. If the loyal nurse came to his rescue, Edmond would reward him handsomely and elevate him to his rightful place—as the head of the billionaire's nursing detail. Ted was a quick judge of character, and in the few short weeks that he worked in Monaco, he observed Edmond's weakness: He knew that Edmond was obsessed with security and terrified of an attack. So he played on Edmond's fears to get what he wanted. It would be a harmless little charade, and it couldn't help but yield large returns. But in the early hours of December 3, 1999, things went badly awry.

Still, no one in the Safra household could have imagined what Ted had in store. Perhaps Ted himself didn't quite know. In any case, no one seems to have suspected that anything was amiss. On December 2, Lily returned from a trip to London, where she had gone for the opening of the Royal Opera House. Edmond had paid to restore it, and Lily attended the lavish party on December 1 with Adriana and her granddaughter Lily. She returned to Monte Carlo the following evening in time to have dinner with her husband, who eagerly awaited her arrival. "We kissed each other," recalled Lily of the last time she saw her husband alive. "We said a prayer together, as we did every evening, and I went to my apartment."

On the way back to Lily's suite of rooms, which comprised a separate wing in the apartment, Lily nearly collided with Ted in the hallway outside her husband's room. "This evening," he told her, "you are going to sleep very well." If the comment disturbed her, she decided not to say. She just chalked it up to Ted's strange sense of humor and wasn't to remember it again until hours later, as she sat shivering in the lobby of the building, waiting for her daughter and son-in-law to arrive.

According to the original indictment, Ted waited until he was well into his night shift before putting his bizarre plan in motion. He took a knife he had brought with him and stabbed himself in the abdomen after applying a local anesthetic. He then alerted Edmond and the Filipino night nurse Vivian Torrente that there were hooded intruders in the penthouse, and that they needed to barricade themselves in Edmond's room. No doubt, Vivian and Edmond saw the frantic nurse bleeding from his self-inflicted wound and were terrified. Vivian urged him to sound the alarm, but Ted claimed he didn't know how the elaborate security system worked. In an effort to summon the authorities and increase the air of danger, Ted lit a fire in a Lucite wastebasket at the nursing station next to Edmond's bedroom, and Vivian tried to calm a groggy Edmond, who had been so medicated before he fell asleep that he had trouble waking up.

It's unclear whether Ted was aware of the irony of using one of Harry Slatkin's perfumed candles to light the fire. After all, it was Slatkin's camera that had resulted in the best job in his life. Perhaps now it would be the dripping wax from Slatkin's candle that would seal his success. Or his doom.

It's also not clear what went through his head as he raced towards the fifth-floor service elevator and down to the lobby of the building, where he dripped blood on the marble floor and alerted the night watchman Patrick Picquenot that the Safras were in grave danger. Upstairs, a terrified Edmond and Vivian locked themselves into Edmond's bathroom bunker to wait for help, which would come too late.

But while Ted may have put the tragic events in motion, it was the bungling of the Monaco police and fire departments that would seal Edmond and Vivian's fates. Police and firefighters acted like a bunch of Keystone cops in a silent film comedy. Before heading to the penthouse where a fire was raging, authorities dispatched emergency workers to comb the several floors of parking that lay under the beaux-arts building to make sure the suspects were not waiting to attack again. The fire department, which sent fifty-five men to contain the blaze, did not communicate with the police department; each spoke on different radio channels, and there was little effort to coordinate their activities. At one point, a group of firefighters were ordered to tackle the fire from the nearby Hermitage, a luxury five-star hotel. They dragged their dusty hoses through the lobby and one of the restaurants of the magnificent hotel, startling a group of late-night revelers as they returned to their rooms. Later, when a different group of firefighters finally arrived in Edmond's bedroom, they couldn't find Edmond and Vivian because the bathroom door was invisible, designed to be part of the decoration of the room. One of the firefighters refused to help extinguish the blaze when he was ordered to the roof of the Hermitage: "I'm not going over there," he said. "I have a fear of heights."

Ironically, Monaco's reputation for safety ended up killing one of its most security-obsessed residents. Unaccustomed to dealing with a violent emergency, the authorities stumbled through a bizarre real-life farce that in the end proved deadly serious.

The moment they received the emergency call at 4:50 a.m., the concern of law enforcement officials became the safety of their own members, not saving those trapped inside the penthouse. As Maurice Albertin, Monaco's chief of police, noted, "It must be kept in mind that Ted Maher had specified to the first police officer on the scene that there were masked men," he said. "With this description, we knew we were confronted with an aggression. We can understand why they [the police] had to make the apartment secure before enabling the firemen to tackle the fire."

Jean-Yves Gambarini, another officer on the scene, remarked that his men had to bar the exits and "collect as much information as possible" before intervening. "I think the operation was carried out correctly in the circumstances," he said. "Unfortunately, what happened happened, but that's not our fault." Another police officer noted that it was the first time in his career that he had arrived on a job armed with three weapons, ammunition, and a bulletproof vest. "It was the first time in my life I've come so heavily armed. I thought there was an aggression."

On the surface, everything appeared to be stacked up against the would-be saviors of Edmond Safra and Vivian Torrente, including the elaborate interior design of the apartment. "Aesthetics were more important than safety arrangements," said Henri Viellard, a fire safety expert who testified at Ted's trial. "Once the fire got going it was totally impossible to operate the blinds." Moreover, fire alarms were not working, emergency doors were locked tight, and the apartment had no emergency sprinklers. In the end, it took security forces three hours to cover the thirty-foot distance between the fire and the bodies.

"The duration of the intervention of the emergency services was abnormally long for a limited-scale fire," noted Viellard and fellow expert Ghislaine Reiss. "The police and fire brigade had delayed taking into account the information provided by the two fire protection services, the police having favored the implausible scenario of attack."

The apartment had been clearly designed to keep people out, but not for escape. Authorities sent to save one of the world's most important bankers were confronted with a double bunker outfitted with bulletproof doors and state-of-the-art locks.

Strangely, none of the Safra bodyguards were on duty in Monaco. Lily testified that she had dispensed with the bodyguards in September, almost immediately after construction was completed on the apartment's new security system. The improved security measures were based on Edmond's system in Geneva, and installed under consultation with HSBC's security experts. "The Safras felt very secure in Monaco," said Samuel Cohen. "They often said, 'What can happen here? It's the most secure place in the world.'"

But sources close to Edmond dispute this version of events. They say that guards continued to be posted at the apartment despite the enhanced security system. On the morning of the fire all the guards were at La Leopolda.

At Ted's trial, Cohen complained about interference with his security arrangements. "Any system of security cannot defend or protect from an inside problem," he said. "If there was a guard in the apartment, Ted Maher would not have had the courage to do what he did."

Perhaps the Safras regretted their decision to rely solely on their state-of-the-art electronic security system. Did this decision cross her mind when she was startled awake by the ringing telephone just before 5:00 a.m.? "*Chérie*, there are aggressors in the house," said Edmond, in a state of panic. "They have injured Ted. Close yourself in and call the police."

Lily immediately dialed Cohen, who had been stationed at La Leopolda since September, and who was already speeding towards Monaco after receiving an earlier call from the police. It was when she got out of bed and rushed to her dressing room that she noticed the smoke under the lampshades for the first time. "Then suddenly, the blinds opened by themselves but only to the level of the railing," she said. Lily tried to pry the shutters upward but it was of little use; they were stuck. The phone rang again. "Have you closed yourself in?" asked Edmond. "Have you called the police and Cohen?"

In the pitch darkness before dawn, Lily peered through the opening of the blinds and noticed the policeman on the roof of the Hermitage across the way. "Get out, Madame, get out straight away," he shouted. Lily struggled to open the shutters wider, but eventually ended up crawling through the small opening to reach the balcony outside her room.

"I don't know how I got out but I did it," she said. "I walked a bit and found myself on a large terrace which was part of the apartment." Lily gingerly made her way along the balcony and hurried down the back stairs of the apartment. "Flames were coming out of the window of the nurses' station," she said. "Police told me go down please. I was taken to the service staircase. They said 'hurry up' but nobody came with me."

Moments after Edmond called Lily on the phone Ted had left with him, Vivian called her boss Sonia. She told her that Ted was bleeding and there were intruders in the apartment. Sonia immediately called the police. Jean-Marc Farca, brigadier chief of police in Monaco, spoke to Edmond forty minutes later. "He was in quite a panicky state," the police chief recalled. "He said someone had been attacked with an axe and they were in trouble. I told him the police were there. I asked him to go out on to the staircase, that there were police there.

He wanted to go out but he was very frightened. Then he spoke to me about the smoke."

The smoke seeped through under the bathroom door. Edmond, shaking uncontrollably from the effects of his disease and utter fear, urged Vivian to continue calling for help, but he refused to leave the bathroom, still fearing the shadowy intruders—sinister men he imagined to be Muslim terrorists or Russian mobsters bent on revenge after Edmond had given evidence about Russian money laundering. Farca again spoke to Edmond to convince him to open the door, but "Mr. Safra's fear was obvious and took away part of his reasoning."

Vivian repeatedly called Sonia, who at one point instructed her to place wet towels on the ground to absorb the smoke. In the background, Sonia could hear Edmond coughing incessantly, and worried they were near the end. "Sonia, it's so dark in here," said Vivian. "I'm feeling dizzy."

In the lobby, where dozens of police and firemen were milling about, waiting for orders, the Safras' butler, Raul Manjate, rushed into the melee waving a set of keys to the apartment. He rushed up and down the stairs several times offering authorities his keys, but no one paid attention to him. At one point, police detained him. "I kept asking if I could go in," he said. "I had the keys. I knew exactly where he was. I said I was willing to die for my boss. They said I wasn't there to die and that there were two armed people in there who could come out and shoot."

Cohen instinctively felt there were no intruders in the apartment when he received the frantic call from Monaco police. But it was enough that his boss was in danger, and he rushed over from La Leopolda to help the authorities. But as soon as he arrived, he was detained by police. It would take him a desperate twenty minutes to explain himself to the authorities, who did not want to let him upstairs.

"Before I showed them my passport, *rien à faire*, I'm sitting on the floor, handcuffed," recalled Cohen. "Nothing happened. Nothing moved."

Police officer Bruno Bouery was the gatekeeper, and he had orders to prevent anyone from going into the apartment until police were certain it was safe. Which is why he later admitted that he detained Cohen and refused to listen to what he was saying.

"I just asked him to raise his arms," said Bouery, referring to Cohen. "We were in a situation of believing there were intruders. I wanted to make sure who he was. I asked him to lie down. He refused. He just put his hand in his pocket. It was a very risky gesture."

Cohen seems to have been too aggressive for his own good. "In front of us there was a man, tall, Mediterranean, he spoke good French," recalled Jean-Luc Belny, another officer who refused to admit Cohen to the apartment. "He kept saying, 'I'm head of Safra's security.' As far as I'm concerned I don't know this person. We therefore took necessary precautions to get this person out. We put handcuffs on him."

When he finally convinced the police to let him go, Cohen rushed up towards the top floor, where he found Lily making her way down the stairs. "The firemen arrived and I told them exactly how and where they needed to go—do ten steps to the right, they find a staircase, go up two flights and they find a door," recalled Cohen. "After fifteen minutes they came back and said they didn't find it. I asked for a mask. The second time they said I had no authority. There was total chaos. People were going up and down the stairs. I saw firemen with a ladder. I shouted which window to go to. They looked at me with the same arrogance. I ran up. I asked them to follow me. I ran up and down—that's what we did. Nobody listened to what I said and they all refused my help."

Lily, who was growing increasingly desperate, used the phone in the lobby to call her daughter, Adriana, and son-in-law, Michel, who lived nearby. But she did not call her frightened husband to urge him to leave the bathroom.

"My mother woke me up shortly before six a.m.," said Adriana. "I could see the fire from avenue des Beaux Arts. My mother was desperate. I saw Cohen, I asked him to do something. He said he had tried but nobody wanted to listen to him."

Adriana, blonde and petite, decided to take charge, and promptly informed the several police officers assembled in the lobby that Cohen was the only person who could save Edmond. "That was his role, to die if necessary," she said. "They didn't understand. It was like an oath."

She also begged police to allow her mother to call Edmond, to try to convince him to open the door of the bathroom. "It was awful that the police didn't give the telephone to my mother so she could speak to him," recalled Adriana years later. "It was important for him to know she was outside. He was always anxious." It's not clear why Lily did not seek out another telephone to communicate with her husband once she was safely out of danger.

By the time Cohen was finally allowed to climb the back stairs to the apartment where Edmond and Vivian were trapped it was too late. They had already succumbed to the effects of carbon monoxide poisoning and died at approximately 6:00 a.m., fifteen minutes before firefighters made their way into the bedroom.

When they extinguished the raging fire in the nurses' station, firefighters made their way to the bathroom where they found the bodies of the petite Filipino nurse and the corpulent banker. Edmond was slumped in an armchair facing the window, his silk pajamas streaked with black, his body covered with soot, his eyes bulging out of his face.

Vivian, neatly dressed in a gray sweater, blouse, and black trousers, was lying on the floor behind the chair. An autopsy would later find "smoke exposure affecting all of the uncovered parts of the body, particularly the face, with soot marks on the lips and mouth. Significant soot deposits around the nasal apertures of the orbital regions." The cause of death was carbon monoxide poisoning, although medical examiners were puzzled by Vivian's autopsy. In their report, they noted the recent bruises on Vivian's stomach and thigh. On dissecting her neck, medical examiners found that the thyroid gland was full of blood which resembled "a moderate blow" like those given in a combat sport, the autopsy concluded.

Later, the question of whether Edmond came to blows with Vivian, perhaps in an effort to prevent her from leaving the bathroom, became the subject of much legal debate as the nurse's surviving family filed a wrongful death suit against the Safras. Lily would later comment that this was absurd: "He was incapable of killing a fly. It hurt me a lot to hear such terrible things, written by journalists who have nothing better to do."

Shortly after finding the bodies, firefighters summoned Lily, who had just become a widow for the second time in her life. "I went up the stairs to where my husband's office was, on the same floor as the apartments," she recalled. "I was told that he was dead and Vivian Torrente, and you can imagine what state I was in at that time."

Rescuers hauled Edmond's heavy lifeless body from the bathroom where the smoke had streaked the leopard-skin rug, the wood-paneled walls, and the metal handrails on either side of the toilet Edmond used to help him sit up. A group of firefighters gently placed his body on the bed. Although most of his corpse was covered in soot, strangely there was none on the necklace that medical examiners later found around his neck. The amulets that he wore as protection against the evil eye emerged intact and gleaming from the fire that killed their owner. They were supposed to ward against the envy and greed that superstitious Jews and Muslims believe to be at the root of evil. But in the end, they proved ineffective.

As she cleaned the soot from his face with the help of her daughter, Lily may have recalled a similar scene thirty years earlier, as she confronted another husband lying on their bed, his blood staining the satin bedspread. But if she remembered Alfredo Monteverde in those terrible moments, she said nothing to anyone.

"He was covered in soot but very calm, his face looked as if he was sleeping. I touched his hand and it was still warm," said Lily, describing Edmond's lifeless body. "I started to clean his face and my daughter helped me. It was horrible. Then I think I was taken to my daughter's home."

AS THE DRAMA was unfolding at the Belle Epoque, across town at the Princess Grace Hospital a young police captain named Olivier Jude, the only member of the Monaco police force who could speak fluent English and had undergone training with the FBI, was sent to interview the first "victim" of the morning's bizarre events. Ted Maher lay in a hospital bed, recovering from his wounds. One of them took one hundred staples to close.

Ted told Jude what he thought he wanted to hear—that two intruders had entered looking for the billionaire banker. In trying to defend himself, Ted had been wounded. But Jude didn't believe the story, especially as it kept changing with each telling. At first, he spoke about two intruders, and then in a subsequent interview he spoke of only one, and then in another interview returned to two. Moreover, during the first interview with Jude, "he seemed too sure of what he was saying," said Jude, who would take five different statements from Maher in the course of the next few days. Jude also suspected that there was something not quite right about Ted's wounds. "The wounds seemed strange and superficial and done with a knife that was the sort of knife used to do odd jobs, not an attack weapon." Still, Ted needed one hundred staples to close the wounds.

It was during Jude's fourth interrogation of Ted, which took place at the police station after Ted was released from the hospital, that Ted finally admitted that he had lied about what had really taken place at the Belle Epoque on December 3. During the four-hour interview, which was duly translated into French by another officer taking notes on a laptop, Ted learned that Edmond and Vivian had died in the fire. At his fifth and final interrogation, Ted signed a long confession in French, a language he barely understood. He claims now that police told him that his wife was in custody and would not be allowed to return to the United States if he did not confess. They also said that Vivian had likely been strangled in the bathroom, and that he was going to be charged with her death unless he signed. Ted signed on the dotted line. Among other things, he confessed to starting the fire, lying about the intruders, and stabbing himself.

Ted later claimed his confession came under duress, after police showed him his wife's passport and threatened him.

After the events of December 3, one of the Safras' staff had contacted Heidi Maher in Stormville and offered to fly her to Monaco to see her husband, who at that time was still considered the glorious hero.

"Upon hearing of the frightening news in Monaco, I called Michelle St. Bernard, Lily Safra's personal secretary, in New York," said Heidi. "She told me that Ted 'was a hero' for trying to save Mr. Safra. However, the suspects in the crime were still at large. I was very concerned about my husband."

St. Bernard made the arrangements for Heidi to travel to Monaco to visit her husband in the hospital. Heidi boarded a Delta Air Lines flight with her brother Todd Wustrau, bound for Nice where they were met at the airport by one of the Safra drivers, a member of the support staff, and head nurse Sonia. Heidi and Todd believed they were on their way to the hospital to visit Ted. While they were in the car, the driver abruptly changed plans and drove them at breakneck speed to the Hotel Balmoral, where Ted and the other nurses lived.

Later, they were summoned to the police station, where they were questioned by authorities. As they prepared to return to the hotel, Heidi and her brother claim, they were violently abducted.

"I was taken off the streets by three people without any identification," recalled Heidi. "They were dressed in black. I was taken by two people, my head between my knees. I was taken in a car to the Hotel Balmoral. I pleaded [to know] who they were and where we were going. They pushed me up the stairs to my husband's room and they were speaking French. They were very upset and went through the luggage and my husband's things."

Heidi said that her kidnappers rifled through her husband's belongings. "They had Ted's small tape recorder on which he stored one of our children's 'I love you Dad' telephone conversations. They played it for me; the emotion was overwhelming. They also took our passports."

When the search was over, Heidi and Todd were left at the Balmoral. A rattled Heidi sought out Sonia and Anthony Brittain, the Safra staff member who had picked her up at the airport. They were "apologetic."

"I learned later that Ted had been shown my passport, which was taken from me during the abduction from the police station, and told that I had been strip-searched and tortured," she said in court papers filed at a courthouse in Dutchess County, near her home in Stormville. "At the time this all happened, his legs and arms were tied to his hospital bed and he was connected to a urinary catheter. Ted neither reads nor writes French. Nevertheless, he was handed a French confession by the Monaco police. He signed it to spare me from what he thought would be further abuse by the Monaco authorities."

When she retrieved her passport from police on December 5, Heidi asked the Safra secretaries to make arrangements for her return to the United States. She had had enough of Monaco and decided to return to New York, even though she had not been able to see Ted. When Heidi and her brother arrived at the Nice airport, Delta Air Lines demanded $2,400 for their return tickets. Heidi charged the return portion of her tickets to her credit card, clearly relieved to leave the scene of her surreal adventures, even if it was on her own dime.

Less than twenty-four hours after his wife's departure, Ted signed a confession. "There was never any pressure on Mr. Maher," recalled Jude, who denied ever having used Heidi's passport to put pressure on Ted. "I would never have had such results if I hadn't established a climate of confidence. I didn't put any pressure on him at any time. I told him if he didn't want to sign, he didn't have to."

Gerard Tiberti, the officer who assisted Jude with Ted's interrogation, confirmed that no pressure was put on Ted. "He is someone who can be considered changeable," said Tiberti, in reference to Ted. "He was extremely nervous. We saw he could change one minute to the next. He could go from extreme kindness to extreme aggression. It was difficult to read him."

Jude said that Ted showed him a photograph of his wife and children, and at no time did Jude have a copy of Heidi's passport. "*He* was showing *me* a photo of his wife and children," said Jude.

The official investigation into the death of one of the world's wealthiest men did not proceed much further than this. The authorities felt that they had captured the culprit—an emotionally unstable American nurse who created an elaborate heroic plot that went badly awry. Monaco authorities breathed a sigh of relief. They could now blame the terrible *scandale* on a deranged outsider and preserve the veneer of respectability, discretion, and security that was the preserve of the world's wealthiest. They were determined that *l'affaire* Safra was not going to affect Monaco's reputation.

LILY ORGANIZED EDMOND's funeral in Geneva in the same way she would organize one of her sumptuous parties at La Leopolda. She completely ignored the fact that Edmond's family had long wished the entire Safra family to be buried at Mount Herzl in Israel and owned a communal plot there. Together with Jeffrey Keil, who had worked so hard on the HSBC deal and was the first of Lily's friends to fly to Monaco after Edmond's death, she compiled a list of the couple's friends. It read like a who's who of international society and finance. Former UN secretary general Javier Pérez de Cuéllar and his wife were on the list, as was Israel's foreign minister David Levy, the Prince Sadruddin Aga Khan, and Sir John Bond, the CEO of HSBC, who had agreed to deliver the eulogy. Never mind that Bond had barely known Edmond. What stood out at the funeral was the importance of the multibillion-dollar deal that Edmond had brokered with HSBC. And this was clearly signaled in Lily's choice of Bond to bid an official farewell to the great banker whose empire he had just acquired.

More than seven hundred guests crowded into the Hekhal Haness, Geneva's largest synagogue. Edmond's brothers Moise and Joseph were among them, although they had not been officially invited and indeed had to strong-arm their way into the house of worship. In what would prove one of the most socially difficult moments for Lily, the Safra brothers had to push their way to the front of the synagogue in order to help carry Edmond's coffin.

"She [Lily] didn't want anyone from the family at the funeral," said one Safra family member who did not want to be identified. "But everyone from our family went anyway. We were not going to stay away from Edmond's funeral because of her."

Joseph, Moise, and their families returned to Brazil immediately following Edmond's funeral. It must have been one of the only times in their lives that these deeply religious Jews decided to dispense with their own mourning rituals by not sitting shiva as a family. They would have their own shiva far away from the widow they despised—at their home in São Paulo.

"You have brought together people from different backgrounds, cultures, religions and social horizons, just as you always have," noted Elie Wiesel in his own speech at Edmond's funeral. "Each of us is dealing with our own memories of you, our own questions of what happened last Friday."

But in the end, few questions troubled Lily or the Monegasque authorities. On the day of the funeral Daniel Serdet, Monaco's public prosecutor, announced that Ted had been charged with arson leading to the death of two people. "He [Ted] didn't intend to kill anyone; he wanted to settle an account with the head of the medical team," was how the prosecutor explained it all away. Ted was sent to jail in Monaco to await his trial.

But the official version of events left many unanswered questions. Edmond's faithful aides and his family in São Paulo would
wonder for years about the bizarre circumstances surrounding Edmond's death. Why were the guards absent? Why were Edmond's
most trusted aides away from Monaco at the time of his death? Why
was Ted Maher hired against their wishes? Why did Maher fabricate
a story about hooded intruders and start a fire, risking his own life
in the process? Why had the Monaco police and firefighters taken
so long to deal with the emergency? Why was Edmond so afraid to
leave the bathroom?

Edmond's family in New York and São Paulo went as far as to hire
their own investigators. But their efforts were met with frustration.
Monaco authorities, worried about drawing even more attention to
the international scandal that was bringing unwanted media attention
to their privileged principality, would quickly decide to close ranks
on *l'affaire* Safra.

The questions lingered, but the big news on December 6, 1999, was
not the burial of the legendary banker or the bizarre circumstances of
his death. It was the completion of the sale of Republic to HSBC as
the Federal Reserve cleared the deal—the final regulatory hurdle to
the multibillion-dollar purchase. After the burial of her fourth husband in Geneva, Lily emerged as one of the wealthiest widows in the
world.

NINE

"Years of Sorrow and Days of Despair"

J AY SALPETER IS a no-nonsense, tough-talking former New York City homicide detective who took early retirement from the force and launched a career as a private detective in 1990. In twenty years on the force, he specialized in investigations into the mob, narcotics, homicide, and white-collar criminals. As a private investigator, he earned a reputation for finding new evidence in old homicide cases. Nobody could hide from Salpeter, not even the elusive billionaire widow Lily Safra. In April 2001, when attorneys for Heidi Maher needed to find and serve Lily with legal papers but had no idea how to find her, they turned to Salpeter.

It is no easy task finding Lily, who jets frequently between her homes in Paris, the Riviera, London, and New York, and retains several public relations experts and lawyers to protect her privacy. In the 1970s, she confounded process servers in London who tried for months to find her at her Hyde Park Gardens flat in order to serve her with the notice that she was being sued, along with Edmond's Trade Development Bank, by her former in-laws.

Several years after his brief brush with Lily on an Upper East Side street corner in the early spring of 2001, Salpeter was hard-pressed to recall how he found out that Lily would be dining at Swifty's or that she would even be in New York at all. Salpeter made a reservation for himself and a colleague at the posh Upper East Side restaurant after he learned that Lily would be honored at an intimate dinner party hosted by Robert Higdon, the representative of Prince Charles's charities in Washington. It was an informal welcome back to New York featuring her new best friends Brian Mulroney, the former prime minister of Canada, his wife Mila, and entertainer Joan Rivers. Old friends—"some of my closest and dearest friends," gushed Lily—Marcela Pérez de Cuéllar (whose husband had been appointed president of the council of ministers of his native Peru), Blaine and Robert Trump, and Evelyn and Leonard Lauder would also be on hand to toast "the lovely Lily Safra, the charmer who also happens to be one of the richest women in the world . . ."

Salpeter didn't care about rich or charming, and he surely wasn't in the habit of reading the society columns in *Women's Wear Daily*. He wasn't intimidated by the rarefied atmosphere of Swifty's or the condescending tones of the wait staff, who seemed eager to rush him out of the restaurant in order to prepare for the private party. Salpeter had a single goal, and he had committed Lily's face to memory.

"You have to imagine the scene here," said a lawyer familiar with the stakeout at Swifty's. "You have Salpeter and his associate, this big black former cop, dining at this bastion of Upper East Side snobbery. Nobody knew what they were doing there, and the wait staff was totally shocked."

On that chilly April evening, Salpeter, a heavyset brick of a man, his brown hair speckled with gray, paid the bill and went to stand outside the restaurant, clutching Heidi Maher's legal papers. He was soon joined by a photographer from the *New York Post*, who had been tipped off, probably by Salpeter himself. The first guest to arrive was

Mrs. William McCormick Blair of Washington, D.C. (known to her socialite friends as Deeda).

"Are you Lily?" asked the former cop. The impeccably dressed, reed-thin, aging socialite with a shoulder-length graying bob could, from a distance, be mistaken for her friend Lily Safra. Deeda managed to ignore Salpeter completely and quickly made her way into the restaurant.

Lily, also impeccably dressed and reed-thin, was the second to arrive, stepping out of a black limousine, accompanied by a security guard.

"Are you Lily?"

It was the unspoken acknowledgment, the fleeting yet at the same time careful look she gave him that told the former cop that he had found his target. He thrust the legal documents into her hand, just as the *Post* photographer snapped multiple frames. Lily touched them, but then decided she would allow them to drop to the ground in front of the restaurant. The papers were retrieved by her security guard. Salpeter had successfully served the richest widow in the world. His job was finished. "It was like taking candy from a baby," he would recall years later. The following day's headline in the *Post* read "Summons Served Between Courses" and featured a photo of an elegant Lily entering the restaurant.

The ambushes by court bailiffs and process servers would prove semiregular events in Lily's life in the months and years after Edmond's death. The lawsuits started shortly after Edmond's funeral in Geneva and a later memorial service in New York. The first came from stunned Safra family members. Still reeling in disbelief from Edmond's mysterious death, they quickly realized that many had their inheritance reduced. In São Paulo, the Safra sisters filed suit against Lily on behalf of themselves and Edmond's nieces and nephews. Lily, her daughter, and lawyer Marc Bonnant were also sued by Ninaca S.A., a Panamanian corporation established as an art trust by

Edmond and his brothers in 1995. In February 1999 Edmond had designated Lily's friend Anita Smaga, her daughter Adriana, and Bonnant as additional trustees, which tipped the board in Lily's favor. The suit demanded $17 million in damages.

Heidi Maher's legal action came next. Seventeen months after her ill-fated trip to Monaco in 1999, Heidi filed a motion against Lily and various Safra employees in the Supreme Court of the State of New York in Dutchess County. The motion was for a pretrial discovery so that her attorneys could establish the facts of just what had happened to her during her ordeal in Monaco in December 1999.

"I suffered shocking and humiliating treatment during the trip which was avoidable and due entirely to the fault of others," said Heidi in her affidavit. "I entrusted my safety and the entire itinerary to the Safra organization. Instead . . . I was diverted without my consent by Safra-related staff to the Monaco police station where I was interrogated for three dreadful days in connection with what I later learned was a criminal investigation of my husband. I was never allowed the promised visit with Ted."

In a letter to the American consul general in Marseilles, one of the members of Ted's defense team protested the treatment of Heidi and her brother by Monaco authorities: "The rights of these American citizens were violated under United States law, International law, and no doubt Monaco law," wrote Michael Griffith, one of Ted's attorneys, in March 2001. "Behavior of this type cannot be tolerated in a civilized world, particularly when United States Government property [passports] were stolen and taken for the purpose of securing an illegal confession under the most despicable circumstances."

In court filings, Heidi demanded to examine and depose everyone from Lily Safra to all of the directors of Spotless & Brite, Inc., the Delaware corporation run out of the Republic Bank on Fifth Avenue that had employed her husband and arranged for her travel to Monaco. According to Heidi's court filings, "We still do not know who orchestrated these events and why. For example, who actually paid for and later canceled the Delta return flight tickets; who is responsible for the sudden change in our limousine's itinerary; who arranged to deceive me into the coercive police interrogation room; and who converted my trip into a Monaco police investigation without my prior informed consent or knowledge. The requested depositions and documents will lead us to the truth and to those truly responsible."

But if she felt she was going to get at the truth with the mighty Safra organization and put Lily Safra on a witness stand in Dutchess County, Heidi was clearly naive.

Stanley Arkin, the very able Manhattan lawyer who had helped Edmond take on American Express, easily disputed Heidi's claims and accused her of wasting the court's time. "Mrs. Maher brought this motion, instead of a lawsuit, because she cannot state an actionable claim against any of the Respondents," said Arkin in his court filings. "Mrs. Maher asks this court to permit her to engage in a far-reaching fishing expedition in the vain hope that she may find a claim for which she can be compensated."

Arkin did a good job of dismissing Heidi's claims, adding that "Mrs. Maher's application is replete with irresponsible unsubstantiated accusations and innuendo."

Later, the parties agreed to an undisclosed out-of-court settlement. Heidi, who had tirelessly campaigned to raise awareness of Ted's plight by writing elected officials, starting a Web site, and denouncing the Safra family to anyone who would listen, seems to have had a sudden and complete about-face. In the months after Edmond's death, when Ted's pay stopped being wired to her, Heidi lost the family home because she could no longer afford the mortgage payments. She and her children were forced to move into her mother's house in Stormville. With her settlement from the lawsuit, she quietly purchased a new house in Stormville and determined that she and her children would have nothing more to do with Ted, whose actions had had such devastating consequences for all their lives. The coup de grâce for Ted came nearly three years later, on the last day of his trial in Monaco. Shortly after the guilty verdict, Heidi decided to end their marriage.

"When [in] Ted's final speech he apologized for what he did to the Safra and the Torrente families I felt like standing up and saying what about me and our children?" said Heidi in an e-mail to writer Dominick Dunne shortly after the end of Ted's trial.

Ted's trial ended almost three years to the day after Edmond's death. While many journalists referred to it as the principality's "trial of the century," Sandrine Setton, one of Ted's four defense lawyers, renamed it the "trial of the imbecility of the century" in her closing arguments. Setton was referring to both Ted's ridiculous plot to make himself the great hero by starting the fire, and the incompetence of the Monaco authorities in their efforts to save Edmond. Georges Blot, another Maher lawyer, even quoted Shakespeare, characterizing Ted as being "full of sound and fury."

As with Edmond's funeral, Ted's trial drew members of the Safra clan from around the world. If Lily had hoped that the family would present a unified front for the world's television cameras and sit together in the courtroom, she was clearly disappointed. As the proceedings began in late November 2002, Lily, through her attorneys, invited Joseph and Moise Safra to sit in her row. They declined.

"One day Joseph Safra went as far as to sit in a row in front of the defense lawyers," noted Dominick Dunne, who covered the trial for *Vanity Fair*. "His beautiful wife Vicki always sat at the back of the courtroom, wonderfully dressed and greatly admired. She and Lily never once looked at each other." Another day, Joseph sat one row behind Lily, but he never acknowledged her.

On the fifth day of the trial, the proceedings turned into an impromptu memorial for Edmond when Joseph Sitruk, the elderly, white-bearded chief rabbi of France, took the stand as a witness for the prosecution. Lily's staff had chartered a private plane to fly the rabbi from Paris to Nice, where one of her drivers met him at the airport for the twenty-minute drive to Monte Carlo.

Following the rabbi's testimony regarding Edmond's charitable work for the Jewish community, the judge asked Ted if he had any questions for the rabbi. Ted asked him "to say a prayer in Jewish for Edmond Safra." The odd request was duly translated into French, and the rabbi was quick to oblige. The elderly rabbi handed his wide-brimmed black hat to an attendant, who placed a black yarmulke on his head. He prayed in Hebrew on the witness stand in front of a six-foot crucifix, which was affixed to the wall, as the Jewish men in the courtroom scrambled to cover their heads with their hands as substitutes for yarmulkes.

It was the first time that Lily lost her composure in public. She wept openly during the prayer, and then followed Sitruk out of the courtroom to thank him for his appearance. Downstairs in the court-house lobby, Joseph and Moise waited to greet the rabbi, and Joseph offered his private plane for the return trip to Paris.

Although the conclusion of Ted's trial surely afforded Lily some relief, it must have been short-lived. Not long after the trial ended, bailiffs acting for the Manhattan lawyer Pompeyo Roa Realuyo, who was representing Vivian Torrente's adult children, served papers on Lily as she prepared to leave the five-star Hotel de Paris in Monaco to board her private jet in Nice. Lily and her entourage of lawyers, sec-retaries, and security guards had occupied much of the fourth floor of the hotel. Although she had so easily dispensed with security for her husband in December 1999, she made a point of employing several guards to patrol the fourth-floor hallways of the hotel while she was there. For this reason, serving her with legal papers would be nearly impossible. Which is why the process server decided to call Lily from a house phone in the lobby.

Lily's lawyer Marc Bonnant, who has long, slicked-back silver hair and smokes cigarettes in a long holder, arrived in the lobby to accept service on Lily's behalf.

But Bonnant did not take it quietly. Fresh from his brilliant clos-ing arguments in the courtroom—"a court performance worthy of

Laurence Olivier"—Bonnant started screaming and yelling at the
process server. The suit, which sought $100 million in damages, was
filed against Lily, the Safra estate, and various insurance companies
connected to the Safras.

The Torrente children—Genevieve, twenty-three, and Jason,
thirty—said they were "victims of a civil conspiracy and fraud per-
petrated by the defendants designed to withhold from them critical
information relating to the circumstances of their mother's death."
Their most important claim was that the autopsy seemed to show that
a struggle ensued between Edmond and Vivian in the locked bathroom. The Torrente children argued that Edmond "imprisoned"
Vivian in the bathroom, and that "the combat-like" mark found on
Vivian's neck, the bruises on her knees, and Edmond's DNA, which
was found under her fingernails, were confirmation "that Mr. Safra's
efforts to restrain her were the direct and proximate cause of death."

Although the autopsy report was concluded on December 5,
1999—two days after the fire at the penthouse—the results were not
made public until Ted's trial some three years later. In the year following their mother's death, the Torrente children claimed that they were
"fraudulently deceived and misled into signing a so-called settlement
agreement with the named defendants wherein critical information,
including the autopsy report was intentionally withheld from them."

Like the Heidi Maher and Safra family lawsuits, the Torrente suit
was quietly settled out of court. For while Edmond might have come
to blows with his nurse in order to prevent her from leaving the bathroom, the autopsy makes clear that both died of smoke inhalation.

"The reason they died was because they waited too long," said
Michael Baden, an expert witness for the defense at the trial. "There
were certain marks on her neck, but there wasn't enough evidence to
reach the conclusion that she had died because of Edmond."

But if at the end of the trial Lily thought she could finally breathe
a sigh of relief, she was deeply mistaken. Following the end of the
trial, there was the matter of Alfredo's company, Ponto Frio, which

Lily now had to oversee without Edmond's expert guidance. It was no secret that she hated Simon Alouan, Ponto Frio's chief executive and Edmond's protégé. Now that she was effectively in charge of the company again as its majority shareholder along with Alfredo's son, Carlos, Alouan knew his days were numbered. She would seek her revenge. Without Edmond there to act as a buffer between Alouan and Lily, the relationship was simply not going to work, and so it was no surprise to him when Lily informed him of her decision to fire him at a board meeting. Lily promptly replaced the hot-headed Lebanese businessman she had despised for so many years with someone over whom she could have complete control—her son-in-law, Michel Elia, who had limited experience running a company of Ponto Frio's size and complexity.

Then, just as the flurry of fittings, lunches, and society functions began again in earnest for Lily, Ted Maher stunned the world with a daring escape from his cell in an old fortress that doubles as Monaco's prison, overlooking the azure waters of the Mediterranean.

On a frigid night in January 2003 and less than a month after his trial, Ted and his Italian cellmate, Luigi Ciardelli, sawed through the metal bars on their window and somehow lowered themselves down the thirty-three-foot drop of the old fortress wall using a rope they had fashioned from forty-six garbage bags. Ciardelli headed to San Remo, Italy. Ted went to the Hotel Artemis near Nice, hoping that he could convince the American consulate there to grant him some sort of safe haven. He called his estranged wife, asking for her credit card number as he attempted to check into the hotel. He also called one of his Monaco lawyers, Donald Manasse. "I've escaped!" he told Manasse. "You can drop the appeal now."

Manasse called the prison to report the escape, and Heidi immediately contacted CBS, which was making a *48 Hours* special on the Safra case, and CBS called the segment producer, who happened to be in Monte Carlo staying at the Hotel de Paris. The Monaco authorities didn't know about the escape until an Anglican priest who had become close to Ted called them to tell them Ted was gone. Ted was rounded up a few hours later. Authorities eventually sentenced him to an extra year in jail, and suspended the director of the prison. No one is quite sure why he tried to escape to Nice, where he spent so many of his free weekends prior to Edmond's death. Did he have some mysterious underworld contact in the French resort city? Were these the dreaded Russian mobsters Edmond had feared so much after he gave evidence to the FBI shortly before his death? Why did Ted return to Nice? Like so much of the story of Ted's involvement in *l'affaire Safra*, the facts remain murky.

A FEW MONTHS after Ted's escape and eventual return to prison, Preston Bailey, the noted New York event designer, was assigned the task of stage-managing Lily's triumphant return to Manhattan society. Just as with the double-header parties at La Leopolda to celebrate the end of Edmond's troubles with American Express, Lily was determined to throw herself an unforgettable return to high society in Manhattan.

It's not that she had ever really left. Even during the drama of Edmond's death, the lawsuits, and Ted's trial and escape, Lily still managed a regular presence at parties on both sides of the Atlantic. With her new super wealth, she bought herself a lavish home in London— "one of the most staggeringly beautiful houses in London," gushed *Women's Wear Daily*, and continued to maintain homes in New York, Paris and the south of France.

In May 2000, five months after Edmond's death, she flew to New York to attend a special United Nations gala in honor of Edmond's work for Israel. In August, she donated a fountain and garden in Edmond's name for Somerset House in London. The spectacular Edmond J. Safra Court, which was the first major public fountain to be commissioned in London since the ones in Trafalgar Square in 1845, has fifty-five jets of water that rise out of the granite-covered ground.

The number five was Edmond's favorite number; he believed that it warded off evil spirits.

A month later, Lily was spotted in "the chicest of black dresses" at a benefit for the American Ballet Theatre at the Metropolitan Opera House in Manhattan. That summer, she was back in London attending a gala at Buckingham Palace, where she was seated to the right of the Prince of Wales, the host of the evening. She also attended her friend Lynn Wyatt's tropical paradise-themed birthday party in the south of France. There were also the flurry of dinner parties she threw for friends in London and New York and at La Leopolda during the summer season on the Riviera.

A month before Ted's trial began in Monaco, Lily was among 115 guests at a fortieth-birthday party for Elton John's partner, David Furnish. It was a black-tie affair, with champagne and white truffle risotto, in both London and Venice (Elton chartered a plane for the London-to-Venice trip). The guests were decidedly more rock-and-roll royalty than the kind Lily was now used to. It's rather difficult to imagine the gilded Lily on the dance floor alongside guests like Donatella Versace, Elizabeth Hurley, Sting, and Isabella Blow. Lily's friend Lynn Wyatt appears to have been right at home, though— "dirty-dancing" with video artist David LaChapelle, "in dangerous *deshabillé* as his shirt hung open, his suspenders dangled at his knees and his trousers slipped down his hips."

After the conclusion of Ted Maher's trial in Monaco in December 2002, Lily's public relations consultants appeared to work overtime to reestablish her important role in society. Triumphant after Ted's conviction, Lily flew to New York to dedicate the synagogue on the Upper East Side that Eli Attia had begun in the 1980s. Following the nasty legal battle with Attia, the beaux-arts—style synagogue, with massive doors of carved brass, was completed by the French architect Thierry Despont. Attia's early work on the house of worship on East Sixty-third Street, off Fifth Avenue, was conveniently forgotten. The Sephardic community for whom it was built was also conveniently forgotten at the dedication even as Lily organized a dinner for three hundred people at the University Club of New York on Fifth Avenue.

Instead of inviting the important members of the New York Sephardic community that her husband had generously supported over a lifetime, the sacred occasion seemed to become just another New York society event. At a later party for the synagogue, it was Lily's golden dress and her "17th century heavy gold necklace recovered from a Spanish ship" that took precedence over the dedication of the Edmond J. Safra synagogue. After the University Club fête, Lily's friends threw other parties to commemorate the grand occasion. One party was held at Swifty's and was hosted by the Iraqi-born financier Ezra Zilkha and his wife, Cecile. Later, Lily was the guest of honor at another lavish party hosted by Joan Rivers at her palatial apartment, which was exquisitely decorated with white lilies, snapdragons and roses for the occasion. "There were Buccellati's silver sparrows at each place setting and silver vases filled with bunches of tiny white roses." Lily arrived wearing "an iridescent claret-colored taffeta coat over claret brocade pants with little satin slippers to match," by Oscar de la Renta.

"Lily is a lovely, courageous woman, who in the last several years has gone through hell since the mysterious death of her husband in a fire in their Monte Carlo apartment and later at the trial during which she handled herself impeccably and emerged in triumph like the lady she is," said her friend Aileen Mehle in her *Women's Wear Daily* column a few weeks after the conclusion of Ted's trial in Monaco.

The "lovely, courageous" Lily also celebrated her legal triumph with the purchase of a new Paris apartment on the exclusive avenue Gabriel, a duplex with marvelous views of the Eiffel Tower from every room—the same apartment that Blaine Trump's family lived in when Blaine was a student in Paris. Again, her friends at *Women's Wear Daily* felt compelled to defend her honor: "These days and nights, she is a happy woman, out lunching and dining with her friends, wearing marvelous clothes, and emerging from the three-year nightmare and the ugly, false and unfounded speculation that followed her in print after the death of her husband, Edmond, in their Monte Carlo apartment, a victim of a fire set by one of his nurses, the now-imprisoned Ted Maher."

Indeed, after years of tension following the bizarre death of her husband, Lily was ready to reassume her place as a leading hostess in New York. Because she believed in doing nothing by half measures, Lily hired Preston Bailey, the most sought-after event planner in Manhattan, to create an evening that would impress even the high-society luminaries who had seen it all.

Bailey is a striking figure on the New York social scene, with his muscular physique and his shaved head—smooth and polished like a billiard ball. He is a former model from Panama who embarked on his career as haute society's foremost event planner when he designed the 1998 wedding of Joan Rivers's daughter Melissa at the Plaza hotel. Bailey turned one of the ballrooms of the hotel into a Czarist winter garden from *Doctor Zhivago*, featuring 30,000 white flowers and 100 trees painted white.

For Lily, he would transform one of her empty Fifth Avenue apartments overlooking Central Park (she owned two) into a French country garden. "We agreed that a lush garden setting would be the perfect antidote to the endless weeks of rain we'd been having, so I set about conjuring an atmosphere that would recall the French countryside," wrote Bailey in an article for *Elle Décor* that devoted one of its glossy pages to the decoration of Lily's party room. "Still, nothing short of a magical evening would wow the guests."

Two weeks before the party, Bailey set about transforming the foyer and forty-seven-foot-long living room in the apartment into a French garden. In the dining room, he attached a grid covered in lemon leaves to the ceiling and hung rose petals sewn together to look like garlands of wisteria in white and lavender. He lined sections of the walls with screens imprinted with photographs of vast landscapes. "I then wove thousands of blossoms into the screens to further blur

the boundaries of the area—used weathered green trellis lit from behind to convey dappled sunlight." The effect was similar to dining
under a huge wisteria tree.

For the centerpieces, Bailey used white peonies flown in from Holland, cymbidium orchids, lavender, sweet pea, blue hyacinths, and
Australian dendrobium orchids. "At each window there were trellis
arbors draped with celadon and pink Fatima orchid 'curtains' outlining the park views."

The sixty guests, who included former British prime minister Lady
Margaret Thatcher, Brian and Mila Mulroney, Michael Bloomberg,
Diane Sawyer, Nancy Kissinger, the Erteguns, Joan Rivers, Princess
Firyal of Jordan, Carolina and Reinaldo Herrera, Robert Higdon,
and Lynn and Oscar Wyatt (who flew in from their home in Texas),
assembled for drinks at Lily's other apartment on a higher floor. For
dinner, they took the elevator to the other apartment. "When the elevator opened 60 jaws dropped at the sight of a fabulous 'conservatory'
fragrant with the smell of all those flowers," gushed Mehle.

"It was a scene of great beauty and those 60 who have been everywhere and done everything could hardly believe their eyes." As
Bailey himself noted, "I waited in the foyer—it was a harbinger of
the lavish things to come, with elephant's ear branches, trellis, and
light patterns bathing the walls and floors—for everyone to arrive.
I was handsomely rewarded with audible gasps, most definitely a
few dropped jaws and I'm not exaggerating, a few soft shrieks of delight."

After dinner, the guests "lounged on wrought iron garden furniture under 10-foot topiary trees built of birch branches and hanging
with pears, lemons and limes."

A month later, Lily was off to England for Elton John's annual
White Tie and Tiara party, an upscale AIDS benefit "that draws every celebrity, moneybags and social figure for leagues around and
then some"—at his country home in Surrey. In "a chiffon dress the
color of moonlight," Lily hired a motorcoach to bring her friends

from London to the party. As usual, Blaine and Robert Trump, Joan Rivers, and Robert Higdon were among her guests.

That fall, Lily wowed them again with the opening of the Edmond J. Safra Hall at the Museum of Jewish Heritage in New York. Elton John performed and Diane Sawyer and Michael J. Fox also presided at the dinner, where Lily greeted her guests in "a black Valentino." In addition to the usual suspects—the Trumps, the Erteguns, the Zilkhas, and the Herreras—legendary New York district attorney Robert Morgenthau, the museum's chairman, also attended.

In the years after Edmond's death, Lily was surely living her dream. She had transformed herself into an elegant hostess, creating memorable parties, wearing beautiful clothes, dining with royalty, and donating huge sums of money to good causes. Which is why she must have received such a devastating shock when, in the summer of 2005, the royal biographer Lady Colin Campbell published a novel about a social-climbing billionairess who murders her second and fourth husbands.

With her imperious manner and drawling upper-class Jamaican accent, Lady Colin is a towering and rather intimidating society blonde who is afraid of no one. Born with a genital disfigurement to a wealthy Jamaican family in 1949, Lady Colin was christened George William Ziadie and raised a boy. When she was twenty-one, she had corrective surgery. She married Lord Colin Campbell, a brother of the Duke of Argyll, in 1974 and divorced him a year later, but held on to the title.

Empress Bianca, Lady Colin's first novel, was not supposed to garner any of the worldwide publicity that it received when it was quietly released in Britain in June 2005, but that was before Lily's society friends read the book and were convinced that it was a thinly disguised roman à clef about her life. Lady Colin is best known for her best-selling tell-all biographies of Diana, Princess of Wales. Known as Georgie to her friends, she argued that *Empress Bianca* was based on one of her cousins and had little or nothing to do with Lily. But the argument may have seemed unconvincing to Lily, especially as Lady Colin's book was dedicated to the memory of Rosy's daughter Christina Fanto, Lily's niece during her marriage to Alfredo Monteverde.

In *Empress Bianca*, the central character, Bianca Barnett, is "a veritable monster of vanity and pretension" and "the most ambitious and mercenary person." She hails from South America, has three children by her first husband, and loses her beloved first son in a tragic car crash. Her second husband, Ferdy Piedraplata, is shot by a hitman who makes the death look like a suicide. The hit is organized by Bianca's lover, a Middle Eastern banker named Philippe Mahfoud, who eventually becomes her fourth husband.

"In life, circumstances sometimes force people to do things they normally wouldn't do," says Philippe to Bianca as he outlines the plan to kill Ferdy soon after Ferdy threatens to divorce her. Philippe enlists a member of the Gambino crime family to carry out the murder in the victim's home in a luxe suburb of the Venezuelan capital Caracas.

The murder further unites Bianca and Philippe, who eventually marry after Bianca divorces her third husband—an interior designer—whom she marries to make Philippe jealous. But years after the murder, relations sour between Philippe and Bianca. Philippe and one of his nurses die in a mysterious blaze in his apartment in Andorra, a tax haven nestled in the Pyrenees between Spain and France. "When police finally managed to cut through, they found Philippe and Agatha sitting on the floor . . . Both were dead. Asphyxiated."

In the novel, police and investigators are paid off by Bianca's highly organized team of lawyers and financiers. Frustrated at the complete absence of justice for her crimes, Bianca's enemies decide to fight her where they know it will hurt the most—in the court of high society. "Wherever she goes and whatever she does, she will know that a healthy proportion of the people around her will either despise her or laugh at her," writes Lady Colin. "All her money, all the influence she has so avidly courted, the people she has just as avidly cultivated and all the manipulations to which she will resort in the future are powerless to bring this punishment to an end. As long as she exists, Bianca now clearly understands, so will it. And the thought of it starts tearing slowly away at her insides."

On July 3, 2005, the *Sunday Telegraph* published an account of *Empress Bianca*. A day later, Lily hired high-powered London lawyer Anthony Julius of the prestigious London firm Mischon de Reya. Julius, who had previously represented Princess Diana in her divorce from Prince Charles, demanded a retraction and apology from the editors of the *Sunday Telegraph*.

The apology was swift, appearing soon after the article. "It was never our intention to suggest that the actions attributed to the fictional character had been carried out by Mrs. Safra in reality," read the newspaper's groveling apology. "We understand that our linking of Mrs. Safra's name with that of the novel's central character has greatly upset her. We very much regret this and apologize unreservedly to Mrs. Safra for any embarrassment caused."

Had Lily read the book?

"I believe that Mrs. Safra read part of the book," said Mark Bolland, Lily's public relations consultant, in a sworn statement. "I understand that she was unable to read any further because she was so distressed by the contents. I believe her advisers also read part of the book."

Bolland, a former public relations adviser to the Prince of Wales, noted that it was his job to promote Lily's charities, protect her privacy, and "keep her out of the papers." Presumably, Bolland meant only the newspapers that refused to kowtow to Lily, and not the society press where she loved to appear.

But not content to focus on the newspapers, Lily turned against the book's London publisher. On July 12, 2005, Lady Colin Campbell's publisher Bliss Books, a subsidiary of Arcadia Books, received a stern letter from Julius. The letter said that "Mrs. Safra regarded the book as defamatory" and wanted it removed from distribution and pulped. It spelled out seventeen direct parallels between the lives of the char-

acter Bianca Barnett and herself. Julius gave Arcadia Books five days
to respond.

Gary Pulsifer, the publisher of Arcadia Books, moved quickly to
withdraw all unsold copies of the book and destroy them. "Our investors want us to settle now, which we'll do," said Pulsifer. "If Georgie
takes it further—sounds like she will—it will be interesting to see
who steps into what witness box." Lily settled with Arcadia on July
25, 2005, after the publisher agreed to destroy all copies of the book.

Lady Colin turned the tables on Lily, suing her on the grounds
that she was depriving the author of her income and foreign sales of
the book, which she defended as a work of fiction based on a distant
relative of her own.

"Lily tried to misuse the laws and then I used them against her,"
said Lady Colin. "I'm an experienced litigant, so I sued her when
Arcadia shut down."

In the early days of the controversy, when the book was released
in London, Lily's friends and foes snapped it up before the ban. A
Brazilian woman close to the story ordered eighty copies of the book
and had them anonymously distributed to Lily's highly placed society
friends, including Nancy Reagan. A handful of copies that survived
the pulping were available on eBay for nearly $1,000 a copy.

The lawsuit against Lily turned into a Mexican standoff, but Lady
Colin did win back the right to rerelease her book in the U.S., provided that she make the seventeen changes demanded by Lily. These
proved to be relatively minor.

"She objected to the fact that Bianca's fourth husband was Lebanese, so I have made him Iraqi," said Lady Colin. "In fact, the character was partly based on my own father, who was Lebanese. On the
advice of my lawyer, I changed everything that Mrs. Safra objected
to."

In late summer 2008, Lady Colin, impeccably coiffed and elegantly
dressed, hosted a group of friends and fans who sipped white wine

and munched on hors d'oeuvres at her Manhattan book launch, which took place at a tony Upper East Side bookshop.

One of Lady Colin's biggest fans turned out to be Ted Maher himself, who read a copy of her book during his last year in prison. He also maintained a correspondence with the grande dame, who publicly stated that she felt he was made a scapegoat by the Monaco authorities, that he was wrongly convicted, and that the real story behind the events of December 3, 1999, has never been properly investigated.

Her claims were unexpectedly bolstered by one of the investigating judges in the Maher case. Jean Christophe Hullin told the French newspaper *Le Figaro* in June 2007 that before Ted's trial in Monaco he had attended a meeting with other high-ranking Monaco officials to discuss Ted. Hullin told a journalist that he had met with Monaco's chief prosecutor and that they had allegedly agreed that Maher would get ten years in jail. His comments have led to an investigation in Monaco, but there is no word on when and if any report will ever be released.

In a rare outburst, Lily lashed out at the allegations that the trial had been fixed. For her, the whole ordeal had come to an end when Ted was convicted and sent to jail. Why did everything need to be rehashed now, some five years later? No doubt this was just more nonsense from "journalists who have nothing better to do," as she had noted in her testimony at Ted's trial when she was confronted by the results of the autopsy report that seemed to suggest Edmond might have caused Vivian's death.

"To say the trial of the one who murdered her husband was fixed, it's totally unbearable to her," said Marc Bonnant, in an interview with the *New York Post*. "Monaco is not a barbarian country. You can't fix trials in Europe."

According to Bonnant, Lily had suffered "years of sorrow and days of despair" since Edmond's death. "Her life is not only made of roses. When you love somebody, the money doesn't make up for their loss. Nothing will heal her wounds. Nothing will take away her pain."

The pain must have returned with a vengeance when Ted Maher was released from jail in the summer of 2007, returning to the United States in the fall. He had spent more than eight years in jail (he was incarcerated shortly after Edmond's funeral) for a crime that he claims he did not commit, and he was angry. Once he stepped onto American soil, Ted told reporters that he had been nothing more than a scapegoat—he had been convicted in order to keep up Monaco's appearance as a safe playground for the rich and famous. He still insisted that two intruders broke into the apartment the night that Edmond died, but there were new elements to his story. Now he spoke about being accosted in Nice a week before the penthouse fire. He now claimed that two gun-toting thugs abducted him off a street in Nice and showed him photographs of his wife in Stormville and his children leaving school.

"He was threatened, and pictures were shown to him by these people of his children coming out of school, and his wife coming out of work," said Michael Griffith, the American lawyer for Ted, who had originally been appointed to the case through Amnesty International. Griffith, a fast-talking Southhampton-based attorney, rose to fame in the 1970s when he represented Billy Hayes, an American student convicted of smuggling hashish out of Turkey in 1970 and the subject of the Hollywood film *Midnight Express*. Since then, he has specialized in helping Americans who find themselves in legal difficulties abroad through his firm, International Legal Defense Counsel.

On December 3, 1999, those same thugs penetrated the Safra penthouse through an open window, said Ted. He tried to fight them, whacking one of the assailants in the head with a barbell that he used for workouts with Edmond. The second one sliced Ted in the left calf and in the stomach.

As the intruders fled through the open window, Ted frantically warned Edmond and Vivian, who told him to set off the alarm. Ted didn't know how, and so he lit a fire with one of Harry Slatkin's scented candles in the Lucite wastebasket in the nurses' station to set off the fire alarm.

"The only alarm that I knew of was a smoke alarm," said Ted.

Although Ted had four lawyers defending him in Monaco, there seemed little coordination or perceptible strategy in his legal defense, especially as Griffith was denied access to his client two weeks before the trial began in late November 2002. Ted's defense was also hampered by profound disagreements among his legal team. One of his attorneys, Donald Manasse, didn't want Michael Baden, the U.S. forensics expert, to testify at the trial because he thought his testimony would not benefit Ted. "Accusing the victim of having murdered someone would not play favorably on the defense," said Manasse, citing the autopsy report that showed Vivian Torrente had bruises on her body. Manasse also said that Griffith did not appreciate the complexities of the Monaco legal system.

Although Griffith concedes that there are "problems" with Ted's multiple versions of events on December 3, 1999, he still maintains that Ted did not stab himself and that he was indeed the victim of armed intruders.

Griffith, who is used to being at the center of gripping international cases involving socialites, murder, and intrigue, confided that Monaco was a difficult place to be a lawyer. His phones, he says, were constantly tapped, and the legal system is overly complex and Byzantine. He sees Ted's predicament as a violation of human rights, and was planning to take his case to the International Court of Justice.

But the press was no longer interested in the story of Ted Maher's innocence or guilt, even as NBC's *Inside Edition* devoted an hour of prime time in the spring of 2008 to Ted's latest version of events, which now involved high-stakes intrigue with mobsters who wanted Edmond Safra dead.

Following his ordeal in Monaco, Maher's return to the U.S. was a lot less glamorous, a lot less remarkable, even though there were moments of some excitement. Ted spoke of his ordeal to his American legal team, literary agents, and, surprisingly, a representative from the Monaco tourist authority, who all gathered at an upscale Midtown Chinese eatery off Park Avenue to welcome Ted back to the United States in the spring of 2008. Ted was hoping to write a book about his adventures in Monaco, and had even floated the idea to a well-placed literary agent in New York. But in the end, no one was interested in his story, which strained belief and had already been exhaustively told by much of the world's media.

Despite his experience as a nurse, Ted was finding it difficult to find a job. "I went to interviews where they said I had more experience than ten nurses, but then I would get a letter saying I needed more experience, which is why I stopped telling people what happened to me in Monaco."

But even a decade after the fact, it's difficult to hide your identity if you were at the center of the mysterious death of one of the world's wealthiest bankers. A simple Google search of Ted's name provides instant information about his involvement with Edmond Safra.

Ted says he is determined to bury the past and to try to get on with his life. "Why should I stick a knife in my heart by telling the truth about what happened to me?" he said. "I've already been stabbed enough."

When he was interviewed for this book, Ted Maher was living in a trailer and having trouble holding onto his job at the Fountainview Care Center, a nursing home in Waterford, Connecticut, after staff members got wind that he was the American nurse at the center of the Safra scandal. After a few days of working at the Waterford facility, where he was managing seventy-five people, his bosses saw his story on NBC. Ted's protestations of innocence fell on deaf ears in an emergency meeting with upper management at the nursing home. How could they have a convicted arsonist on the staff of a long-term care facility for the elderly? A few days after the meeting at the Fountainview, Ted was fired, despite Griffith's entreaties with the managers of the facility. Although he was a convicted felon in Monaco, Ted's record was relatively clean in the United States.

"America has turned out to be another prison," said Ted, his deep blue eyes flashing in anger. During his first few months in the United States, Ted was convinced that he was being followed by shadowy figures.

Following his return, Ted was prevented by court order from seeing his children in Stormville, whose names had been changed after the divorce from Heidi was finalized in 2006 while he was still in jail. He was arrested by Poughkeepsie police in August 2007 when he ignored a restraining order and tried to see his children. "I came by the area that I knew to be my life," he said. "I was pulled over and put in jail for twenty-four hours because of the restraining order against me." The bail was set at $5,000, which was paid for by Ted's sister Tammy, who remains close to him.

Still, despite the difficulties, he seemed optimistic, quoting his hero Teddy Roosevelt—"You do what you can with what you have where you are"—and working on completing his pilot's license.

"Things aren't so bad in my life," said Ted. "I'm not working at Burger King. I'm not fearful of anything in my life after what I've been through. I can do anything that I put my mind to."

Still, he lives for the day when he can clear his name and get revenge against authorities in Monaco, who "robbed me of 2,886 days of my life."

But the more Ted spoke, the more his stories sounded like fantasy. Which was a good thing for both Lily Safra and the authorities in her new country of citizenship, Monaco.

Epilogue:
"We Know Everything and
We Know Nothing"

⁂

R IO DE JANEIRO'S most prestigious Jewish cemetery is located
off Avenida Brasil, a potholed stretch of highway that passes
through myriad shantytowns and decaying suburban warehouses. It's
a large, sunbaked plot of concrete where the graves are arranged in
orderly rows. The tropical heat and torrential afternoon downpours
in summer have dislodged the concrete in many places, and tough
weeds—some of them dotted with colorful flowers—shoot through
the cracks.

Except for Edmond Safra, who is buried in Geneva, many of the
most important people in Lily Safra's life are buried here at the cemetery everyone calls Caju, after the cashew trees that used to grow in
the outlying district where the cemetery is located.

There is Wolf White Watkins, Lily's father, whose remains occupy
plot number 40. Wolf died in Montevideo in 1962, but he is buried in
the Rio suburbs—an appropriate choice, perhaps, because it was in
those same suburbs that he finally made at least part of the fortune he
had dreamed about as a young man in London. What he didn't know
was that the fame and fortune he so craved in his own life would be
the legacy taken up by his youngest child—the beloved daughter he

had named after his favorite opera star and pushed to marry a rich man. Lily married two rich men, and in the end she amassed a fortune beyond her father's wildest dreams.

Lily's mother, Annita Watkins, managed to get a glimpse of what her very able daughter was capable of doing. She died in 1971 in Rio de Janeiro, two years after Lily inherited Alfredo Monteverde's fabulous fortune and moved to London to protect her interests. Annita is buried nearby, in plot number 424. There are several stones on her grave—no doubt remembrances from "her children, son-in-law, daughters-in-law, cousins and nieces and nephews," who are mentioned in the inscription carved into the stone.

A short way away lie the remains of Wolf and Annita's second son, Daniel. He died of a heart attack in March 2002, unable to enjoy the new apartment he had just bought with his wife, Malvina, across the street from the imperial palace—the summer home of the Brazilian royal family—in Petropolis, a picturesque town nestled in the mountains outside Rio. Malvina lives alone in the apartment overlooking the palace. She refused repeated requests to be interviewed for this book.

Daniel, who was born in 1921, had always been close to Lily even though he was thirteen years older. It was Daniel who was designated as Lily's caretaker. He signed her school reports at the Colegio Anglo-Americano in Rio de Janeiro and pledged that the family would take care of the school's tuition fees. Later, when Lily was an adult, Daniel was charged with all those unpleasant tasks that Lily was perhaps too sensitive to handle on her own. He identified Alfredo Monteverde's body at the Rio morgue and signed the death certificate. It was Daniel who was an important witness when Alfredo made his last will and testament in 1966, and it was Daniel who was named trustee and guardian of Carlinhos in the event of the deaths of both Alfredo and Lily.

Artigas Watkins is also buried at Caju. Artigas, who was six years older than Lily, died in Teresopolis, a mountain town outside Rio where he had a condo, on November 14, 2006. Everyone knew he was close to Alfredo—especially Alfredo's accountants, who were regularly asked to set aside envelopes stuffed with cash for him. To be sure, he was a bona fide employee of Ponto Frio, working as a security guard at one of the company's warehouses in the industrial outskirts of Rio de Janeiro. But Artigas may have made far more than any other security guard in the city. He was constantly at the Ponto Frio offices in downtown Rio or at the house on Rua Icatu. Like his younger sister, Artigas had an appetite for money that seemed insatiable, and he stuck close to Alfredo, who never denied him cash. Lily's imminent divorce from his benefactor no doubt gave him pause. Was he worried about his own future when he heard that Alfredo was planning to divorce his sister? What would happen to him and the rest of the Watkins family without the regular cash infusions from Ponto Frio?

"Artigas practically lived at the office asking Fred for money," said Vera Chvidchenko, Alfredo's secretary from 1960 to 1969. "He was very able when he needed money."

Was it by accident or design that Artigas was at his brother-in-law's home on August 25, 1969, the day he died? According to one of the servants, nobody quite knows what he was doing there that day. Perhaps he needed cash. In any case, he seems to have slipped out before someone fired the two gunshots that killed Alfredo and shattered the stillness of that August afternoon.

Near the entrance of the cemetery, Lily's eldest son, Claudio Cohen, is buried with little Raphael Cohen, her grandson, who died in the car crash on the highway to Angra dos Reis. There are a handful of rocks on the white headstone, perhaps indicating the regular visits of mourners.

Nearby is the grave of Claudio's wife, Evelyne Sigelmann Cohen, whose young son Gabriel effectively became Lily's charge after his mother's death. Evelyne, who worked so diligently to ensure the best for her little boy before her own death, would surely be proud of the young man who is now enrolled in a good East Coast university. Perhaps she would even have found it in her heart to forgive Lily for taking him away from Antonio Negreiros, the man who had become the most important person in her life following Claudio and Raphael's deaths in 1989.

IN THE END, Lily managed to obtain a measure of revenge for the tragedy that befell her eldest son and his family when she fired Simon Alouan from Ponto Frio. Alouan, who is today one of the most successful businessmen in São Paulo, refused to sell his shares in Ponto Frio, and for many years after he left the company, he remained an important fixture in the appliance empire that Alfredo created—a thorn in Lily's side when she tried to sell the company with Carlos in 1998.

At the time, Lily approached Carlos, who was recovering from his terrible accident in Italy, to convince him to join her in the sale. Carlos had endured a difficult relationship with Lily after the death of Alfredo. In an interview at his five-story townhouse in South Kensington, he recently admitted for the first time that he blamed himself for Alfredo's death. It was nine-year-old Carlos who first discovered the body on the afternoon of August 25, 1969, and the event clearly left him traumatized.

"I thought his [Alfredo's] death was my fault, and I thought I was being punished by being sent to boarding school," said Carlos. "I spent my adolescence with psychologists."

He was also extremely upset by Edmond's death, thirty years later. "Since I was thirteen years old, he was my second father," said Carlos, whose relationship with Edmond effectively ended after he married a Muslim in the late 1980s.

Despite Carlos's rather dangerous hobby of collecting and racing vintage Ferraris, the Monteverdes lead a fairly quiet life with their two daughters in London. Isis, a former model, lives the life of a moneyed socialite. She takes art and exercise classes and attends fabulous parties. Every New Year's Eve, the family heads to Mauritius to celebrate with their society friends Lee Radziwill, the younger sister of Jacqueline Kennedy Onassis, famed interior designer Nicky Haswell, and the Picassos.

According to Isis, Lily, whom she refers to formally as Madame Safra, has been a very good grandmother to her two girls. "I respect her," said Isis about her mother-in-law. "But my family is me, Carlos, the girls and that's it."

But there's nothing like a business opportunity to bring families back together. Since Alouan sold his minority shares in Ponto Frio two years ago, Lily has been eager to sell her part in the company. In March 2009, she again teamed up with her stepson to sell their combined interests in the company. Despite a worldwide recession, Lily and Carlos managed to sell Ponto Frio in June 2009 to Brazilian supermarket magnate Abilio dos Santos Diniz for just over $400 million.

Perhaps it wasn't the best deal they could have made for Alfredo's old company, but they must have felt a sense of relief to see it go. For years, Carlos admitted he had only a passing interest in his father's old company. "Sometimes I call to find out about the business, but my big preoccupation is to strengthen the foundation, extending the primary education component," he said in an interview. "It's my way of contributing to my country."

Maria Consuelo Ayres, the first employee Alfredo hired when he started Globex in 1946, managed that foundation until her death in February 2009. The nonagenarian secretary was in charge of the Alfredo João Monteverde Foundation, the philanthropic organization he set up for the company's workers, providing them with health care, educational opportunities, and recreation for their families. Today, the foundation helps more than nine thousand of the company's employees spread out over 370 stores throughout Brazil.

Maria Consuelo was extremely loyal to Alfredo, but she was a corporate survivor, and after his death, when she saw that Lily was firmly in charge of the company, Maria Consuelo toed the line. She helped organize Alfredo's funeral, looking the other way when Geraldo Mattos was forced to make certain financial "contributions" to avoid undue scrutiny and publicity. Still, Maria Consuelo was clearly conflicted in her old age. She never believed that Alfredo really would have killed himself, but she could not contemplate any other scenario.

So she continued to show her devotion to Alfredo by working diligently at the foundation. She also sought to protect Carlos's interests in Brazil. She held his power of attorney in the country and represented him at Ponto Frio board meetings that he was too busy to attend. For years, she tried to track down information about Carlos's birth family in Rio.

"Maybe if you find them, I can help them in some way," Carlos had told her. But the task was simply too complicated even for the very able Maria Consuelo. By the end of the custody trials in Brazil and England in the early 1970s, Maria Consuelo had tracked down several birth certificates for Carlos.

To show their respect for her loyal services, Ponto Frio executives provided Maria Consuelo with a company car and driver, who would pick her up every day from her apartment in northern Rio and take her to Ponto Frio's suburban offices. Maria Consuelo, a heavyset woman whose girth caused her to take pained, deliberate steps, worked at the company until her death at ninety-two. She needed the job, she said, because she was the sole support of her younger sister, who suffered from Alzheimer's disease.

Today, Maria Consuelo lies in the Catholic cemetery adjacent to the old Jewish burial ground at Caju. Her remains lie in a vault in a high-rise tower, an ingenious effort on the part of cemetery directors to accommodate as many people as possible.

Despite all her hard work for Ponto Frio, few of the company's top executives attended her funeral or memorial mass in Rio de Janeiro. Only the old Ponto Frio accountant, Ademar Trotte, now an elderly man who manages his own firm on gritty Avenida Venezuela across from the federal police building in downtown Rio, attended the funeral along with Conrado Gruenbaum, Alfredo's old attorney.

With Maria Consuelo's passing, Conrado is the last of the old guard at Ponto Frio. Alfredo brought him into the company in 1957. Now well into his seventies, Conrado is a thin, wiry, and elegant man, who is bronzed from all the time he spends walking on the beach near his home in Rio. He is the director of the Rio Association of Store Owners, a powerful local business group located a few blocks from Ponto Frio's first store on Rua Uruguaiana, which today occupies nearly a whole city block next to the teeming old Arab market.

When I interviewed him in 2008, Conrado refused to answer any questions about Alfredo or Ponto Frio, where he still worked a few days a week. When I asked him about Alfredo's death and the version of events that he related to police on August 25, 1969, Conrado smiled and answered every question the same way: "It's off the record," he repeated. "I can't say."

By contrast, Vera Chvidchenko, Alfredo's secretary in the 1960s, had a great deal to say. For the first time in more than four decades, she spoke about her visit to the coroner's office the day after Alfredo died. "I never believed that Fred committed suicide," said Vera in an interview at her office in Rio. Neither, it seems, did the coroner, who did not find gunpowder residue on his hands, and who told Vera that if Alfredo did commit suicide, the shots that entered his thorax could only have been fired with his left hand. But somewhere along the way to the police station or the coroner's office or both, money changed hands, Vera said.

Shortly after Alfredo died, Vera left Ponto Frio to study law. She said she soured on the company after its director Geraldo Mattos forced her to sign over a building that she had purchased on Alfredo's behalf in downtown Rio. Alfredo, who put up the cash, asked her to put the deed in her name for tax reasons. "Of course, I could have demanded a great deal of money to surrender the building after he died, but I didn't ask for anything," said Vera, who still works as a senior partner in a downtown law firm. "I was just completely disgusted with everything they did with the company after Fred died. I didn't want to be a part of it anymore."

But Vera holds no grudge against Lily and is grateful for the bottles of perfume that Lily gives her every time she comes to Brazil on a visit, which is not often anymore.

In the end, even Geraldo Mattos didn't have the stomach for the new Ponto Frio. Geraldo, who was summoned to meetings in Geneva with Edmond after Alfredo died, didn't like what he was seeing. The meetings were held in a boardroom of Edmond Safra's Trade Development Bank. Edmond sat next to a shredder and regularly destroyed his memos to the Brazilian company in Geraldo's presence.

Although he once promised Alfredo that he would stay with the company until Carlos turned twenty-one, Geraldo tendered his resignation to Lily and Edmond in Geneva in March 1974, less than five years after Alfredo died. "This is the last trip that I make to Geneva," he wrote on an airline menu, which his daughter Sonia found amongst his old papers when he died. "This is a decisive moment in my life. I believe that what I should have done, I did. I want to continue to be successful and to create something for my children."

Lily called Geraldo her "thief-director" because he had held onto several million dollars worth of shares that were signed over to him by Alfredo when he was in a state of euphoria. Geraldo's family denied that this was the case, but did acknowledge that part of his job after Alfredo died was to send profits from the company offshore to an account that his widow controlled.

"My father was in charge of Ponto Frio after Fred died, but the new owners treated him badly," said Geraldo's daughter Sonia.

With the $5 million in a settlement that he was able to obtain from the company after his resignation, Geraldo, a balding, heavyset executive with a perfectly trimmed mustache, opened his own small chain of appliance stores in Rio. Although he was successful for a few years, he sold the firm to a businessman who, unbeknownst to him, was tied to Edmond Safra. The businessman refused to pay, and Geraldo spent the rest of his life in costly litigation. He never told his family that he had lost everything; they found out after his death when they had to pay tens of thousands of dollars in remaining litigation fees.

Laurinda Soares Navarro also feels that she lost everything after the death of her beloved boss. Although Lily had asked Alfredo's old housekeeper to accompany her to London, Laurinda politely declined. She needed to look after her two sons, Adilson and Ademir. But a few years after Alfredo died, Laurinda lost Ademir to an assassin's bullet—a victim of the drug violence that now regularly rips through Rio de Janeiro's teeming favelas. Today Laurinda, who recently retired from her cleaning job at Rio's Catholic University, lives alone in a small apartment on the outskirts of Rio de Janeiro, attended by her son Adilson, a taxi driver, who still lives in the old favela with his own family. When I interviewed her for this book, Laurinda, seventy-seven, had tears in her eyes when she spoke about Seu Alfredo, and kissed one of the black-and-white photographs from the autopsy that I showed her.

"We know everything and we know nothing," was how she summed up August 25, 1969, the day Alfredo died and the day her life changed forever.

TODAY, THE HOUSE on Rua Icatu that was the scene of so much tragedy in 1969 is full of life again. Marcelo and Klara Steinfeld, who bought the house from Lily, raised their children there, and after Klara's death, Marcelo married a younger, lively Argentine woman who spends a great deal of her time tending the garden and grooming the couple's dogs. The Steinfelds are not fazed by the events that took place in their master bedroom four decades earlier, although they concede that Lily's life has been marked by "too much tragedy" since Alfredo's death.

The street itself has probably changed little from Alfredo's day.

It is still a quiet neighborhood of lush mango trees, dotted by color-ful orchids and hibiscus, where tamarind monkeys stop in bemused attention to stare at passersby as they climb up the mountain. Some of the houses are bigger, though, and they are set back behind large mechanized wrought-iron gates, monitored by doormen carrying walkie-talkies—a sign of the violence that has gripped the city in the years since Alfredo's death.

SEVERAL YEARS AFTER Edmond's death Lily sold the Monaco pent-house that she had so painstakingly decorated with mirrored walls covered in peach-colored treillage at the entrance and faux Fragonard murals and swans hand-painted on the elevator doors. Although she now identifies herself as a citizen of Monaco (Brazil has been con-veniently forgotten) and still uses the principality as her home base, nobody could blame her for selling off the penthouse, with its terrible memories of the fire and Edmond's death.

But despite her attempts to liquidate the recent past, it haunts her still, mostly in the unanswered questions that remain after Ted Ma-her's trial in 2002. "It was never explained satisfactorily why she [Lily] had taken the keys to the apartment away from all the em-ployees shortly before the tragedy," wrote Dominick Dunne. "The greatest unexplained question will always be why there was no guard on duty that night since the Safras maintained a private cadre of 11 guards trained by the Mossad."

A decade later, it is impossible to corroborate anything Maher has said. Were there intruders in the apartment? It's impossible to say since the surveillance tapes were mysteriously erased. Did Ted act alone or was he a pawn of a much bigger conspiracy?

Over the years, Ted's statements about December 3, 1999, became so confused that it's impossible to say with any certainty what exactly took place on that winter morning in one of the world's most privi-leged and security-obsessed enclaves.

For their part, Edmond's brothers and sisters want nothing to do with Monaco. Edmond's death still weighs heavily on them a decade after his passing. "It was a really stupid death," said one family member who did not want to be identified. "What can I say? Nobody investigated. Nobody found anything. To this day, we are still disgusted with everything that happened. No one in the family has returned to Monaco since the trial, and we will never return there."

And what of relations with their billionaire sister-in-law, Lily Safra? Hard to say, since the Safras have never spoken about her publicly. The cryptic press release they issued after Edmond's death was the first and last word on the woman they are still linked to in name.

But only in name.

"Every family has issues, but everything is settled now," said the Safra family member, matter-of-factly. "There was no court; everything was settled out of court."

For Samuel Bendahan, Lily's third husband, little was ever settled—in a court or outside of one. Bendahan, now seventy-four, has spent a lifetime trying to figure out why his fairy-tale marriage came apart at the seams. His answer? Edmond Safra, the man he says ruined his entire life. Bendahan claims that the stress he suffered when he was jailed in New York and the protracted legal actions that followed were directly responsible for the onset of his stomach cancer.

Strangely, he feels no ill will towards his former wife, who he believes was simply forced to do Edmond's bidding because of the large sum of money she had inherited from Alfredo and which Edmond controlled. After the end of the lawsuits against him, Bendahan retreated to his property in southern Spain. He never married. His goal in speaking so openly about his former wife is his own public redemption. He was not the "gigolo" third husband of Lily Safra, but a businessman from a distinguished Jewish family who fell in love with a young widow who was once also passionate about him.

"Even I am [now] surprised about how little I knew about Lily's past," wrote Bendahan in an e-mail. "In computer parlance, what I saw is what I got, and what I saw was most pleasing and fulfilling. Our time together was far too good to have to rely on 'What was your favorite subject at school? What was he like in bed?'"

Following the settlement of all the other lawsuits against Lily after Edmond's death, Lily turned to other matters. For years there were rumors that she had received offers to sell her villa in the south of France. In one of the earliest rumors, Microsoft chairman Bill Gates was said to be interested in the property. Then the Russian oligarchs got involved. Press reports recounted how she had sold the property to Roman Abramovich, Russian billionaire and owner of the Chelsea Football Club. But the rumors proved to be false.

However, the home was provisionally sold to another Russian billionaire before the worldwide recession put a dent in Lily's plans. In 2008, Lily reached a deal with Mikhail Prokhorov, who offered her $500 million for the estate—a staggering sum of money that would have made La Leopolda the world's most expensive residential property. Prokhorov, the former owner of Norilsk Nickel, put down a 10 percent deposit in the summer of 2008 but backed out of the deal in February 2009. He demanded his deposit back after he lost money in the severe economic downturn, but Lily refused. For her part, she had not wanted to sell the house at any price but reached an agreement after repeated requests on Prokhorov's behalf. At first, Prokhorov said no deal was made, but the *Financial Times* found a deposit from a subsidiary of a company called Atenaco, which Prokhorov controlled.

Prokhorov, a self-made billionaire, was no stranger to controversy. In January 2007, he was detained by French police in the ski resort of Courchevel in a case of suspected high-class prostitution although no charges were brought against him.

Lily, who had already moved out the furniture and had agreed to a penalty if she reneged on the deal, refused to be moved by the economic crisis and the Russian billionaire's economic woes. In a press release, she noted that she would not return Prokhorov's deposit. She said that she would distribute the $55 million to numerous charities, including the Michael J. Fox Foundation for Parkinson's Research in New York (€2 million) and the Claude Pompidou Institute for Alzheimer's Disease in Nice (€8 million). Her biggest contribution of €10 million was destined for Harvard University, for the Edmond J. Safra Foundation Center for Ethics.

"By transforming the purchase deposit into an act of giving, I would like to encourage all who can do so to support medical research, patient care, education and other important humanitarian causes during these times of economic uncertainty," she said in a press release.

Dividing her time between her apartment in New York City and homes in London and Monaco, Lily continues to give generously to her pet causes and is a regular fixture at society events in Europe and New York. Through the Edmond J. Safra Philanthropic Foundation, which she has chaired since Edmond's death, she is an important supporter of medical research into cancer, AIDS, and humanitarian relief and education around the world. She endowed the Edmond J. Safra Foundation Center for Ethics at Harvard and has given away more than 16,000 scholarships to needy students in Israel for university education since the 1977 founding of the International Sephardic Education Foundation, the charity she created with Edmond and Nina Weiner.

Lily was a lead supporter of the American Red Cross's relief effort in New Orleans after the 2005 hurricane. Her support allowed Dillard University in New Orleans to offer temporary classes in the aftermath of the hurricane and helped the school rebuild the campus for the fall 2006 semester. She is a member of the board of the Michael J. Fox Foundation for Parkinson's Research and she financed the construction of the Safra Family Lodge at the National Institutes of Health in Bethesda, Maryland, in 2005. The Safra Family Lodge, an English arts and crafts manor surrounded by a beautiful garden, provides a retreat for the families of patients who are receiving care at the clinical center. The garden is named after Claudio and Evelyne Cohen, and includes a fountain dedicated to the memory of Raphael Cohen, Lily's grandson.

Lily's generosity has been honored all over the world. In 2004, the French government gave her the rank of Commandeur in the Ordre des arts et des lettres and a year later she was named a Chevalier de la Legion d'honneur by then president Jacques Chirac. She is an honorary fellow of King's College London and the Courtauld Institute of Art, whose programs she has generously supported. She also holds honorary doctorates from Hebrew University of Jerusalem and Brandeis University, where she established the Lily Safra Internship Program at the Hadassah-Brandeis Institute, which allows six undergraduates and two graduate students to conduct research in Jewish and women's studies every summer.

In the United States, she supports a myriad of community organizations and is a member of the Chairman's Council of the Museum of Modern Art, the Kennedy Center's International Committee on the Arts, and a trustee of the Museum of Jewish Heritage in New York. In Washington, she established the Edmond J. Safra Visiting Professorship at the National Gallery of Art.

She is a regal presence at philanthropic galas, where she inevitably shows up in gorgeous couture, her short hair beautifully styled. With no man in her life these days (at least no one she is ever seen with publicly), the grand dame now appears at many events accompanied by her granddaughter, who is beautiful and blonde and whose name also is Lily. At other events, she has been photographed with her daughter, Adriana, and her other grandchildren. Her son Eduardo, who owns an antiques business in the more fashionable part of Buenos Aires, is absent from any recent photos, although he appeared at Ponto Frio's sixtieth-anniversary celebrations in Rio de Janeiro in 2006. He was pictured in the Rio society columns, among the city's glitterati, wearing a Ponto Frio T-shirt at the company party that drew hundreds of people.

In spite of the money and glamour, the parties and charities, and her public profile, the life of Lily Watkins Cohen Monteverde Bendahan Safra has had more than its share of tragedy. The woman herself remains inscrutable.

"DO YOU KNOW Dona Lily?"

The question was directed to no one in particular. Marcos, the tall, sunburned administrator of the Caju cemetery, put a hand up to his forehead to shield his eyes from the blistering afternoon sunshine.

Marcos hails from Lebanon and claims to have gone to school with Edmond Safra. He says he has repeatedly tried to get in touch with Lily Safra over the years through her son-in-law, Michel Elia, who used to oversee Ponto Frio. Yes, he knows that these are very busy and important people, but they owe a sacred duty to the dead, he says. The headstones of the Watkins, Cohens, and Monteverdes all need upkeep. It costs little more than $50 to clean a headstone, $15 to re-carve each of the fading letters, he said.

"They haven't paid anything in years, and look at the headstones now," said Marcos, who wore a yarmulke and short-sleeved, button-down shirt as he took a visitor through the Caju cemetery. "The stones are dirty and falling apart. Some of the letters need to be re-done. They all need to be cleaned. What am I supposed to do?"

Marcos stopped at the grave of Alfredo Monteverde, which is situated a short distance from the graves of the Watkins family towards the back of the cemetery. The headstone of Lily's second husband, whose death became the seminal event in her life, is dirty and the letters are fading.

Alfredo's remains lie close to those of his mother, Regina Rebecca Monteverde, who died in 1976, the same year that Lily finally married Edmond Safra in a low-key ceremony in Geneva. After the death of her beloved son, Regina was a broken woman. She tried everything to investigate what she always believed to be his murder, and tried to prevent her former daughter-in-law from taking over Globex, which Regina always considered a family company because it was built from the gold that the Monteverdes brought to Brazil from Romania.

"Even though she could be really nasty to Fred, he was really her whole life," said Alfredo's old secretary Vera, who remained close to Regina until her death. "He was the most important thing in her world."

He was also the most important man in Lily's life—even more significant than her father and Edmond Safra. Although they were married for just over four years, Lily inherited a vast family fortune that enabled her to live the fairy tale she had dreamed of when she was a teenager in a lilac organza dress, hoping to catch the eye of a young man with money at the CIB socials. It was only after Alfredo's sudden death that Lily was quickly able to launch herself into the rarefied world of couture gowns and sumptuous parties on two continents.

Despite his immense importance in the course of Lily's life and his dominance of Rio business circles in the 1960s, Alfredo Monteverde has been largely forgotten. There were only two stones on his tombstone when I visited recently, which probably means that he has had few visitors at the cemetery.

But in 2007, Alfredo enjoyed a renaissance of sorts. Across town from the gritty cemetery, in a well-appointed Copacabana apartment, an elderly woman with a continental accent gathered up a bundle of T-shirts, all of them with a silk-screened impression of Alfredo Monteverde. The photo of the founder of Ponto Frio was taken when he was a young man, on the ski slopes in Switzerland or France. He is suntanned and handsome, his gaze full of hope and possibility.

The elderly woman, who prefers to remain anonymous, has poured thousands of dollars into keeping Alfredo's memory alive. When Ponto Frio celebrated its sixtieth anniversary in 2006, few of the current executives thought to honor the founder. So she rented airplanes to fly giant banners that featured two penguins, the Ponto Frio mascot, proclaiming, "They've forgotten our founder." The planes flew over Rio's beaches on the weekends, when they would be crowded with sunbathers. The woman also took out full-page ads in the country's biggest newspapers with the same message.

"All of this is costing me so much that I had to sell one of my Picassos to put all of it together," said the woman with a wink as she examined the hundreds of white T-shirts that she planned personally to distribute through Rio de Janeiro's poorest communities.

In a country of nearly 200 million people, it might have appeared a feeble gesture to raise awareness of a man, long dead, who had built a massive fortune but never forgot the poor. But to those who knew him and loved him, Alfredo Monteverde was no ordinary man. And his death, which has never been investigated to their satisfaction, still weighs on them, even more than forty years after the fact.

When the first full-page ad of the Alfredo remembrance campaign was published in *O Globo*, Victor Sztern, who was a young man of seventeen when Alfredo died, bought a copy and headed to the cemetery at Caju. Victor, a heavyset businessman who is in his late fifties and owns his own coffee export business in Rio, has never forgotten the man who took him under his wing when his own parents died. Victor placed a copy of the newspaper on top of Alfredo's grave and said a prayer.

The newspaper was not allowed to remain on Alfredo's tombstone for long. Marcos's assistants at Caju cleaned it up before it joined the refuse that makes its way into the cemetery from passing cars and mourners.

"We would clean up the rest of these graves, if we could get a hold of Dona Lily or Michel Elia," said Marcos, who was growing increasingly annoyed as he finished his tour of the graves.

But for now, at least, the graves of the people who were so important in the plot of the great novel that has been the billionaire widow's life so far remain unkempt, neglected, and forgotten.

According to Marcos's calculations, Lily Safra owes the cemetery just over $3,000, and he's not about to continue the upkeep of the graves until the lady pays up.

Acknowledgments

I CAUGHT A GLIMPSE of Dominick Dunne on the first day of the Sotheby's auction of property from the collections of Lily and Edmond J. Safra in New York. In his tortoiseshell glasses and impeccably tailored English suit, he appeared to be deeply absorbed in the catalogue, which featured exquisite European furniture and objets d'art. But upon closer inspection, he was really surveying the crowd for the moneyed glitterati he regularly covered for *Vanity Fair*.

It was November 2005, and I was preparing to leave for Brazil to begin the research for this book. Dominick had already been writing about Lily and the events in Monaco for at least five years. Standing outside the auction room on the second floor of Sotheby's on York Avenue, I resolved that I was not going to speak to him until my own work on Lily Safra was complete. I didn't want to be influenced by his reporting; I wanted to be discreet.

Three years later we met at a dinner, and Dominick was keen to talk about Lily, whom he found endlessly fascinating. I demurred, but a year later we met again and agreed to meet for lunch at Patroon in Midtown Manhattan, where I tentatively handed him part of the manuscript for this book. Our lunches turned into a routine. He always arrived early and would be seated at his table, observing the well-dressed lunchtime crowd, many of whom stopped by to pay their respects to the legendary journalist and author. Over lobster rolls and Diet Cokes, we talked about the Safra case and other stories we were both following. He spoke about his own book *Too Much Money*, which he was in the process of editing, and which was based on real-life Manhattan socialites.

Lingering over espresso, I summoned up the nerve to hand him a manila envelope with the remaining chapters of my book. I was encouraged by his enthusiastic response to what he had read so far. After lunch, I walked him the few blocks to his apartment on East Forty-ninth Street. It was the last time I saw him. He seemed tired and weak, so I blurted out the only thing I could think of that might make him feel better.

"We all have to keep going," I told him. "We all have to keep searching for the truth."

He perked up right away, and took my hand: "You betcha," he said. "But, it's up to you now."

Three weeks later, in late August 2009, Dominick Dunne passed away after a long battle with bladder cancer. I handed in the manuscript to my publisher. I remain forever grateful to him for his generosity and confidence in me.

THE RESEARCH FOR this book was often frustrating and logistically challenging, taking place on three continents. In Rio de Janeiro, my efforts were often confounded by officious bureaucrats and messy archives. I can no longer remember how many times I trudged to the Instituto Médico Legal, the coroner's office in the down-at-heels Lapa neighborhood, in search of Alfredo Monteverde's autopsy report. First, I was told that the 1969 documents did not exist. On another visit, I was told they did exist, but that they were on microfilm. However, I couldn't view the microfilm because the machine was broken. When I offered them a hefty deposit to take the film elsewhere for viewing, they refused. They also refused my repeated offers to pay for the repair of the machine. As with most things in Brazil, at the moment you lose faith that anything will work in your favor, that's when things magically turn around. And so the Brazilian magic—the *jeitinho brasileiro*—worked for me a year into my research when the autopsy report, complete with detailed police photographs of the corpse, materialized after a chance encounter with a young lawyer.

I am a great believer in that Brazilian *jeitinho*—the magic that saw me through four difficult years of research. I am deeply thankful to my neighbor in Copacabana, Gastão Veiga, who vividly recalled his old neighbor and business associate Wolf White Watkins and Lily as a young woman. Rio socialite Ruth de Almeida Prado was also very helpful, and I will never forget interviewing this aged grande dame in her sprawling penthouse, across the street from the Copacabana Palace Hotel, as she sat riveted to a Formula One race on television.

I also want to thank the staff of the National Archives in Rio de Janeiro, who met my difficult requests for information with good humor and rare efficiency. The staff of the Colegio Anglo-Americano, particularly the school's de facto historian Renée Grossman, generously gave me access to old school records.

Although many people I tried to interview simply refused to speak about the Safra and Monteverde families, others were extremely generous with their time and stories. Maria Consuelo Ayres, president of the Fundação Alfredo Monteverde, was one of these sources, and she spoke to me at length about the early days of Ponto Frio, and the events of August 25, 1969. Thank you to Albert Nasser, Ana Bentes Bloch, Al Abitbol, Victor Sztern, Lourdes Mattos, Sonia Mattos, Rosy Fanto, Masha Monterosa, and Guilherme Castello Branco for their stories of Alfredo, Lily, Edmond, and their families. Marcelo Steinfeld opened up his home on Icatu Street in Rio and allowed me to wander through the second-floor master suite where Alfredo Monteverde spent his final moments.

I am greatly indebted to Laurinda Soares Navarro for welcoming me into her home on several occasions and reliving some of the most traumatic events of her life.

There were dozens of others in both Brazil and Argentina who were extremely helpful with contacts and making introductions to the rarefied universe of South American high society. I am grateful to them and to the medical examiners and retired police officers who guided me through autopsy and ballistics reports in Rio. They are not named here at their own request.

My dear friend Nélida Piñón was an inspiration and a support, and, when I was writing the manuscript, provided me with an office that had a spectacular view of Rio.

Samuel Bendahan, Lily's third husband, was a great source of insight and information. He was extremely patient and generous with his time, and brutally honest about his own life with Lily. I thank him for trusting me to tell his story for the first time.

In New York, I relied on several sources who wish to remain anonymous.

Eli Attia, Edmond's architect, was extremely generous with his time. Michael Griffith, one of Ted Maher's attorneys, was always ready to answer trial-related questions. I am also grateful to Ted Maher for his cooperation and to the other members of his legal team in Monaco.

At HarperCollins, I want to thank Claire Wachtel for her vision and careful editing. I am also very grateful to Julia Novitch and Beth Silfin. For years, David Kilgour has been a brilliant editor and good friend. I thank him for seeing me through this book. Thanks also to my agent Dorian Karchmar and my good friends Serena French, Jean McNeil, Sasha Josipovicz, and Milosh Pavlovicz.

Lauren Ramsby, my first editor at the *New York Post*, has been a great supporter of me and my work. Thank you also to Steve Lynch, Paul McPolin, and all of my colleagues at the Sunday *Post*, who are among the finest journalists I have ever encountered.

I am also grateful to Kenneth Whyte, editor and publisher of *Macleans*, who published my news stories from South America during the critical years of research for this book. Thank you also to Priscilla

Painton, formerly of *Time*, for her encouragement, and to Deborah Frank at *Departures* and Jeffries Blackerby at the *New York Times*.

Finally, I want to thank my family, who encouraged the move to the other end of the world during the research for this book, even though the frustrations and challenges of life in a foreign country often seemed overwhelming.

Notes

INTRODUCTION: "THE PLOT OF A GREAT NOVEL"

1 *The drama that would lead to the death of Edmond Safra*: Transcripts of Ted Maher's trial in Monaco, Le Tribunal Criminel de la Principauté de Monaco, November 21, 2002. Testimony of Pierre Picquenot, "Death in Monaco," Dominick Dunne, *Vanity Fair*, December 2000.

4 *"Enemies?"*: Marcelo Steinfeld, interview by author, October 17, 2007.

4 *"Telephone calls between third parties and the occupants"*: Edmond Safra's autopsy report, Court of the First Instance of Monaco, Office of the Attorney General, December 5, 1999.

5 *"I saw their relationship"*: Eli Attia, interview by author, January 6, 2008.

6 *"he would telephone his far-flung business associates"*: "Death in Monte Carlo," *The Economist*, December 11, 1999.

6 *"a slim blonde charmer"*: New York Post, March 12, 1981.

6 *"Lily answered a toast from her host"*: New York Post, March 12, 1981.

7 *Mehle wrote that Lily and her friend Lynn Wyatt*: Aileen Mehle, Suzy, *Women's Wear Daily*, April 4, 1997.

7 *Brooke Astor "wore her sable hat"*: Aileen Mehle, Suzy, *Women's Wear Daily*, February 2, 1994.

7 *The Safras had "exquisite taste"*: Aileen Mehle, Suzy, *Women's Wear Daily*, September 13, 1996.

7 *"perhaps the most beautiful home in all of London"*: Aileen Mehle, Suzy, *Women's Wear Daily*, July 25, 2001.

7 *"one of the most wonderful private houses on the Cote d'Azur"*: Aileen Mehle, Suzy, *Women's Wear Daily*, September 3, 1996.

8 *"Lily was an extremely generous woman"*: Vera Contrucci Pinto Dias, interview by author, October 16, 2007.

8 *on behalf of the Alzheimer's Association*: Details of the Alzheimer's Association's Rita Hayworth Gala from the organization's auction catalogue, *A Sparkling Silver Celebration*. The event took place at the Waldorf-Astoria hotel in New York City, October 28, 2008.

9 *"I think that since childhood her dreams"*: Samuel Bendahan, interview by author, October 2, 2007.

9   *"Every girl dreams of her Prince Charming"*: Ana Bentes Bloch, interview by author, March 11, 2009.

10   *Ted Maher's agreement . . . reads*: The confidentiality agreement is dated August 16, 1999, and signed by Anthony Brittan. It was widely quoted in press reports and also used as an exhibit at his 2002 trial in Monaco.

11   *"Lily Safra litigates with a bottomless pit"*: Lady Colin Campbell, interview by author, August 30, 2008.

14   *"Those who were there at the scene"*: The press statement issued by the São Paulo branch of the Safra family was widely quoted in press reports following the Maher verdict in December 2002.

14   *"This story is all about money, power, and corruption"*: Ted Maher, interview by author, March 5, 2008.

15   *"I don't know how she has coped"*: Carlos Monteverde quoted in "A Nora de Lily," Bruno Astuto, *RG Vogue*, November 2007. Translated from the Portuguese by the author.

15   *"She is really the prettiest of women"*: Aileen Mehle, Suzy, *Women's Wear Daily*, April 29, 1992.

16   *"I have always believed"*: Gastaõ Veiga, interview by author, April 26, 2006.

ONE: "THE MOST ELEGANT GIRL"

17   *"Lily was a social climber"*: Gastaõ Veiga, interview by author, April 26, 2006.

22   *"He made a tidy fortune"*: Marcelo Steinfeld, interview by author, October 17, 2007.

24   *"For ten years we have worked with Mr. Watkins"*: Hilmar Tavares da Silva, October 12, 1950. Da Silva's letter to federal authorities is part of the Watkins family's application for Brazilian citizenship, National Archives, Rio de Janeiro. Translated from the Portuguese by the author.

27   *In "Description of the Engraving," Lily wrote*: Lily Watkins, school papers, Colegio Anglo-Americano, Rio de Janeiro. Translated from the Portuguese by the author.

27   *"She was a beautiful girl"*: Ana Bentes Bloch, interview by author, March 11, 2009.

30   *"I can easily say that Lily was the most beautiful and the most elegant debutante"*: Lygia Hazan Gomlevsky, interview by author, March 13, 2009.

30   *"Lily used to wear the most exquisite dresses"*: Ana Bentes Bloch, interview by author, March 11, 2009.

32   *"Her parents must have been"*: Ana Bentes Bloch, ibid.

TWO: "EVERYTHING IN ITS PLACE"

43   *"Fred was an incredible businessman"*: Victor Sztern, interview by author, August 22, 2006.

43   *"Fred was brilliant"*: Gastão Veiga, interview by author, April 26, 2006.

43   *"We'd be on his boat"*: Vera Contrucci Pinto Dias, interview by author, October 16, 2007.

43   *"one of the most important figures in commerce and industry"*: Editorial, *Luta Democratica*, August 26, 1969.

44   *"I do not get tired, as I work with great pleasure"*: Alfredo Monteverde to Rosy Fanto, October 8, 1950.

45   *"Sometimes we had people who would come into the office"*: Maria Consuelo Ayres, interview by author, August 27, 2006.

47   *At the Millfield School*: Charles Greville, "When it comes to Raising Funds, They Certainly Know All There is To Know About it At Millfield," publication and date unknown.

48   *"I spent a lot of time undoing Fred's whims"*: Ademar Trotte, interview by author, March 12, 2009.

48   *"Geraldo had a difficult time"*: Lourdes Mattos, September 13, 2006.

50   *For despite his phenomenal success*: letter from Alfredo Monteverde to Rosy Fanto, July 2, 1956.

50   *"The women arrived at Fred's house"*: Rosy Fanto, interview by author, July 27, 2006.

50   *"Sylvia is wonderful"*: Alfredo Monteverde to Rosy Fanto, October 8, 1950.

51   *"We never understood Fred's attraction to Sylvia"*: Maria Luisa Goldschmid, interview by author, October 25, 2007.

51   *"Fred drove right through reception"*: Maria Luisa Goldschmid, ibid.

51   *"Fred fell in love with an image"*: Rosy Fanto, interview by author, July 27, 2006.

52   *"We'd be playing poker at his penthouse"*: Al Abitbol, interview by author, September 20, 2006.

52   *"He was a crazy genius"*: Marcelo Steinfeld, interview by author, October 17, 2007.

52   *"Every woman in Rio turned her head"*: Alvaro Pães, interview by author, May 8, 2006.

54   *"We set up the store as part of Fred's larger company"*: Ademar Trotte, interview by author, March 12, 2009.

54   *"She had the best of everything in her store"*: Vera Contrucci Pinto Dias, interview by author, October 16, 2007.

55   *"They were never among the first team"*: Danuza Leão, interview by author, March 11, 2009.

57   *"He could move heaven and earth for the people he loved"*: Victor Sztern, interview by author, August 22, 2006.

57   *"Money was just paper to her"*: Al Abitbol, interview by author, September, 20, 2006.

58   *"Fernando didn't even think of charging them"*: Vera Contrucci Pinto Dias, interview by author, October 16, 2007.

58   *"Regina always said that Fred"*: Masha Monterosa, interview by author, November 7, 2006.

58   *"We finally thought Fred had found the best woman"*: Maria Luisa Goldschmid, interview by author, October 25, 2007.

58   *Whenever brother and sister were together*: Rosy Fanto, interview by author, July 27, 2006.

59   *"Rosy, dear, as usual I am filling a whole letter"*: Alfredo Monteverde to Rosy Fanto, July 2, 1956.

60   *"I want to be able to walk a short distance"*: Laurinda Soares Navarro, interview by author, May 11, 2007.

62   *"If I'm not staying, no one else is going to stay"*: Laurinda Soares Navarro, interview by author, May 11, 2007.

62   *"Tell me"*: Maria Consuelo Ayres, interview by author, August 27, 2006.

62   *"Fred commented to my husband"*: Lourdes Mattos, interview by author, September, 13, 2006.

63   *"Shortly before Fred died Regina told me"*: Masha Monterosa, interview by author, November 7, 2006.

63   *"It was a bit of creative accounting"*: Ademar Trotte, interview by author, March 12, 2009.

64   *"But it was the wrong thing to do"*: Laurinda Soares Navarro, interview by author, May 11, 2007.

THREE: "SHE BEHAVED BEAUTIFULLY"

Much of this chapter relies on information found in the police report on Alfredo Monteverde, August 25, 1969, Tenth District Precinct, Rio de Janeiro Police. Translated from the Portuguese by the author.

67   *"Seu Artigas was at the house"*: Laurinda Soares Navarro, interview by author, May 11, 2007.

67   *"He wasn't in one of his depressions"*: Maria Consuelo Ayres, interview by author, August 27, 2006.

68   *"He told my husband"*: Lourdes Mattos, interview by author, September 13, 2006.

68   *Most of Alfredo's executive team at Ponto Frio*: Lourdes Mattos, ibid.

68   *"I know that Lily did not accept the divorce"*: Maria Consuelo Ayres, interview by author, August 27, 2006.

69   *Although they were by no means destitute*: Maria Consuelo Ayres, ibid.

70   *Had he mixed his medications with the Mandrax*: Laurinda Soares Navarro, interview by author, May 8, 2007.

71   *"My father is dead. He's angry"*: Laurinda Soares Navarro, ibid.

72   *Laurinda saw Lily stop to open the drawer*: Laurinda Soares Navarro, ibid.

72   *It was the elevator operator*: Vera Chvidchenko, interview by author, January 28, 2008. Chvidchenko described the scene at the Ponto Frio offices after the staff found out about Alfredo's death.

73 *"I saw Fred stretched out on the bed"*: Ademar Trotte, interview by author, March 12, 2009.

74 *The Ponto Frio executives who assembled at the house*: Lourdes Mattos, interview by author, September 13, 2006; Maria Consuelo Ayres, interview by author, August 27, 2006.

75 *It would be several hours after they found the body*: Police report dated August 25, 1969; Conrado Gruenbaum, interview by author, December 18, 2007.

75 *It's not clear why Conrado*: Conrado Gruenbaum, interview by author, ibid.

76 *Nevertheless, they spent hours analyzing*: Laurinda Soares Navarro, interview by author, May 8, 2007; Maria Consuelo Ayres, interview by author, August 27, 2006. Information also comes from the police and autopsy reports. The description of Alfredo's room is taken from the photographs accompanying the police reports, August 25, 1969.

77 *But there were obvious gaps*: Laurinda Soares Navarro, ibid; Maria Consuelo Ayres, ibid.

77 *"He wasn't there when we discovered the body"*: Laurinda Soares Navarro, interview by author, May 8, 2007.

77 *There were other elements missing*: Maria Consuelo Ayres, August 27, 2006; Laurinda Soares Navarro, ibid.

78 *The police photographs show a dead body*: Laurinda Soares Navarro, ibid.; Rosy Fanto, interview by author, August 10, 2006.

78 *"He shot himself twice"*: Al Abitbol, interview by author, September 20, 2006.

79 *Samy Cohn, another wealthy*: Samy Cohn, interview by author, December 5, 2006.

79 *Do you want the body embalmed*: Rosy Fanto, interview by author, July 27, 2006. Rosy's recollections of Alfredo in this chapter are mostly from this interview.

82 *The Ponto Frio executives worked into the wee hours*: Lourdes Mattos, interview by author, September 13, 2006; Sonia Mattos, interview by author, January 10, 2008; Laurinda Soares Navarro, interview by author, May 8, 2007; Maria Consuelo Ayres, interview by author, August 27, 2006.

82 *"It's just like Fred"*: Maria Consuelo Ayres, interview by author, August 27, 2006.

82 *"Geraldo said that Fred's death was very strange"*: Lourdes Mattos, interview by author, September 13, 2006.

83 *his secretary Vera received a call*: Vera Chvidchenko, interview by author, January 28, 2008.

83 *"The newspapers omitted most of the details"*: Hélio Fernandes, interview by author, March 10, 2009.

84 *Shortly after Alfredo died, there were some rumors*: Lourdes Mattos, interview by author, September 13, 2006; Sonia Mattos, interview by author, January 10, 2008; Maria Consuelo Ayres, interview by author, August 27, 2006.

86 *"Received the revolver, four bullets intact"*: Police receipt, 10th District Precinct, Botafogo, Rio de Janeiro, August 26, 1969. There is some debate about who signed the police receipt for the return of the revolver and the bullet. It is impossible to tell from the scrawled signature on the receipt.

89   *"It was the day after her husband's funeral"*: Rosy Fanto, interview by author, July 27, 2006.

91   *But like so many others who questioned*: Maria Consuelo Ayres, interview by author, August 27, 2006; Rosy Fanto, interview by author, August 10, 2006; Masha Monterosa, interview by author, November 7, 2006.

91   *But as the investigating lawyers would find*: Letter to Dr. Alfredo Lamy Filho from investigators, signature indecipherable. March 18, 1970.

93   *"Although the initial police report"*: Report by medical examiner Alexandrino Silva Ramos Filho, March 16, 1970.

FOUR: "EDMOND SAID HE WOULD FIX EVERYTHING"

97   *"Every Jew had money outside the country"*: Marcelo Steinfeld, interview by author, October 17, 2007.

97   *"For years, Fred was Edmond Safra's biggest account"*: Maria Luisa Goldschmid, interview by author, October 25, 2007. Goldschmid and Maria Consuelo Ayres both said that Edmond Safra's brothers were frequently at the Ponto Frio offices in Rio de Janeiro.

98   *Their friend Albert Nasser*: Albert Nasser, interview by author, December 3, 2006.

99   *"We all thought that when Fred died"*: Ruth Almeida Prado, interview by author, April 30, 2006.

99   *"My son died on August 25, 1969"*: Regina Rebecca Monteverde's affidavit dated 1971, court documents, 1971 F. No. 2064, High Court of Justice, Chancery Division.

100   *"but in the manner that a railway baron"*: Samuel Bendahan, interview by author, October 2, 2007.

101   *Lily was careful not to declare*: Samuel Bendahan, interview by author, October 7, 2007; Willard Zucker to G. C. Sutton, 13 December 1971, re: Mrs. L. Monteverde.

101   *"She wasn't exactly an intellectual"*: Rosy Fanto, interview by author, July 27, 2006.

104   *In rare interviews*: "The Mystery Man of Finance," *BusinessWeek*, March 7, 1994. "Collector of Banks is Going Public," *New York Times*, September 27, 1972.

104   *"You need honesty and hard work"*: In "Safra, um banqueiro de 4,2 bilhões de dolares de ativo," *Jornal do Brasil*. Translated from the Portuguese by the author, May, 14, 1978.

104   *"That is what my father taught me"*: "The Mystery Man of Finance," *BusinessWeek*, March 7, 1994.

105   *he convinced his father's chauffeur*: Albert Nasser, interview by author, December 3, 2006.

105   *"Edmond, you are going to grow up"*: Albert Nasser, ibid.

105   *Years later, Madame Tarrab*: Albert Nasser, ibid.

106   *"Sephardic assimilation was slowed"*: Daniel J. Elazar, *The Other Jews*: *The Sephardim Today* (Basic Books, 1992), p. 146.

107 *"If they ask you"*: Bryan Burrough, *Vendetta: American Express and the Smearing of Edmond Safra* (HarperCollins, 1993), p. 35.

107 *"I'm in no hurry"*: "The Mystery Man of Finance," *BusinessWeek*, March 7, 1994.

107 *The Safras moved to Rio de Janeiro*: Edmond Safra, application for Brazilian citizenship (1954 to 1957), National Archives, Rio de Janeiro.

109 *There were also so-called hold-mail accounts*: Burrough, p. 43.

110 *"He went there to buy a hat"*: "The Mystery Man of Finance," *BusinessWeek*, March 7, 1994.

110 *Charles Knox initially established the hat company*: Landmarks Preservation Commission, New York, September 23, 1980, Designation List 137, LP1091.

111 *"He knew more about the history"*: Eli Attia, interview by author, January 6, 2009.

112 *So, at the bank's grand opening*: "Kennedy Cuts Ribbon at a New Bank on Fifth Avenue," *New York Times*, January 25, 1966.

113 *"If someone brings a friend"*: "A TV spectacular sets off a 'run' on New York bank," *Wall Street Journal*, April 12, 1973.

114 *But attracting new depositors*: Burrough, p. 50.

115 *"I'm now competing with the big boys"*: "Collector of Banks is Going Public," *New York Times*, September 27, 1972.

116 *"Who is that beautiful woman?"*: Albert Nasser, interview by author, December 3, 2006.

118 *"The relationship between the bank and the first-named defendant"*: Rosy Fanto's affidavit dated October 6, 1971, court papers, 1971 F. No 2064, High Court of Justice, Chancery Division. All subsequent information pertaining to the London legal case is quoted from the court transcripts.

120 *Alfredo was, at various times, put on a combination*: Dr. Giacomo Landau, affidavit dated June 6, 1971.

122 *demanding the guardianship of Carlos Monteverde*: All information from the legal battle over the adoption of Carlos Monteverde by Lily Monteverde is taken from Brazilian court transcripts, 1970–1973.

126 *They finally found a lawyer*: João Augusto Miranda Jordão to Rosy Fanto, July 16, 1973.

128 *In the summer of 1970, Lily rented a yacht*: Court papers, 1971 F. No 2064, High Court of Justice, Chancery Division.

129 *"They really knew how to enjoy themselves"*: Marcelo Steinfeld, interview by author, October 17, 2007.

130 *"The Safras put a lot of pressure on Edmond not to marry Lily:"* ibid.

FIVE: TWO WEDDINGS

134 *"Much to my surprise"*: Samuel Bendahan, letter to Mark Haymon, Esq., dated March 19, 1972.

134   *"Mrs. Cohen had preferred to let us be alone"*: Samuel Bendahan, letter to Mark Haymon, Esq., March 19, 1972.

135   *"Much to my stupefaction"*: ibid.

135   *"Lily's latest gigolo"*: Marcelo Steinfeld, interview by author, October 17, 2007.

135   *"She was only using the guy"*: Marcelo Steinfeld, ibid.

136   the *"black money" as she called it*: Samuel Bendahan, interview by author, October 7, 2007.

136   *photos of "poor darling Freddy"*: Samuel Bendahan, interview by author, February 5, 2008. These photographs of Alfredo were also mentioned by Maria Luisa Goldschmid, Alfredo's former secretary, who visited Lily shortly after she arrived in London, and recalled seeing them in Lily's living room.

139   *When he died in 1907*: Obituary of Judah Bendahan, London's *Jewish Chronicle*, December 6, 1907.

140   *Life with Lily seemed blissful in those early days*: Lily Monteverde to Samuel Bendahan, December 30, 1971.

140   *refers to herself as Madame Claude*: Lily Monteverde to Samuel Bendahan, undated note.

141   *"My adorable husband"*: Lily Monteverde to Samuel Bendahan, January 8, 1972.

141   *to have children with her ("lots of them!")*: Lily Monteverde to Samuel Bendahan, January 4, 1972.

141   *"my love, my darling, my beloved"*: Lily Monteverde to Samuel Bendahan, January 8, 1972.

141   *Still, there were strains*: Samuel Bendahan, letter to Mark Haymon, Esq., March 19, 1972.

142   *"Mrs. Monteverde was of course incensed"*: Samuel Bendahan, ibid.

143   *the man she called her "Red Indian"*: Lily Monteverde to Samuel Bendahan, undated note.

143   *"beautiful Alain Delon's [sic] hat"*: Lily Monteverde to Samuel Bendahan, undated note.

143   *"She had traveled with these!"*: Samuel Bendahan, interview by author, October 7, 2007.

143   *"As a very last precaution I did insist"*: Samuel Bendahan, letter to Mark Haymon, Esq., March 19, 1972.

143   *"very concerned about the disparity"*: Samuel Bendahan, interview by author, October 7, 2007. Bendahan also discussed the financial arrangements with Lily regarding the servants during this interview.

144   *"held an idealistic view of marriage"*: Samuel Bendahan, letter dated March 19, 1972.

145   *"Dear mum and dad*: Carlos Monteverde to Lily Bendahan and Samuel Bendahan, February 13 and February 27, 1972.

146   *"How does it feel to be part of a mad family"*: Samuel Bendahan, letter dated March 19, 1972.

146 *"We arrived in Rio"*: Samuel Bendahan, ibid.

146 *"She was so happy on that trip"*: Elza Gruenbaum, interview by author, December 18, 2007.

147 *Lily found an even grander stone villa*: Samuel Bendahan, letter to Mark Haymon, Esq., March 19, 1972; property records, Vallauris, France, March 1972.

148 *set out the terms of purchase*: Willard Zucker, intent to purchase to Mme. Gilberte Duarte Ex. Esders, March 6, 1972.

148 *He was furious at her extravagance*: Samuel Bendahan, interview by author, October 28, 2007.

148 *the shares being held in equal parts*: Samuel Bendahan, letter to Mark Haymon, Esq., March 19, 1972.

148 *"And this continued well into my day"*: Samuel Bendahan, interview by author, October 7, 2007.

149 *"We were excited to be together"*: Samuel Bendahan, interview by author, December 9, 2007.

149 *"a dramatic decline"*: Samuel Bendahan, letter to Mark Haymon, Esq., March 19, 1972.

149 *Werner, her London chauffeur*: Samuel Bendahan, interview by author, October 7, 2007.

150 *"endless telephone calls"*: Samuel Bendahan, ibid.

150 *Lily began to receive a "fusillade" of calls*: Samuel Bendahan, ibid.

150 *"He offered me his warmest congratulations"*: Samuel Bendahan, interview by author, October 26, 2007.

150 *"she was subjected to a barrage"*: Samuel Bendahan, letter to Mark Haymon, Esq., September 24, 1973.

150 *"On the airplane to London"*: Samuel Bendahan, ibid.

151 *went around inspecting every lampshade*: Samuel Bendahan, ibid.

151 *"I now no longer had to press her to speak"*: Samuel Bendahan, letter to Mark Haymon, Esq., March 19, 1972.

151 *she begged Bendahan to hide a painting*: Samuel Bendahan, interview by author, October 26, 2007.

153 "thief-director": Lourdes Mattos, interview by author, September 13, 2006.

154 *Bendahan heard a knock on the door*: Samuel Bendahan, letter to Mark Haymon, Esq., March 19, 1972, and interview by author, October 26, 2007.

155 *"I have tried to reach my wife"*: Samuel Bendahan, letter to Mark Haymon, Esq., March 19, 1972.

155 *"This is in effect how our marriage broke up"*: Samuel Bendahan, letter dated September 24, 1973.

155 *"Edmond told me that he couldn't sleep at night"*: Albert Nasser, interview by author, December 3, 2006.

156 *"He called Alouan and asked him"*: Albert Nasser, interview by author, December 3, 2006.

157 *"I can only think that my wife is either very sick"*: Samuel Bendahan, letter to Mark Haymon, Esq., March 19, 1972.

157 *In a chatty letter*: Lily Monteverde to Samuel Bendahan, January 5, 1972.

157 *and suffered hallucinations*: Lily Monteverde to Samuel Bendahan, two letters dated January 8, 1972 and one letter dated January 15, 1972.

158 *Lily later met up with Eduardo*: Samuel Bendahan, notes 1972, on photographs from his honeymoon.

159 *"were persistent and categorical"*: Samuel Bendahan, interview by author, October 26, 2007.

159 *he was arrested by a plainclothes policeman*: Samuel Bendahan, interviews by author, October 24 and October 26, 2007.

160 *he accused her of transferring funds illegally*: "Inglês é detido nos EUA sob acusação de extorquir brasileira," *O Globo*, translated from the Portuguese by the author, January 31, 1975.

160 *In the weeks of arduous divorce negotiations*: Samuel Bendahan, interview by author, October 7, 2007.

160 *"Imagine how popular"*: Samuel Bendahan, interview by author, October 7, 2007.

161 *Lily and Edmond didn't formally extricate themselves*: "British Case Wastes Time: Judge," *New York Post*, July 21, 1976.

SIX: "THE BILLIONAIRES' CLUB"

165 *She simply adored Claudio*: Samuel Bendahan, interview by author, October 7, 2007. Bendahan also provided information about Lily's relationship with her other children.

168 *"For years, every ambassador"*: Ana Bentes Bloch, interview by author, March 11, 2009.

169 *"I told her that if she didn't want anyone to gossip"*: Guilherme Castello Branco, interview by author, December 4, 2007.

171 *"An event like Rio has never seen"*: Perla Sigaud, society column, *O Globo*, May 7, 1983. Translated from the Portuguese by the author.

172 *Years later, when they wanted to impress the Safras*: Peter Truell, "A Fallen King in Search of a Lesser Throne," *New York Times*, May 3, 1998.

173 *"The wedding was truly spectacular"*: Ricardo Stambowsky, interview by author, December 3, 2007.

175 *"It was dawn"*: Guilherme Castello Branco, interview by author, December 4, 2007.

176 *"Life sometimes sends us difficult times"*: Perla Sigaud, society column, *O Globo*, May 7, 1983. Translated by the author from the Portuguese.

178 *"You don't even know these people"*: Burrough, p. 92. Many of the details about the Safra-American Express debacle are from Burrough's book *Vendetta*.

179 *"It was an economic decision"*: Interview with a source close to the negotiations of the sale of Trade Development Bank to American Express, January 6, 2009.

181 *"TDB ran like nothing we'd ever seen"*: Burrough, p. 98.

181 *"Safra's a brilliant guy"*: Nicholas D. Kristof, "Safra Quits as Chief of Bank Unit," *New York Times*, October 23, 1984.

183 *"Mr. Safra, a private sometimes eccentric"*: David B. Hilder and George Anders, "Safra to Quit as American Express Head of International Banking, Sources Say," *Wall Street Journal*, October 22, 1984.

183 *Edmond arranged for the restaurant to be decorated*: Meredith Etherington-Smith, "Eyeview," *Women's Wear Daily*, November 28, 1984.

183 *"I feel as free as a bird"*: Albert Nasser, interview by author, December 3, 2006.

184 *"Nothing in this agreement shall impose"*: Burrough, p. 138.

185 *"a discreet, efficient and rapid channel"*: *Final Report for the District of the Independent Counsel for Iran/Contra Matters*, August 4, 1993, United States Court of Appeals for the District of Columbia Circuit.

186 *"Mrs. L. Monteverde's"*: letter by Willard Zucker, December 13, 1971.

188 *"Safra . . . exhorted his aides"*: Burrough, p. 185.

189 *"Lily and Edmond Safra's doubleheader"*: Dennis Thim, "The Gilded Lily," in "Eye," *Women's Wear Daily*, August 8, 1988.

191 *"La Leopolda was surely never this grand"*: ibid.

191 *Security was tight*: John Fairchild, *Chic Savages* (Simon & Schuster, 1989), p. 196.

192 *"the grounds were guarded as heavily as the White House"*: Dennis Thim, "The Gilded Lily," in "Eye," *Women's Wear Daily*, August 8, 1988.

192 *"With the opening of a place like this"*: ibid.

193 *"The Safra event itself"*: Fairchild, p. 196.

195 *"Edmond brought Alouan to Brazil"*: Albert Nasser, interview by author, January 27, 2008.

195 *"Alouan was very rough"*: Guilherme Castello Branco, interview by author, December 4, 2007.

197 *the paid obituaries took up nearly two broadsheet pages*: Paid obituaries of Claudio and Raphael Cohen, *O Globo*, February 19, 1989.

198 *"I want to know why you are here"*: Albert Nasser, interview by author, January 2008. Adriana's comments were also repeated by several people who attended the funeral of Claudio and his son who did not want to be identified.

198 *"I was so comfortable with him"*: Bruno Astuto, "A Nora de Lily," *RG Vogue*, November 2007. Carlos' comments about his step-brother Claudio Cohen and relationship with the Safras after he married Isis, from *RG Vogue*, November 2007.

199   *"it was Lily who took Claudio's death the hardest*: Ruth de Almeida Prado, interview by author, April 30, 2006.

200   *This time, nobody bought the clunky PR move*: "Behind the American Express Smear," *New York Post*, August 9, 1989.

201   *It's unclear who at American Express knew about the smear campaign*: Kurt Eichenwald, "Executive at American Express Quits," *New York Times*, August 4, 1989.

SEVEN: "WHEN I GIVE LILY A DOLLAR,
LILY SPENDS TWO DOLLARS"

204   *"It was the anxiety"*: Antonio Negreiros, interview by author, April 27, 2006.

205   *Evelyne dictated her instructions*: Evelyne Sigelmann Cohen, will, dated September 2, 1992, 23rd Notary Office, Rio de Janeiro. Translated from the Portuguese by the author.

205   *"Evelyne died on a Friday"*: Antonio Negreiros, interview by author, April 27, 2006.

208   *"I try to remain unknown as much as possible"*: Edmond Safra in "Safra, um banqueiro de 4,2 bilhões de dolares de ativo," *Jornal do Brasil*, translated from the Portuguese by the author, May, 14, 1978.

209   *"the beauty of the night"*: Aileen Mehle, Suzy, *Women's Wear Daily*, April 29, 1992.

209   *She wore "pinky red chiffon by Valentino"*: Aileen Mehle, Suzy, *Women's Wear Daily*, July 15, 1992.

210   *"Joseph Safra had just thrown a huge party"*: Interview with a source close to the Safra family, January 12, 2009.

210   *were fond of "elaborate decorations"*: Fairchild, pp. 91–92.

210   *As Edmond himself noted in an exchange*: Fairchild, p. 92.

211   *"It is the capital of the world"*: Fairchild, ibid.

211   *"Banker Edmond Safra and his wife, Lily, served so much caviar"*: Fairchild, p. 91.

211   *"Darling, I bought you an airplane today"*: Ana Bentes Bloch, interview by author, March 11, 2009. Her late husband, Adolfo Bloch, overheard the Safras' conversation at a luncheon with Lily and Edmond.

211   *the old money families*: Fairchild, p. 90.

211   *"The number of bodyguards"*: Aileen Mehle, Suzy, *Women's Wear Daily*, August 12, 1991.

212   *Nasser spent seventy-five days*: The kidnapping of Ezequiel Edmond Nasser in São Paulo in 1994 is well documented in press reports in Brazil and the United States, including "The Safras of Brazil: Banking, Faith and Security," Simon Romero, *New York Times*, December 8, 1999.

213   *"so glorious and impeccable"*: Aileen Mehle, Suzy, *Women's Wear Daily*, September 13, 1996.

213   *"There is no security system"*: Samuel Cohen, transcript from Ted Maher's trial, Le Tribunal Criminel de la Principauté de Monaco, November 25, 2002.

214 *Cohen trained with the Mossad*: Dominick Dunne, "Verdict in Monaco," *Vanity Fair*, February 2003.

215 *"As was the case with a number of Attia's projects"*: *Eli Attia Architects v. Safra*, No. 94 CIV. 2928 (SDNY 1996).

216 *"He [Edmond] told me that the bill was the responsibility"*: Eli Attia in "Case vs banker is building," *New York Post*, December 5, 1995.

216 *But in court papers*: *Eli Attia Architects v. Safra*, No. 94 CIV. 2928 (SDNY 1996).

217 *"We were having dinner with Lily and Edmond"*: Albert Nasser, interview by author, December 3, 2006.

218 *"The . . . party was a celebration"*: *W*, September 1996.

219 *"Lily was distraught after the accident"*: Interview with a source close to the Safras, January 2009.

221 *Edmond "called his brothers several times a day"*: Sem Almaleh testimony, Maher trial transcript, Le Tribunal Criminel de la Principauté de Monaco, November 27, 2002.

221 *"that Edmond wouldn't speak to his brothers"*: Albert Nasser, interview by author, December 3, 2006.

222 *"He was a brother"*: Joseph Safra, Maher trial transcript, Le Tribunal Criminel de la Principauté de Monaco, November 27, 2002.

222 *"Lily cut him off after thirty years"*: Albert Nasser, interview by author, January 27, 2008.

222 *The Safras moved with their entourage of aides*: Information about Edmond's doctors and the experience in Toronto with Dr. Bruce Sutton is from interviews with un-named sources who were close to the couple, January 2009.

223 *Edmond was taking a potent cocktail of antidepressants*: Nursing schedule from Mo-naco, obtained by the author.

224 *the deal would "mark the end of independence"*: Alan Cowell, "HSBC to Pay $10.3 billion for Republic," *New York Times*, May 11, 1999.

225 *"I am taking this action"*: Jesse Angelo, "Safra's Act of Pride—Coughs Up $450 m to protect holders," *New York Post*, November 9, 1999.

EIGHT: "NOT OUR FAULT"

230 *He was also a highly respected and dedicated nurse*: From testimony of George Morelli, Maher trial transcript, Le Tribunal Criminel de la Principauté de Monaco, Novem-ber 21, 2002.

231 *In addition, Ted would have to sign*: Confidentiality agreement, August 16, 1999, signed by Anthony Brittan.

232 *Behind her back*: Ted Maher, interview by author, March 5, 2008.

232 *"Ted was strange in some ways"*: Sonia Casiano Herkrath, Maher trial transcript, Le Tribunal Criminel de la Principauté de Monaco, November 21, 2002.

233   *"I considered it the best job"*: Ted Maher, Maher trial transcript, Le Tribunal Criminel de la Principauté de Monaco, November 21, 2002.

233   *"In the day, he [Edmond] moved fairly well*: Lily Safra, Maher trial transcript, Le Tribunal Criminel de la Principauté de Monaco, November 29, 2002.

233   *According to the nightly schedule*: Ted Maher, interview by author, March 5, 2008.

233   *In addition to massaging his feet*: From the nursing schedule for Edmond Safra in Monaco, December 1999, obtained by the author.

234   *"Ironically, he was doing so much better"*: Sonia Casiano Herkrath, Maher trial transcript, Le Tribunal Criminel de la Principauté de Monaco, November 21, 2002.

235   *"We kissed each other"*: Lily Safra testimony at Maher trial, Le Tribunal Criminel de la Principauté de Monaco, November 29, 2002.

235   *"This evening"*: Lily Safra testimony at Maher trial, ibid.

236   *Later, when a different group of firefighters*: Maher trial, Le Tribunal Criminel de la Principauté de Monaco, November 26, 2002.

237   *the concern of law enforcement officials became the safety*: From testimony of various police officers at the Maher trial, Le Tribunal Criminel de la Principauté de Monaco: Jean-Luc Belny (November 25, 2002), Bruno Bouery (November 25, 2002), and Jean-Marc Silvi (November 25, 2002).

237   *Another police officer noted*: Testimony of Olivier Jude, Maher trial, Le Tribunal Criminel de la Principauté de Monaco, November 25, 2002.

237   *On the surface, everything appeared to be stacked up*: Henri Veillard, Maher trial transcript, Le Tribunal Criminel de la Principauté de Monaco, November 27, 2002.

238   *"The duration of the intervention of the emergency services"*: Testimony of Henri Veillard, November 27, 2002.

238   *Strangely, none of the Safra bodyguards*: Samuel Cohen, Maher trial transcript, Le Tribunal Criminel de la Principauté de Monaco, November 25, 2002.

238   *Cohen complained about interference*: Samuel Cohen testimony, Maher trial, Le Tribunal Criminel de la Principauté de Monaco, November 25, 2002.

239   *"Chérie, there are aggressors"*: Lily Safra testimony, Maher trial, Le Tribunal Criminel de la Principauté de Monaco, November 29, 2002.

239   *"Have you closed yourself in"*: Lily Safra testimony, ibid.

239   *"I don't know how I got out but I did it"*: Lily Safra, Maher trial transcript, Le Tribunal Criminel de la Principauté de Monaco, November 29, 2002.

239   *"He was in quite a panicky state"*: Jean-Marc Farca testimony, Maher trial, Le Tribunal Criminel de la Principauté de Monaco, November 22, 2002.

240   *"Sonia, it's so dark in here"*: Sonia Casiano Herkrath testimony, Maher trial, Le Tribunal Criminel de la Principauté de Monaco, November 21, 2002.

240   *"I said I was willing to die for my boss"*: Raul Manjate testimony, Maher trial, Le Tribunal Criminel de la Principauté de Monaco, November 25, 2002.

241   *"Cohen seems to have been too aggressive"*: Jean-Luc Belny testimony, Maher trial, Le Tribunal Criminel de la Principauté de Monaco, November 25, 2002.

241 *"The firemen arrived"*: Samuel Cohen testimony, Maher trial, Le Tribunal Criminel de la Principauté de Monaco, November 25, 2002.

241 *"My mother woke me up shortly before six a.m."*: Adriana Elia testimony, Maher trial, Le Tribunal Criminel de la Principauté de Monaco, November 27, 2002.

243 *"He was incapable of killing a fly"*: Lily Safra testimony, Maher trial, Le Tribunal Criminel de la Principauté de Monaco, November 29, 2002.

243 *"I went up the stairs to where my husband's office was"*: Lily Safra testimony, ibid.

243 *"He was covered in soot"*: Lily Safra testimony, ibid.

245 *"Upon hearing of the frightening news"*: Heidi Maher, affidavit, Supreme Court of the State of New York, Dutchess County, April 13, 2001.

246 *"There was never pressure on Mr. Maher"*: Olivier Jude testimony, Maher trial, Le Tribunal Criminel de la Principauté de Monaco, November 25, 2002.

247 *Jude said that Ted showed him a photograph*: Olivier Jude testimony, ibid.

247 *Lily organized Edmond's funeral in Geneva*: Interviews with Edmond Safra's former employees, who did not want to be named. Dominick Dunne, "Death in Monaco," *Vanity Fair*, December 2000.

248 *"She [Lily] didn't want anyone from the family"*: Interview with a Safra family member who spoke on condition of anonymity, March 9, 2009.

248 *"You have brought together people"*: Jon Henley, "Feud that Led to Billionaire's Death," *The Guardian*, December 7, 1999.

NINE: "YEARS OF SORROW AND
DAYS OF DESPAIR"

252 *an informal welcome back to New York*: Aileen Mehle, Suzy, *Women's Wear Daily*, April 20, 2001.

252 *"You have to imagine the scene"*: Michael Griffith, interview by author, March 19, 2009.

253 *"It was like taking candy"*: Jay Salpeter, interview by author, March 2, 2009.

253 *"Summons Served Between Courses"*: Neal Travis, "New York," *New York Post*, April 20, 2001.

254 *"I suffered shocking and humiliating treatment"*: Heidi Maher, affidavit, Supreme Court of the State of New York, Dutchess County, April 13, 2001.

254 *"The rights of these American"*: Letter from Michael Griffith to Martha Melzow, Consulate of the United States of America in Marseille, France, March 17, 2001.

256 *"When [in] Ted's final speech he apologized"*: Dominick Dunne, "Verdict in Monaco," *Vanity Fair*, February 2003.

257 *"a court performance worthy of Laurence Olivier"*: Dunne, ibid.

258 *The Torrente children*: Torrente v. Estate of Edmond Safra, Supreme Court of the State of New York, December 2, 2002.

258   *"The reason they died"*: Michael Baden, interview with author, March 20, 2009.

259   *"I've escaped"*: Michael Griffith, interview by author, March 19, 2009.

260   *"one of the most staggeringly beautiful houses"*: Aileen Mehle, Suzy, *Women's Wear Daily*, March 8, 2002.

261   *A month later, Lily was spotted in the "chicest of black dresses"*: Aileen Mehle, Suzy, *Women's Wear Daily*, May 2, 2001.

261   *"in dangerous* deshabillé*"*: Aileen Mehle, Suzy, *Women's Wear Daily*, October 29, 2002.

262   *"17th century heavy gold"*: Aileen Mehle, Suzy, *Women's Wear Daily*, December 18, 2002.

262   *another lavish party hosted by Joan Rivers*: Aileen Mehle, ibid.

262   *"she is a happy woman"*: Aileen Mehle, Suzy, *Women's Wear Daily*, February 3, 2003.

263   *"We agreed that a lush garden"*: Preston Bailey, "Thousands of Rose Petals and a Whole Lot of Trellis Make a High-Rise Room a Garden for a Night," *Elle Décor*, October 2003.

264   *"When the elevator opened"*: Aileen Mehle, Suzy, *Women's Wear Daily*, June 11, 2003.

264   *"I waited in the foyer"*: Bailey, "Thousands of Rose Petals," *Elle Décor*, October 2003.

264   *After dinner, the guests "lounged"*: Aileen Mehle, Suzy, *Women's Wear Daily*, June 11, 2003.

264   *"that draws every celebrity"*: Aileen Mehle, Suzy, *Women's Wear Daily*, July 18, 2003.

267   *"I believe that Mrs. Safra read part of the book"*: Mark Bolland, Witness Statement of Mark Bolland, in the High Court of Justice, Queen's Bench Division, December 12, 2005.

268   *"If Georgie takes it further"*: Gary Pulsifer in "Dominick Dunne's Diary: Did Someone Say Safra?" Dominick Dunne, *Vanity Fair*, September 2005.

268   *"Lily tried to misuse the laws"*: Lady Colin Campbell, interview by author, August 29, 2008.

268   *"She objected to the fact that Bianca's"*: Lady Colin Campbell, ibid.

269   *"To say the trial"*: *New York Post*, August 18, 2007.

270   *"He was threatened"*: Michael Griffith, interview by author, May 17, 2007.

271   *"Accusing the victim of having murdered someone"*: Donald Manasse, interview by author, October 19, 2009.

272   *"Why should I stick a knife"*: Ted Maher, interview by author, March 5, 2008.

273   *"America has turned out to be another prison"*: Ted Maher, ibid.

EPILOGUE:
"WE KNOW EVERYTHING AND WE KNOW NOTHING"

277   *Artigas had an appetite for money*: Maria Consuelo Ayres, interview by author, August 27, 2006; Vera Chvidchenko, interview by author, January 28, 2008; and Ademar Trotte, interview by author, March 12, 2009.

277 *"Artigas practically lived"*: Vera Chvidchenko, ibid., and Ademar Trotte, ibid.

278 *"I thought his [Alfredo's] death was my fault"*: Carlos Monteverde in Bruno Astuto, "A Nora de Lily," *RG Vogue*, November 2007.

279 *"But my family is me, Carlos"*: Astuto, ibid.

279 *"Sometimes I call to find out about the business"*: *RG Vogue*, ibid.

280 *"Maybe if you find them"*: Maria Consuelo Ayres, interview by author, August 27, 2006.

281 *"I never believed that Fred"*: Vera Chvidchenko, interview by author, January 29, 2008.

282 *even Geraldo Mattos didn't have the stomach*: Sonia Mattos, interview by author, January 10, 2008.

282 *"My father was in charge of Ponto Frio"*: Sonia Mattos, ibid.

283 *"too much tragedy"*: Marcelo Steinfeld, interview by author, October 17, 2007.

285 *"It was a really stupid death"*: Interview with a Safra family member, March 9, 2009.

285 *"Even I am [now] surprised"*: Samuel Bendahan, e-mail message to author, February 9, 2009.

287 *She said she would distribute the $55 million*: "Mrs. Lily Safra to make charitable donations on three continents," press release, March 6, 2009.

Index